The Grammar of School Discipline

Race and Education in the Twenty-First Century

Series Editors: Kenneth J. Fasching-Varner, University of Nevada, Las Vegas; Roland Mitchell, Louisiana State University; and Lori Latrice Martin, Louisiana State University

This series asks authors and editors to consider the role of race and education, addressing questions such as "How do communities and educators alike take on issues of race in meaningful and authentic ways?" and "How can education work to disrupt, resolve, and otherwise transform current racial realities?" The series pays close attention to the intersections of difference, recognizing that isolated conversations about race eclipse the dynamic nature of identity development that plays out for race as it intersects with gender, sexuality, socioeconomic class, and ability. It welcomes perspectives from across the entire spectrum of education from Pre-K through advanced graduate studies, and it invites work from a variety of disciplines, including counseling, psychology, higher education, curriculum theory, curriculum and instruction, and special education.

Recent Titles in Series

The Grammar of School Discipline: Removal, Resistance, and Reform in Alabama Schools by Hannah Carson Baggett and Carey E. Andrzejewski

Implications of Race and Racism in Student Evaluations of Teaching: The Hate U Give, edited by LaVada Taylor

Technology Segregation: Disrupting Racist Frameworks in Early Childhood Education, by Miriam B. Tager

Surviving Becky(s): Pedagogies for Deconstructing Whiteness and Gender, edited by Cheryl E. Matias

Latinx Curriculum Theorizing, edited by Theodorea Regina Berry

Intersectional Care for Black Boys in an Alternative School: They Really Care About Us, by Julia C. Ransom

Culture, Community, and Educational Success: Reimagining the Invisible Knapsack, edited by Toby S. Jenkins, Stephanie Troutman, and Crystal Polite Glover

Whiteness at the Table: Antiracism, Racism, and Identity in Education, edited by Shannon K. McManimon, Zachary A. Casey, and Christina Berchini

The Classroom as Privileged Space: Psychoanalytic Paradigms for Social Justice in Pedagogy, by Tapo Chimbganda

Curriculum and Students in Classrooms: Everyday Urban Education in an Era of Standardization, by Walter S. Gershon

Race, Population Studies, and America's Public Schools: A Critical Demography Perspective, edited by Hayward Derrick Horton, Lori Latrice Martin, and Kenneth Vasching-Varner

The Grammar of School Discipline

Removal, Resistance, and Reform in Alabama Schools

Hannah Carson Baggett and
Carey E. Andrzejewski

Foreword by
Cheryl E. Matias

LEXINGTON BOOKS
Lanham • Boulder • New York • London

Published by Lexington Books
An imprint of The Rowman & Littlefield Publishing Group, Inc.
4501 Forbes Boulevard, Suite 200, Lanham, Maryland 20706

www.rowman.com

6 Tinworth Street, London SE11 5AL, United Kingdom

Copyright © 2021 The Rowman & Littlefield Publishing Group, Inc.

Kevin King is a visual artist and Mobile, Alabama, native who currently resides in Montgomery, Alabama, with his wife and daughter. Kevin is the founder of The King's Canvas Gallery and Studio located in West Montgomery. The King's Canvas is a creative space that serves an underdeveloped and underexposed art community in West Montgomery. Their goal is to provide opportunity and access for marginalized artists in our city, using art as a means to develop people in the areas of art, entrepreneurship, financial literacy, and life-skill development.

All rights reserved. No part of this book may be reproduced in any form or by any electronic or mechanical means, including information storage and retrieval systems, without written permission from the publisher, except by a reviewer who may quote passages in a review.

British Library Cataloguing in Publication Information Available

Library of Congress Cataloging-in-Publication Data Available

ISBN 978-1-7936-0175-9 (cloth : alk. paper)
ISBN 978-1-7936-0177-3 (pbk : alk. paper)
ISBN 978-1-7936-0176-6 (electronic)

∞™ The paper used in this publication meets the minimum requirements of American National Standard for Information Sciences—Permanence of Paper for Printed Library Materials, ANSI/NISO Z39.48-1992.

Dedication
In loving memory of our friend and colleague, Dr. Brittany Larkin.

Contents

Acknowledgments ix

Foreword xi
Cheryl E. Matias

Prologue xvii

Introduction: Any Given Day in an Alabama Alternative School 1

PART I REMOVAL 7

1 Methods of Removal (*with Nicholas P. Triplett*) 9
2 Motives for Removal 37
3 A Portrait of Removal: Cotton County Schools
(*with Jasmine S. Betties and Sangah Lee*) 57

PART II RESISTANCE 69

4 Removed for Resistance 71
5 Who Are the "Bad Kids"? Portraits of Alternative School Students
(*with Sean A. Forbes*) 81
6 Resistance and School-Based Practitioners 95
7 Hitting Kids "Just Doesn't Sit Well": Resistance to Corporal
Punishment (*with Benjamin Arnberg*) 109

PART III REFORM		119
8	Efforts toward Reform	121
9	A Portrait of Reform: Timber County Schools (*with Nanyamka A. Shukura, Sangah Lee, and Jasmine S. Betties*)	129
PART IV REPAIR		145
10	The 4th R	147
11	Self-Portraiture, Problematic Positions, and Politics	155
References		167
Index		201
About the Authors		207

Acknowledgments

We would not have begun, much less completed, this project had we not benefited time and time again from the wisdom, patience, support, and guidance of our scholar-mentors, namely Dr. Cheryl Matias, Dr. Heather Davis, Dr. Jessica DeCuir-Gunby, and Dr. Patricia Marshall. They have modeled integrating theory, method, and school-based engagement in their scholarship, and we have tried to follow their example. They have also taught us to see whiteness and white supremacy at work in every aspect of our lives. Their influence has shaped every element of the research presented here. Similarly, our research has depended on the high school students and school-based practitioners who invited us into their school worlds, offering us the gifts of their time and their stories. Trusted colleagues, especially Dr. Sarah Bausell and Dr. Kamden Strunk, have also supported this project, reading early drafts, attending conference presentations, and giving critical feedback. The contributions and insights of the editorial team and reviewers at Lexington Press have been invaluable. Finally, our families and friends have graciously listened to us as we (sometimes endlessly) narrated our sense-making of the educational landscape of Alabama. We are forever in their debt.

Foreword

Cheryl E. Matias

University of Kentucky

If there is one thing 2020 taught us, it is that we cannot take humanity for granted. How pompous of us to live our daily lives without a care for how we truly live as human beings and how we treat others? How we get too preoccupied with the daily minutiae that we often overlook our approach to humanity and if it indeed aligns with humanizing compassion, empathy, and love? Yet, despite this obvious overlooking we continue to pretend, moreover, we arrogantly proclaim to care, love, and be empathetic to others, even amid their obvious destruction. Human life and Black Lives Mattering should have always mattered, and it is grossly embarrassing that we had to face a global pandemic in Covid-19 and bear witness to even more murders of Black Americans like George Floyd and Breonna Taylor to finally cop up to the fact that not all lives matter, particularly Black lives. This is of grave importance because as we, humanity, attempt to assert our morality, we cannot and will never reconcile our sense-making of morality, or lack thereof, when we remain complicit in immoral behaviors. Plainly, never will morality embrace us if we refuse to embrace others.

That we strive to be good human beings is not contested. In fact, we oftentimes herald this striving for goodness as a litmus for positive engagement in religion, politics, and education. Instead, what is contested is how we present ourselves as good even while we, whether consciously or subconsciously, engage, reify, and maintain practices that ultimately hurt others. This is how whiteness works. For the Miss Anne caricature (white mistress of a plantation), she lives life presuming herself to be a moral being while reading bible verses to enslaved Black children. For the Becky caricature (young white woman who believes herself to be antiracist, but engages in racist behaviors), she feels morally astute in teaching Black and Brown

K-12 students while never living in close proximity to them or even having meaningful relationships with people of Color. Many teachers or school administrators, many of whom are white, believe themselves to be equitable, non-biased, and even antiracist educators but still draw from racial bias to justify their maltreatment of Black and Brown students. *Those* children are deemed disobedient, disruptive, or defiant to authority just because they refuse to kowtow, more precisely, bow down to white supremacist authority. As if the only *good* role for Black students to play in an anti-Black racist school is to shut up, sit down, and nod politely; a respectability politic that is unidirectional.

This is the moral dilemma. How is it one proclaims themselves to be a moral human being when they engage in immoral behaviors? *The Grammar of School Discipline* answers this exact question because as Baggett and Andrzejewski canvased school discipline in schools in Alabama, they also unearthed the disgusting reality of whiteness that then plagues schools in ways that hurt students of Color, particularly Black students. In the Black Belt, for example, the common employment of corporal punishment "brutalizes students, particularly Black students, in educational contexts where they should feel safe" (116). Suffice it to say that the commonplace understanding that educators are righteous to enforce discipline by hitting students, many who are disproportionately Black, in a setting that professes safety for all, is a disgusting perversion. Then we wonder why students of Color, particularly Black students, do not academically excel, refuse to become teachers, or even refuse to respect the educational system. To complicate the matter further, too many educators and administrators in the field of education refuse to bear witness to the racial reality of anti-Black racism in schools. This egregious blindness perpetuates whiteness in education just as it perpetuates immorality in teaching. Therefore, silencing the disciplinary actions that take place in schools is a testament to how schools maintain white supremacy and brush their racist behaviors under the rug. Notwithstanding this culture of silence, this vital book clearly demonstrates how schools engage in anti-Black punitive measures that not only disrespect Black students but also seek to literally "whip" them into shape.

Yet, oddly amid it all, the dominant narrative used to justify this maltreatment of students is that of care, love, and compassion. In this twisted sense of reality, schools continue to practice zero tolerance, stringent school discipline, and swift removals from class instruction, proclaiming that such measures improve the safety of all. In fact, those practices are not for the safety of all, more than they are about saving the intactness of whiteness. Authors Baggett and Andrzejewski masterfully connect today's school discipline policies and practices to the same disciplinary actions against people of Color of yesteryear. That removal from class instruction is emblematic of the forcible removal of Indigenous and Black peoples from their sovereign nations and lands is in and of itself evidence of historical wrongdoing existing in today's educational context. Clearly, we are not learning from our past, nor are we facing the realities of white supremacy presenting anew. If education is to be emancipatory in any sense of the term, it must honestly attend to its past, like mandatory bussing to boarding schools, as ways to better inform our actions today. As the authors contend, the removal of students of Color is just an evolved way to continue controlling the movement, place, and bodies of people of Color. Or, as they claim, a surveillance of some sort, brought forth by the ever-elusive white gaze of white supremacy, that will forever burn the letter "C" for yesteryear's "Colored" onto the hearts of Black students. This is white supremacy par excellence.

Though Baggett and Andrzejewski do not place blame throughout their book, I do. In fact, trepidatious as they were to even implicate themselves, as white scholars, in how they might have inadvertently maintained whiteness in school disciplining procedures, they do indict the past schooling behaviors of Alabama as "a great shame to our nation" (164). However, in this calling out they also call us in to remind us that Alabama is also the "site of great resilience and resistance," and thus, "what happens in Alabama happens everywhere" (164). They are kind, compassionate educators knowing that all too often teachers are blamed for the wrongdoings of the nation's educational system. I, too, am sensitive to that as a former K-12 teacher. Yet, I still indict teachers, administrators, teacher educators, and professors of education, as well as the state departments of education and national department of education. It is not enough to proclaim yourself moral leaders of education if you do not engage in the messiness of confronting and dismantling anti-Black racism in education. It is not enough to publicly wear a safety pin and declare yourself a white ally in the fight against white supremacist schooling practices without ever engaging in the critical examination of whiteness directly. It is not enough to pretend to be committed to anti-racism (simply against racism) when one refuses to engage proactively in racial justice (toward the justice of people of Color). Simply put, *do better*. If we can scrutinize the policing practices and brutality that more often than not utilize racial profiling, racial bias, and anti-Black racism, then we can also scrutinize schooling practices that utilize racial bias, stereotypes, and whiteness to deem what constitutes defiant behavior and thus worthiness of suspension. In fact, beyond the rates in suspensions, detentions, and alternative schooling placements, racial bias has also been found in who gets referred to special education, who does not get referred to gifted and talented education, and who gets tracked into remedial as opposed to honors and Advanced Placement courses in high school. Educators call this phenomenon a racial achievement gap or, more apropos, a racial opportunity gap. Regardless of what one calls it, one thing remains consistent: race is always the determining factor in positioning students favorably or unfavorably in schools. Therefore, to not directly address race, anti-Black racism, whiteness, or white supremacy in schools is to maintain a culture of silence of how racism continues to manifest in K-12 schools today; this book refuses that culture of silence.

Too often educational researchers feel justified, almost righteous, to racially disaggregate their data, which are then used as racial statistics to justify the failures of students of Color. Slide after slide, they show graphs of how students of Color, particularly Black students, have lowered: (1) graduation rates, (2) standardized test scores, (3) presence in honors and Advanced Placement courses, and (4) college acceptance rates. However, in these ceaseless reports and PowerPoints, rarely do these researchers engage in the presence of racism and white supremacy directly, as if both are mere *fantasmas* (ghosts or illusions), unreal to the world in which we exist. Their lack of racial theory to dig deep into the presented data tells the resoluteness of whiteness. Because as they forthrightly share these racialized statistics, they do so with such pomposity and arrogance, claiming expertise of something they know not of, especially as they present these raced data sets without any racial theory to truly understand their manifestations. Metaphorically speaking, 'tis like presuming oneself an expert oncologist without providing any research or literature on cancer. Therefore, research devoid of such directness is trash.

Unlike those types of research, this book directly engages in the roots of racism. As Baggett and Andrzejewski highlight how Black students are "surveilled, adultified, infantilized, brutalized, and dehumanized," they do so with particular attention to how those same ideas are "long-standing and deep-rooted, created and perpetuated by a system of white supremacy, a system that protects white racial domination by whatever, even contradictory, means necessary" (4). Meaning, unlike others, this book is courageous in that it directly ties today's school discipline processes, rhetoric, narratives, and justifications to long-held white supremacist ideological frames. By doing so, the racialized data is not divorced from its racist past. Instead, the past is what informs the present, which in any field of understanding is the proper way to understand social patterns as social scientists. In today's popular parlance, the discussions around fake news and what constitutes its falseness typically draw from one's refusal to adhere to scientific or historical fact. If research utilizes racial data without employing any racial theory to understand that data is fake news, then research like the racialized data and racial theories found in this book is the real deal, even if it is difficult to hear.

In the end, Covid-19 has taught us many things: the need to wear a mask, social distancing, and quarantining. However, beyond those obvious public safety measures, it has also taught us many things about how we view, engage, and treat humanity. The rising divorce rate indicates that perhaps love was not really present in the first place. The rise in child abuse and domestic violence reminds us that although folks smile around town, presumably having it all, still lurking in their own homes is a dark violence. The rise in Covid-19 infections and death toll found predominately in communities of Color serve as lasting testaments to the racism in the United States, and to our complicity in this racism, as we turn a blind eye to global protest and fail to simply say Black Lives Matter. More importantly, the vehement, aggressive backlash to the movement made by people who have no stake in the matter clearly shows how deeply rooted the hatred for Black people is. The increase in mental health conditions only tells us that, in our isolation, we do need each other; Zoom is not enough. In this day and time, we are living an existential crisis whereby we live thinking we knew the world we lived in, even at times wishing or praying for that world to return to normal, yet also realizing that what constituted normalcy is, and was never, normal in the first place. Was it normal to witness another Black murder by police? Was it normal to feel like you had to live life everyday hiding conditions, realities, and abuses that stem from home? Was it normal to never consider the humanity of another human being? Is that the normal to which we want to return? Much like the authors, I too believe that in order to live anew, think anew, and be human anew we must "repair the damage done to our humanity in the times when we have been complicit in the oppression of people of Color" (163). To make good our vow, as human beings, to care, love, and empathize with humanity in ways that are honorable and good, we must first recognize and repair the trauma. Whether the trauma is made by school disciplining measures or self-isolation, the point is that if we, as human beings, do not take an honest look in the mirror to see not who we *believe* we are but who we *truly* are, we forever commit ourselves to the ill-formed grammar of humanity.

Prologue

Alabama, the state from and about which we write this book, is home to a public education system that ranks near or at the bottom of the United States each year, with problems so entrenched they are taken for granted, having become part of the "grammar" of schooling. As Tyack and Tobin (1994) explained over a quarter century ago:

> the basic "grammar" of schooling, like the shape of classrooms, has remained remarkably stable over the decades. By the "grammar" of schooling we mean the regular structures and rules that organize the work of instruction. Here we have in mind, for example, standardized organizational practices in dividing time and space, classifying students and allocating them to classrooms, and splintering knowledge into "subjects." (454)

We see similar stability in the "structure and rules that organize" school discipline policies and practices in Alabama. We have come to think of this structure as a grammar in its own right: a framework that dictates what is allowable in school discipline policies and practices.

In this book, we focus on the three Rs of the grammar of discipline: the persistent *removal* of students from classrooms, *resistance* by students and school-based professionals, and efforts at *reforming* school discipline practices. Trends in disciplinary tactics and consequences have shifted, for example, with the rise and then retraction of zero tolerance policies, the introduction of vast numbers of school-based police, and the implementation of programs aimed at changing the behaviors of students and even of school-based practitioners. Yet, outcomes have remained the same: students are still removed from schools in Alabama, even in the midst of resistance and reforms aimed to provide relief from the devastating impacts of that removal, thus revealing this stubborn grammar. To a large extent, resistance and removal are mutually reinforcing, especially as students' acts of resistance are often used as the rationale for their removal. Reforms, even well-intentioned, have yet to make a dent in the removal of students from Alabama schools or reframe perceptions about student behavior.

In this book, we add a focus on what is often missing from the research literature and discourse about the grammar of schooling (and similar arguments, such as the deep structure of schooling, Tye 1998): the anti-Black racism that is part and parcel of public education (for a discussion of racial grammar in the U.S., see Bonilla-Silva 2012). Although school discipline policies and procedures affect many students across our state, we take up and direct our attention to how exclusionary discipline is situated in a long history of anti-Black racism in Alabama, a racism that is dynamic and pernicious, much older than the public school buildings bearing the names of Confederate leaders. We examine the mechanisms by which policies, practices, and practitioners remove Black students from Alabama classrooms, also exploring how this removal in the name of discipline is taken for granted. And, we describe resistance, resilience, and efforts toward reform by and in communities who are most affected, efforts which are also rooted in Alabama's history and spirit of civil rights activism.

To explain the grammar of school discipline, we draw on literature from different fields—for example, research in the fields of education, sociology, criminal justice, developmental psychology, educational psychology, and others—and our work over the last five years with students and practitioners in Alabama public schools. In doing so, we reject explanations for racial discipline disparities that are localized to students, families, and communities. Black students do not misbehave more than white students. Black students' behaviors are not rooted in a "culture of poverty," nor are they a product of parents who "don't care" about education. There is nothing innate about Black students that requires they receive harsher and more frequent discipline than their white peers. Explanations blaming Black students for their own punishment and removal are rooted in racist stereotypes about deficiency and inferiority, layered with presumptions about criminality, innocence, and intellect. At the core of this book is an invitation to our reader to examine their own explanations for school discipline outcomes, to identify how modes of thinking about students and families are constrained by the grammar of school discipline, and to situate those explanations and modes of thinking in Alabama's anti-Black historical and sociopolitical context. As we present these portraits of removal, resistance, and reform, we also invite our reader to consider who benefits from this grammar.

Introduction

Any Given Day in an Alabama Alternative School

Mr. Owlson: Ms. Block,[1] we've got too many sleepers.
Ms. Block: Yes, sir.
Mr. Owlson: Can we get those hoods removed so I can see who I'm looking at?
Ms. Block: Yes, sir.
Mr. Owlson: That student needs to sit up and take that hood off his head.
Ms. Block: Yes, sir.
A few minutes lapse.
Mr. Owlson: Ms. Block, let me see that student with the hood in the front office.
Ms. Block: Whitmore?
Mr. Owlson: The one who's got the grey hood on . . . the one who's sleeping. I need to see him.
Ms. Block: Yes, sir, he's headed that way.

We overheard this chatter on the walkie-talkie system as we arrived to our classroom at the alternative school, a place like many in Alabama where students are sent as punishment for disciplinary incidents, removed from their traditional schools and the instruction, social interaction, and extracurriculars therein. Alternative schools are often students' last stop before being pushed out of school altogether. We were engaged in ongoing instruction in an agriscience class, working to develop students' critical consciousness and action research skills around issues of food systems and food security. At the school, all teachers were required to have their radios on at all times, and all broadcasts were made over a single general channel in the school. This meant that all teachers and all students heard all broadcasts, all day. Most of the broadcasts came from the building principal, who monitored classrooms, via a series of cameras, on a TV screen in the front office.

In broadcasting this message, the principal used two technologies—one visual, one aural—to control and to publicly shame both the student and the teacher. The conjunction of the video camera system and the radio broadcasts functioned not only as a form of student surveillance but also as a reminder that everyone was being watched, including teachers. In these moments of surveillance, it became apparent that there was no safe place for the teacher or the student, as this type of surveillance serves to decrease the sense of safety that students, and particularly students of Color, feel in schools (Johnson et al. 2018). Moreover, the linkages created among the administrator, the camera, and the walkie-talkie made impossible the relational foundation on which a classroom functions. There was no room, in this space, for the interactions that might have needed to occur between teacher and student, interactions that would have allowed the teacher to establish and maintain rapport with students in meaningful ways. There was also no opportunity for communication among students.

During class changes, when students were prompted to line up single file in the hallway as they moved from room to room, we heard continual verbal reprimand of students for wearing hoods or sagging pants and for talking in the hallway, talking in the classroom, talking in the lunchroom, talking at all. We noted the common practice throughout the semester of students sent home for the so-called disciplinary incidents like nose rings, possession of cell phones, talking back, talking, laughing, crying, existing in the wrong place at the wrong time (e.g., in the hallway on the way to the restroom, outside of their designated classrooms), many of which were captured and punished via this system of surveillance: the administrator, his cameras, and his walkie-talkie.

As Whitmore, a Black teenager wearing locs and a gray Alabama hoodie, walked up to the front office from Ms. Block's class, he paused to stick his head in our classroom and smile. A few students smiled back, waved, or gave him a head nod. We prepared to venture outside into the school garden, exiting our classroom into the hallway and passing a group of elementary school-aged students lined up to go to the bathroom, almost all of whom were Black children. They whispered to one another, giggling and fidgeting, as young children do. They waited along the wall as the teacher instructed them: "Remember your ducktails." The children placed their hands behind their backs, palms up, fingers wiggling, meant, ostensibly, to mimic the movements of a duck wagging its tail feathers. Hands behind their backs, palms up, fingers out. Hands behind their backs...

We rounded the corner and headed up to the front of the school, where we saw Whitmore speaking with not only the principal but also the School Resource Officer (SRO)—the police officer who was on duty at the school that day. They stood near the front office and talked: the principal asking why he was wearing his hood up, the SRO telling him he needed to "straighten up or else . . ." and Whitmore protesting that he was tired, that schoolwork was boring, and nobody cared if he did it anyway.

We'd been wrapped up in the dramas and dreams of students at this alternative school, an open secret in the school system, almost invisible on the public-facing school system website but widely known to community members. Over the past several semesters, we'd listened to students' stories of their teenage lives: weekend and after-school events including walks to the store for soda and candy and parties with local rappers and grandparents. They discussed cycles, abortions, births, contraception. They described a mother's cancer, operation, and chemo treatments; an uncle's (cousin's, father's, brother's, friend's) death by gun violence; a custody battle, with an adoptive mother, for one student's own child. Students expressed the thrill of a new job at the barbeque joint, the satisfaction of payday, and the goals of saving for their "own place." They told of their child's seizures and endless doctors' appointments. They divulged the secrets of a life in foster care, uncertainty, and angry outbursts resulting from being bounced to three foster placements in the course of one semester, all with a toddler in tow. They delighted in newfound interests in planting, watering, and tending crops of tomato plants and some ridiculously spicy ghost peppers special ordered from a catalog. They dwelled on the events that led them to this school, full of "bad kids." They wished they could attend theatre class, football games, proms. Their desire to take back whatever perceived disciplinary incident had occurred, to have a redo, another chance, was the frequent topic of conversation. They regretted, they blamed, they sensed and named the injustices that had led them to the school. They took responsibility for disciplinary incidents that, in our view, should never have warranted a placement at an alternative school—"defiant," "disorderly," "disobedient" behavior, not worthy of disciplinary consequences. And ultimately, they atoned, in this "bad school" full of worksheets, online credit recovery modules, points sheets to reward and punish based on perceptions about behavior, fights, silence, surveillance, and ever-present criticism from those who were "in charge."

On any given school day, thousands of Alabama public school students are removed for school discipline incidents. They may be sitting in school sites devoted to in-school suspension, suspended or expelled out of school in their homes and neighborhoods, in alternative education placements, or incarcerated in youth development centers, juvenile justice facilities, or adult prisons. Regardless of their spatial or geographical location, these students have been functionally removed from their regular classroom contexts, including their teachers and peers.

OVERVIEW

In this book, we explore this removal by drawing on and narrativizing several sources of numeric school discipline data retrieved from the Alabama State Department of Education (ALSDE) website; data provided to us from ALSDE; and data retrieved from the Office of Civil Rights (OCR) Data Collection website. These narratives paint a bleak picture of school discipline policies and practices in Alabama. We juxtapose devastating patterns in the numeric data with the richness of narrative data presented in the form of portraits that evidence our "search for goodness" (Lawrence-Lightfoot 1983, 23) and our desire not to become complicit in the same ethos of removal that we critique. We also use these portraits to define the other parts of the grammar of school discipline—the resistance and reform that are ever-present in public schools in Alabama. Portraiture affords us the opportunity to add depth and dimension to the dismal gestalt of school discipline in Alabama, as revealed in the publicly available numeric data and the data not publicly disclosed, together with the details of both heartbreaking and cheerful individual experiences (Lawrence-Lightfoot and Davis 1997). We zoom in to specific contexts and individuals, drawing on data that are intimate and writing that is impressionistic, to offer portraits of the particular. These portraits enable us to examine how students and school leaders navigate and resist oppressive school discipline policies and practices and how community members, school leaders, and legal advocates partner together in efforts to reform school discipline in Alabama.

We intend these portraits to also prompt reconsideration of the tendency to position students unidimensionally as only marginalized and victimized by the policies and practices of school discipline; our portraits also reveal their joy, capability, resistance, and resilience. Likewise, our portraits of school-based practitioners defy a unilateral positioning of them as complicit and villainous; we position them also as resistant and transformative. In this way, we pursue a nuanced and complex treatment of the grammar of school discipline in Alabama. Portraiture affords us the opportunity to emphasize how students, educational practitioners, and stakeholders, indeed all people, can be agentic and provocative in their respective contexts. We hope these portraits "provoke readers, participants, and ourselves into reevaluating our respective points of view." We consider our efforts in portraiture to be "a small but meaningful form of social justice" (Chapman 2007, 159).

Throughout the book, we use critical theories to frame and focus on a number of ideas: that Black students are simultaneously surveilled, adultified, infantilized, brutalized, and dehumanized as they are removed. We explain how these ideas can exist in tandem with one another, as they are long-standing and deep-rooted, created and perpetuated by a system of white supremacy, a system that protects white racial domination by whatever, even contradictory, means necessary. These ideas and arguments are not new; before us come many scholars of Color and abolitionists who have laid the groundwork for what we weave together in this book to frame our analysis of the grammar of discipline in Alabama. We also engage in self-portraiture to trouble our position as white scholars who are engaged in work with and about Black students and practitioners, exploring the tensions we navigated while conducting research and teaching the students and practitioners about whom we have written.

At the onset of this book, we want to make clear that we are committed to the idea and ideal of public education. As participants and stakeholders in that system, our critique is not aimed at individual teachers or administrators. We do not wish to vilify school-based practitioners—we are school-based practitioners—despite our hope that this text will catalyze rethinking school-based practices. Nor is our aim to "narrow the problem [of school discipline] to bad schools or flawed policies" (Meiners 2016, 10). Rather, our aim is to push and nurture public education toward its ideals by inquiring into and contextualizing the processes of removal, amplifying the voices of removed students and school leaders who resist efforts to remove students. We do this so readers might hear their voices, imagine their experiences, and be motivated to take transformative action in schools. We highlight community efforts toward reform to emphasize the solidarity possible when community stakeholders organize and come together to advocate for themselves and one another, and we imagine what might be accomplished through efforts to repair the harms done by the grammar of school discipline.

Readers, particularly those who are school-based practitioners, can anticipate an opportunity to reflect on and render visible the elements and functions of the grammar of school discipline: the taken-for-granted, routinized policies and practices in their own contexts. For example, under what conditions are students like Whitmore removed from their regular classrooms and peers? How are students, particularly Black students, stereotyped, adultified, criminalized, and dehumanized to justify harsh or exclusionary discipline? How does surveillance function as a mechanism to identify which students are to be removed, and how is that surveillance connected to stereotypes about race? And, who benefits when large numbers of students are removed from Alabama schools?

We encourage practitioners, who take up this text, to engage in scrutiny and careful thinking about what constitutes student (mis)behavior and to distinguish it from the predictable behavior of children and adolescents. For instance, when, if ever, should dress code and uniform violations, profanity, or hearty laughter in the hallway be treated as punishable? And, when students do enact behaviors that are commonly understood to be problematic, might they be doing so in efforts to resist harmful and oppressive policies and practices, including discipline, but also ineffective and irrelevant curriculum and instruction? In other words, how might behaviors that are regularly characterized as defiant, disobedient, and disruptive be reframed as productive resistance on the part of students? What might Whitmore have been communicating in wearing his hood up, or putting his head down on his desk? Teachers could have a significant impact on the application of discipline by making commitments to understanding the ways that stereotypes about students inform their perceptions about student behavior. School administrators could be instrumental in helping to reframe student (mis)behavior as everyday acts of resistance and communication, encouraging anti-removal commitments in their respective school contexts.

We hope that readers will use this text as an opportunity to cultivate vocabulary and bravery to speak out about anti-Black racism and the removal of Black students from classrooms and schools and make moves toward repair. Efforts toward reform, such as the alternative school placement that Whitmore received in lieu of suspension or expulsion, must be analyzed for their perpetuation of inequities in schooling—the very things we say we want to avoid when designing and implementing reforms. We also hope readers will take up broader questions about the ways in which the idealized purposes of education—critical thinking, engaged citizenry, an informed body politic, and maybe even the possibility of revolution—are eroded by privileging compliance, conformity, and quietude. We cannot at once hope for education that meets the needs of all students *and* defer or deny education to some via discipline.

Finally, we hope that readers will join us in thinking about repair: the redress of harms that have been done to students via their removal, the rejection of their resistance, and perpetual efforts at reform, in addition to the repair of our humanity and the humanity of schools. When practitioners enact anti-Black racism, the injuries do not just affect Black people; practitioners also harm our own humanity and the institutions we serve. By enacting oppression, we deprive ourselves of our full humanity (Matias 2016). Moreover, discipline, surveillance, and punishment are not humanizing ideas. They are not natural. Rather, they are learned, cultural, and particular. Ultimately, those ideas are premised on preserving a hierarchy; we punish some to the benefit of others.

NOTE

1. All names of counties, cities, school systems, schools, and individuals, with the exception of the authors, are pseudonyms.

Part I
REMOVAL

Chapter 1

Methods of Removal (*with Nicholas P. Triplett*)

In Alabama, large numbers of students are removed from their regular classrooms and schools every day, sometimes for many days at a time (OCR n.d.; PARCA 2020). Removal, in the context of school discipline policies and practices in Alabama, occurs in public schools when students are suspended from their classrooms, either in-school settings or outside-of-school settings; when they are expelled from their schools for a semester or more; when they are referred to alternative schools which may be geographically remote and removed from community centers (Baggett and Andrzejewski 2017), where students sometimes complete online, credit-recovery modules in lieu of face-to-face instruction (Baggett and Andrzejewski 2020a), and where students face stringent rules about silence and compliance (Anderson and Baggett 2020). Removal also happens when students are referred to law enforcement officials, including those who may be stationed in their schools (i.e., School Resource Officers or SROs), for things that happen at school; arrested for school-based incidents; and when they are taken out of classrooms to be paddled or otherwise disciplined using corporal punishment (OCR 2016). Scholars characterize these practices as "exclusionary discipline," which has severe, deleterious effects on students, families, and communities, especially communities of Color (Noltemeyer and McLoughlin 2010; Skiba, Arredondo, and Williams 2014; U.S. Department of Education 2018; USGAO 2018). In this chapter we highlight increased use of these kinds of consequences for what may once have been considered normal student (mis)behavior that is increasingly criminalized in schools, and for student conduct misinterpreted as misbehavior, aligning what we know nationally about the racialized nature of school discipline with trends in Alabama. We take particular interest in ways that students are punished via exclusionary practices for (mis)perceived incidents and the ways that Black students, in particular, are affected by these practices. In the following chapter, we explore explanations for this removal as an extension of a historically rooted legacy of removal in the Deep South. In the final chapter in this part, we render an account of one school system in Alabama where removal is routine.

OBJECTIVE AND SUBJECTIVE INCIDENTS

Extant research regarding different kinds of disciplinary infractions supports distinguishing between those student behaviors and corresponding incident labels that researchers define as *objective* and those they define as *subjective*, or "vaguely defined, *more* open to individual interpretation, and dependent on the tolerance and perceptions of the adult who is witnessing and reporting the behavior" (Theriot and Dupper 2010, 207; emphasis added). Objective disciplinary incidents include possession of weapons or drugs, for which there are often zero tolerance policies in place. Decades of research connect the implementation of zero tolerance policies with an increase in exclusionary discipline, with scholars noting that these types of policies do little to impact the rates of violence at school (American Psychological Association Zero Tolerance Task Force 2008; Curran 2016; Skiba and Peterson 2000). These policies have been so heavily critiqued that many school systems have retracted them (Lacoe and Steinberg 2018). Other types of disciplinary offenses, categorized as subjective in much of the scholarship about school discipline, include incidents for which there are no incontrovertible, tangible forms of evidence, such as disobedience, insubordination, defiance, and disruption. Irby (2018) explains:

> Most school administrations use a combination of two overarching approaches to establishing discipline policies and practices. One approach . . . is to apply severe consequences to high-level incidents such as fighting, drugs, and weapons possessions. . . . Yet teachers spend most of their day-to-day discipline efforts addressing low-level, often subjective disciplinary incidents . . . interactions [which] require adults to regulate dress and appearance (Morris 2005), promote adherence to traditional authority and social mores (e.g., reduce use of profanity), mitigate academic complacency (e.g., refusal to complete work), deter noneducative uses of cellphones and social media technologies, and reduce hallway hanging. (Skiba et al. 2002, 696)

It has been widely reported that incidents considered subjective are disproportionately assigned to students of Color, and particularly Black students, and that subjective incidents largely account for the racial disparities in school discipline in the United States (Annamma et al. 2020; Blake et al.

2011; Forsyth et al. 2015; Girvan et al. 2017; Gregory, Bell, and Pollock 2014; Gregory and Weinstein 2008; Public Counsel 2015; Skiba et al. 2002, 2014; Wentzel 2002). There is no evidence to suggest that Black students misbehave more, or are more defiant, disruptive or disorderly than their white peers, and there is clear evidence to the contrary, indicating that different racial/ethnic groups exhibit similar patterns and amounts of misbehavior (Finn, Fish, and Scott 2008; Gregory and Weinstein 2008; Huang 2020). When racial/ethnic differences in (mis)behavior have been detected, those differences have been insufficient to explain the magnitude of racial/ethnic discipline disparities (Eitle and Eitle 2004; Peguero and Shekarkhar 2011; Skiba and Williams 2014; Wallace, Goodkind, Wallace, and Bachman 2008). Moreover, both objective and subjective discipline are entangled with racial stereotyping, such that there are no behaviors that school-based practitioners can assess objectively. These stereotypes become even clearer when accounting for Black students' narratives about their experiences with disciplinary consequences (see, e.g., the counternarratives provided by Gibbs Grey and Harrison 2020, as well as McElrath et al. 2020).

While racial stereotypes exist for all students, we take particular note of the ways profiling and criminalization of Black students happens. Black students in public schools are more likely to be accused of committing disciplinary infractions, more likely to be punished, and more likely to experience harsh and exclusionary consequences (U.S. Department of Education 2018; USGAO 2018). Black people are surveilled and criminalized on highways, in stores, in community spaces, at universities, indeed, even in neighborhoods (e.g., "shopping, driving, swimming, napping, studying, residing, etc. while Black"). This surveillance and criminalization is historically rooted (Muhammad 2010). In schools, Black students are similarly surveilled and criminalized. Despite there being no evidence indicating Black students bring weapons or drugs to school at rates higher than their white peers, because Black students are more likely to be surveilled and profiled (Ferguson 2001; Noguera 2009), they may be more likely to be caught for these so-called objective incidents. Teachers often interpret Black students' behaviors as oppositional or defiant (Allen and White-Smith 2014; Gregory and Weinstein 2008; Wentzel 2002). Research suggests that, when asked to look for student misbehavior, teachers are more likely to monitor Black boys (Gilliam et al. 2016).

Research about school discipline and its consequences, perhaps especially research about the school-to-prison pipeline, is often focused on Black boys. Black girls also experience the harsh consequences of school discipline at the intersection of racism and sexism (Annamma et al. 2019; Blake and Butler 2011; Gibbs Grey and Harrison 2020; Harrison 2017), experience hypersurveillance and sexualization (Townsend et al. 2010), and are often traumatized and pushed out of schools via disciplinary practices (Hines-Datiri and Carter Andrews 2020; Morris 2016; Walker, Matias, and Brandehoff 2017). Nonbinary and genderqueer Black students also face harsh disciplinary consequences and contexts (Bellinger et al. 2016; Morgan et al. 2014; Snapp et al. 2015), as do queer Black students (Bellinger et al. 2016; Kosciw et al. 2018), with research suggesting that peer victimization plays a role in disciplinary consequences (Palmer and Greytak 2017). According to a GLSEN report, almost 45 percent of Black LGBTQ students reported some type of disciplinary consequence in the 2017 National School Climate Survey (NSCS), including detention and exclusionary consequences like out-of-school suspension and expulsion (Truong, Zongrone, and Kosciw 2020).

Scholars have argued that practitioners are more likely to report Black students for offenses such as defiance based on the influence of "troublemaker" stereotypes of Black students (Okonofua and Eberhardt 2015). Cultural stereotypes about Black people as criminal and dangerous (Muhammed 2010) also inform school-based practitioners' interactions with students (Okonofua, Walton, and Eberhardt 2016), as do stereotypes of Black children with "absent fathers" (Owens and McLanahan 2020), who "sag their pants" (Gregory and Fergus 2017), or who have stereotypically "Black names" (Okonofua and Eberhardt 2015). There are higher suspension rates in schools where leaders attribute student discipline issues to deficit thinking about poverty and "poor parenting" (Rausch and Skiba 2005). Further complicating racial disproportionality in the use of exclusionary discipline is that school leaders are loathe to engage in conversations about race and racism (Khalifa and Briscoe 2015; McMahon 2007).

Also contributing to discriminatory discipline are stereotypes about white students as "inherently innocent" (Diamond and Lewis 2019, 838). In other words, even though discipline policies and practices are written and enacted under the premise of objectivity and "colorblindness"[1] (Kennedy, Acosta, and Soutullo 2019, 130), there can be no objectivity in school discipline when the judgments of school-based authority figures (whether incidents are labeled subjective or objective) are experienced through the filters of racial stereotypes. Stereotypes about Black students mean they are more persistently and closely surveilled than their white peers and their behavior and demeanor are likely to be interpreted as problematic and deviant. Thus, the pretense of objectivity is used as a tool to direct attention away from racialized, inequitable treatment. Labeling disciplinary incidents as objective thus serves to camouflage the racialized nature of identifying and punishing Black students.

In Alabama, practitioners are charged with categorizing disciplinary incidents listed and defined in a statewide glossary. Intended to guide practitioners in recognizing and naming student (mis)behavior (see table 1.1 for a list), definitions of what constitutes each classification of behavior,

Table 1.1 All School Incidents Defined and Collected by the Alabama State Department of Education*

State-Defined Incidents	Subjective Offenses
Alcohol possession—sale/transfer—use	
Arson	
Assault	
Bomb threat	
Burglary/Breaking and entry	
Criminal mischief (vandalism)	
Defiance of authority	x
Disobedience—persistent, willful	x
Disorderly conduct (other than those listed)	x
Disruptive demonstrations	x
Drugs other than alcohol and tobacco possession—sale/transfer—use	
Electronic pager/unauthorized communication device	
Fighting	
Fire alarm, tampering with or setting off	
Gambling	
Harassment (Note: Bullying reported here)	
Homicide (on school campus)	
Inciting other students to create a disturbance	x
Kidnapping	
Larceny/theft/possession of stolen property	
Motor vehicle theft or unauthorized use	
Profanity/vulgarity	x
Robbery	
Sexual battery	
Sexual harassment	
Sexual offense	
Threats/intimidation (other than bomb)	x
Tobacco possession—sale/transfer—use	
Trespassing	
Truancy/unauthorized absence	
Weapon possession—sale/transfer—use	
Other incidents **	x

Notes: * All descriptions taken verbatim from the State Department of Education School Incident Report (SIR) Resource Guide—Overview and Major Reporting Elements (2010).
** Other incidents—"any offense which are not enumerated in the SIR which were a violation of local board of education policy and resulted in one or more SDE-defined disciplinary actions."

or incident, vary across teachers, administrators, schools, and systems. The ways that practitioners categorize and code behaviors, as well as available consequences for each incident, vary widely across schools (Anderson and Ritter 2020; McElrath et al. 2020), and, in our experience, even within schools. Indeed, "the act of interpreting and coding referrals, which determines how incidents get recorded on students' permanent records and informs future educators' perceptions of the students, depends completely on the judgment of the person writing and reading the referral" (Kennedy, Acosta, and Soutullo 2019, 139).

Further complicating these practices that push students out of school is that, despite the separation of incidents into classes (often referred to as Class I, Class II, and Class III violations, or Class A, B, C, etc., which mirror the ways that misdemeanors and felonies are classified in legal and penal systems), the same consequences might be enacted upon students for subjective or objective incidents that are categorized differently. Inconsistent alignment between class of incident and severity of consequence introduces another vulnerable time point in the discipline process for Black students. For example, a student might receive days of in-school suspension for a dress code violation (a Class I Minor Violation in some places), for defiance (also a Class I violation), and also for fighting or disobedience (both Class II Intermediate Violations).

Taken together, the disproportionate assignment of disciplinary incidents to Black students and the ratcheting up of exclusionary disciplinary consequences have created a culture of removal of Black students in the United States, and in Alabama, public schools. In the following section, we offer an overview of the nature, history, and consequences of exclusionary school discipline writ large.

EXCLUSIONARY DISCIPLINE

To restate, exclusionary school discipline punishes students for (mis)behavior by removing them from the classroom via in-school and out-of-school suspension, expulsions, referral to and placement in alternative schools, and referral to law enforcement. We also consider corporal punishment policies and practices, widely used in Alabama, to be exclusionary since practitioners remove students from their classrooms and then inflict physical violence on them. A large body of research literature has established a relationship between exclusionary discipline and a host of negative outcomes in school and beyond (Fabelo et al. 2011; Noltemeyer, Ward, and McLoughlin 2015; Nicholson-Crotty, Birchmeier, and Valentine 2009). Research has documented relationships among disciplinary exclusion, denied academic instruction (Noguera 2008), lower academic achievement (Arcia 2006; Cobb-Clark et al. 2015; Gregory, Skiba, and Noguera 2010; Raffaele-Mendez 2003; Skiba and Rausch 2004), increased dropout (American Academy of Pediatrics 2013; American Psychological Association 2008) and grade retention (Balfanz, Byrnes, and Fox 2014; Marchbanks et al. 2013; Suh and Suh 2007), and increased interaction with law enforcement and the juvenile justice system (Fabelo et al. 2011; Skiba et al. 2014). Exclusionary discipline is also linked to detriments to students socially, emotionally, and behaviorally; impairment of relationships with school adults (Anyon, Zhang, and Hazel 2016; Christie, Nelson, and Jolivette 2004); and damaging effects on schools and the school environment (Kupchik and Ward 2014; Perry and Morris 2014). Finally, exclusionary discipline has long-term economic, social, and behavioral consequences for students (Marchbanks et al. 2013; Wolf and Kupchik 2017), for mothers (Powell and Coles 2020), and for families (Kupchik 2016).

Below, we briefly review a chronology of exclusionary discipline policies and practices. Before doing so, we wish to be clear that although the form of disciplinary removal shifts over time, the basic premise remains the same: remove some students from schools for the benefit of others. Given the steady presence and persistent use of exclusionary tactics across Alabama public schools, we argue that exclusion, or removal, is part of the grammar of school discipline: that which defines policies and practices of school-based discipline in taken-for-granted ways.

A Chronology of Exclusionary Discipline

Exclusionary discipline practices are long-standing, deep-rooted, and connected to regimentation and oppression embedded in schools. As Tyack (1976) explains, the adoption and enforcement of compulsory schooling between the mid-eighteenth century and the mid-nineteenth century brought expectations that students serve certain roles as they assimilated into the culture of schools and into broader, already defined societal roles. Compulsory schooling was touted as a way to socialize youth in ways that parents were failing to, especially those families who were poor or who were viewed as immigrants or racialized others. In the latter half of the nineteenth century, discipline and criminalization of those students who failed to attend school became commonplace (Gleich-Bope 2014), giving rise to the new roles of truancy officers and counselors (Tyack and Berkowitz 1977), and establishing a clear connection between educational and court systems (Monahan, VanDerhei, Bechtold, and Cauffman 2014). The norms of compulsory schooling were born of particular views about religion, history, language, and values, but "all children were required to fit" into this framework (Sensoy and DiAngelo 2017, 166). Thus, ironically, students were and still are coerced into attending school, but punished via exclusionary means once there if deemed unfit or defying the dominant norms of schooling.

Although the particular forms of exclusion have shifted over time, removal has shown itself to be omnipresent in schools. Some theorize that the rise of suspensions, for example, began in the 1960s and 1970s with school desegregation orders and subsequent increases of fighting among students (Palmer 2013). There is no doubt, however, that the use of suspensions and expulsions increased dramatically with the rise of zero tolerance policies in the mid-1990s. These policies became intricately woven into schooling contexts due to a confluence of sociopolitical events and subsequent legislation, deemed a "punitive turn" in the ways U.S. society approaches policy and people (Nolan 2011). Schools, increasingly militarized (Robbins 2008; Saltman and Gabbard 2003) and prisonlike (Meiners 2011), now serve as sites where police officers work in tandem with security and surveillance technologies to control and discipline students (for compelling accounts of the wide reach of the security industry into public schools, see Cassella 2003b; Robbins 2008). These systems socialize and prepare students for a carceral, surveillance state (Meiners 2007), encouraging compliance and docility rather than critically involved citizenship (Kupchik 2010).

This punitive turn may have begun with the escalation of the War on Drugs (also characterized as a "War on our Own People," Fornili 2018) during the 1980s and 1990s. Alarmist rhetoric about crime and drugs stoked fears across the United States. Images of gang-filled hallways, graffiti, fights, and drug deals in schools saturated the media and pop culture. Amid this context, the passage of the Drug-Free Schools Act in 1986 set the stage for institution of zero tolerance of any drugs and alcohol on school grounds. The Violent Crime Control and Enforcement Act of 1994 began to lend financial support, and incentives, to school systems to employ school-based police. The Gun-Free Schools Act in 1995 linked funding for education to the enactment of zero tolerance policies, including mandatory expulsion for students who brought weapons to school. At the same time, a prominent Princeton professor (Dilulio 1995) conjured the idea of the juvenile "superpredator," predisposed to criminal activity including drug use and distribution, assault, rape, and gang affiliation (Bennett, Dilulio, and Walters 1996, 27). This mythical persona (Jennings 2014), largely assigned to young Black men, was taken up and recycled by the media and adopted in criminal justice and legal circles to justify harsh treatment of youth. The myth of the superpredator added to the "moral panic" (Farmer 2010) around dangerous youth and thus solidified a shift in ideology, policy, and practice from rehabilitation to criminalization and punishment of youth. Zero tolerance policies in schools began to proliferate across the country (Stinchcomb, Bazemore, and Riestenberg 2006), whereas once they "required predetermined, nonnegotiable punishments for specific acts of misbehavior . . . [they] morphed into a broad, sweeping set of harsh disciplinary practices that exclude children from learning for a range of misbehaviors, even the most trivial" (Browne-Dianis 2011, 25). Students find themselves in more trouble for minor incidents than they ever have before, caught in what has been termed a "net deepening" effect (Irby 2013).

The mass shooting at Columbine High School in 1999 fueled the expansion of more punitive approaches to student behavior, including a greater use of exclusionary discipline as consequences and the increased presence of school-based police (Addington 2019). Though pre-Columbine legislation established the place of police in schools (Mallett 2016), the Department of Justice began "COPS in Schools" programs in the 1990s, generating an influx of funding for more school-based police (Vitale 2017) and further contributing to carceral and punitive school climates. The general public's fears about unsafe schools grew in the wake of Columbine and have continued with other school shootings like those at Sandy Hook Elementary School and Marjory Stoneman Douglas High in Parkland. The responses to these tragedies have included a growing number and increasingly escalated calls by some educational stakeholders for even more surveillance and armed police in schools, met with resistance from youth organizers in the campaign for #policefreeschools. In Alabama, the COPS program has granted funds to police units for decades, and as recently as July of 2020, to support and sustain the expansion of SRO programs in schools (DOJ 2020). Some, including legislators in Alabama, have even called for arming school administrators and teachers (Mazzei 2019), an idea nearly three-quarters of teachers oppose (Brenan 2018).

Consequences of Exclusionary Discipline

Punitive, exclusionary approaches are often favored by the public because they are seen to keep order in schools and to ostensibly keep children safe (Noguera 1995), paralleling a tough-on-crime approach in U.S. sociopolitical rhetoric. They are also perceived by some to be cheaper, faster, and more effective than approaches premised on restructuring school climates and cultures, relationship building with students and communities, and remediation for students. School security and punishment, including the use of SROs, are actually quite costly (e.g., see Kupchik 2016; Langberg, Fedders, and Kukorowski 2011) and happen at the expense of the well-being of students and their families. Evidence suggests that even students who are not directly disciplined suffer in school environments where exclusionary practices are the norm (for a review of the "collateral consequences of exclusionary punishment," see Perry and Morris 2014). Finally, accountability measures tying school funding and teachers' salaries to students' test scores have led some to posit that exclusionary discipline functions to expediently remove underperforming students (Bryk et al. 1998; Fuentes 2003).

Punitive approaches, including exclusionary discipline and school-based policing implemented in the wake of violence committed by white students (Addington 2019; Triplett, Allen, and Lewis 2014), have devastating impacts for students of Color and particularly for Black students. There is ample evidence that exclusionary discipline is, at its heart, an anti-Black project. National trends support this conclusion, indicating not only that teachers and administrators attribute more disciplinary incidents to students of Color but also that Black students are disproportionately removed from classrooms and excluded from instruction through suspension, expulsion, and referral to alternative schools due to those disciplinary attributions. Black students receive harsher punishments of all types of exclusionary discipline, for less serious incidents than their white peers (USGAO 2018). These trends are consistent across the United States, despite the fact that all student groups, regardless of race or ethnicity, exhibit similar levels of (mis) behavior (Finn, Fish and Scott 2008; Huang 2020; Kupchik and Ward 2011; Rocque 2010; Wallace et al. 2008). Black students are also more likely to receive corporal punishment in schools (Whitaker and Losen 2019), especially in those areas where Black people were lynched (Ward et al. 2019). These discipline disparities (Whitford, Katsiyannis, and Counts 2016) are so great that, in a study of 70,000 school districts in the United States, researchers determined Black students to be more than three times more likely than white students to be suspended or expelled (U.S. Department of Education, Office for Civil Rights 2012). Zero tolerance policies in schools exacerbate the sheer amount of exclusionary discipline and the degree to which exclusionary discipline is disproportionately applied to Black students (Hoffman 2014), in addition to increased surveillance by SROs and surveillance technology. In recent years, some school districts have reconsidered zero tolerance policies and their catastrophic impacts on the life trajectories of the students they punish (Ward and Delessert 2014). Exclusionary policies and practices remain in place, however, in many schools across the United States including in Alabama.

In the following sections, we provide an overview of the specific methods used to remove students from their classrooms and schools in Alabama, drawing specifically on disciplinary school incident data for the 2015–2016 academic year, a year during which Alabama public schools enrolled 743,893 students in grades K-12. The Alabama State Department of Education (ALSDE) made detailed reports of the 2015–2016 academic year available to us. These reports provided evidence of the relationships between types of disciplinary incidents and consequences, and the Office of Civil Rights (OCR) issued reports detailing relationships among student demographics and disciplinary consequences. We describe each type of exclusionary discipline and the consequences thereof, examine the incidents for which it was used as a punishment, and describe how its use disproportionately affected Black students.

SUSPENSIONS

Suspending students from their classrooms is a routine response to disciplinary incidents across the United States (Christie et al. 2004). Students may be required to attend an in-school suspension room or wing of the school, or they may be sent out of school for some length of time. Out-of-school suspension practices were critiqued as early as the 1970s, with detractors arguing that out-of-school suspension pushed students out of school (Nielson 1979); these critiques gave rise to the use of in-school suspension as an alternative. Most troubling about these practices is that the removal of students from their schools and classrooms—whether via out-of-school or in-school suspension—has no bearing on improving school safety or changing student behavior (Losen and Skiba 2010). The practice of suspension also decreases student achievement (Anderson, Ritter, and Zamarro 2019) and increases the likelihood that students drop out of school (Balfanz et al. 2014), which one might intuit given that students are unable to fully learn and connect if they are not physically in class with their teachers and peers. The relationship between exclusionary discipline and noncompletion of high school has been characterized as school "pushout" (Morris 2016), as practices like in-school suspension and out-of-school suspension send messages to students that they do not belong in class. These messages are devastating, since "among the most valuable relational resource from which all students benefit is being fully desired by students, teachers, and families alike for their presence in school" (Irby 2014, 784). Students who are suspended are more likely to face additional suspensions (Raffaele Mendez 2003) and may also be more likely to be caught up in criminality—both criminal victimization and involvement in criminal activity—as adults (Wolf and Kupchik 2017). These findings indicate that suspensions should be abolished altogether in U.S. schools, yet teachers often support the use of suspensions, even calling for increases in implementation in some contexts (Will 2019).

Suspensions also take a toll on students' families, especially in the era of mass incarceration and the "criminalization of families" (Elliott and Reid 2019). About their work in one school system in Alabama, Kupchik and Mowen (2016) explain that parents of students who had been suspended or expelled described job difficulties and financial strain when they had to attend frequent meetings about their children at school, meetings that were often scheduled during the workday in central offices far from their homes. Families often felt obligated to miss work or pay someone, like a babysitter, to supervise their children who had been suspended out-of-school. Families explained the emotional toll of school punishment: sense of "failure as a parent" (65) and frustration at school-based practitioners for only seeing the "bad in their children" (66). Finally, families described a feeling of hopelessness, of "giving up" because they felt alienated from schools and school officials, and hostility in response to negative perceptions about them and their children (70).

Students across Alabama are routinely suspended for discipline incidents via both out-of-school and in-school suspension, and the use of out-of-school suspension in Alabama continues to be above the national average according to reporting by the OCR. As in nationwide disciplinary data, Alabama schools are more likely to suspend Black students than their white peers (Crain 2017). Numeric data from the OCR indicate that in Alabama schools during the 2015–2016 school year, 61,627 public school students (approximately 8 percent of all students enrolled in Alabama public schools) were suspended out of school. Of those, 40,276 were Black (approximately 65 percent). The total enrollment of Alabama school systems that reported using out-of-school suspension was approximately 33 percent Black that year, indicating that Black students were overrepresented in out-of-school suspension. In fact, of the 136 reporting school systems that used out-of-school suspension, 128 did so in ways that disproportionately affected Black students (i.e., the percent of suspensions assigned to Black students was larger than the percent of the enrollment that was Black). The disproportionality in 39 of those systems was more than double, suggesting that the discriminatory nature of the use of out-of-school suspension should be readily apparent to those working in the school systems. For example, in one Alabama public school system where the enrollment was approximately 24 percent Black, approximately 57 percent of the students suspended out-of-school were Black.

Likewise, OCR data show that Black students were overrepresented in in-school suspension. Whereas approximately 34 percent of the 725,653 students enrolled in Alabama public school systems that used in-school suspension as a consequence were Black, approximately 51 percent of the 59,856 students who experienced in-school suspension were Black. Moreover, 121 of the 130 systems that reported using in-school suspension did so in ways that disproportionately affected Black students, and 28 systems did so in ways that meant that the percent of in-school suspension assigned to Black students was more than double the percent of the system enrollment that was Black. For example, in one system where 491 (approximately 7 percent) of the 7,010 enrolled students were Black, 42 of the 104 (approximately 40 percent) students suspended in-school were Black.

Numeric data provided by the ALSDE indicate that the reasons for suspension vary widely, ranging from dress code violations and disobedience to fighting (see figure 1.1; subjective incidents are marked with an asterisk). Here, we focus in on those incidents that are related to perceptions about behavior, those broadly characterized as subjective (see table 1.1. for a list of all school-based disciplinary incidents in Alabama, including those that we consider subjective, which are consistent with the broader research literature). During the 2015–2016 school year, 118,816 of the 225,573 days of suspensions (approximately 53 percent), both in- and out-of-school, in

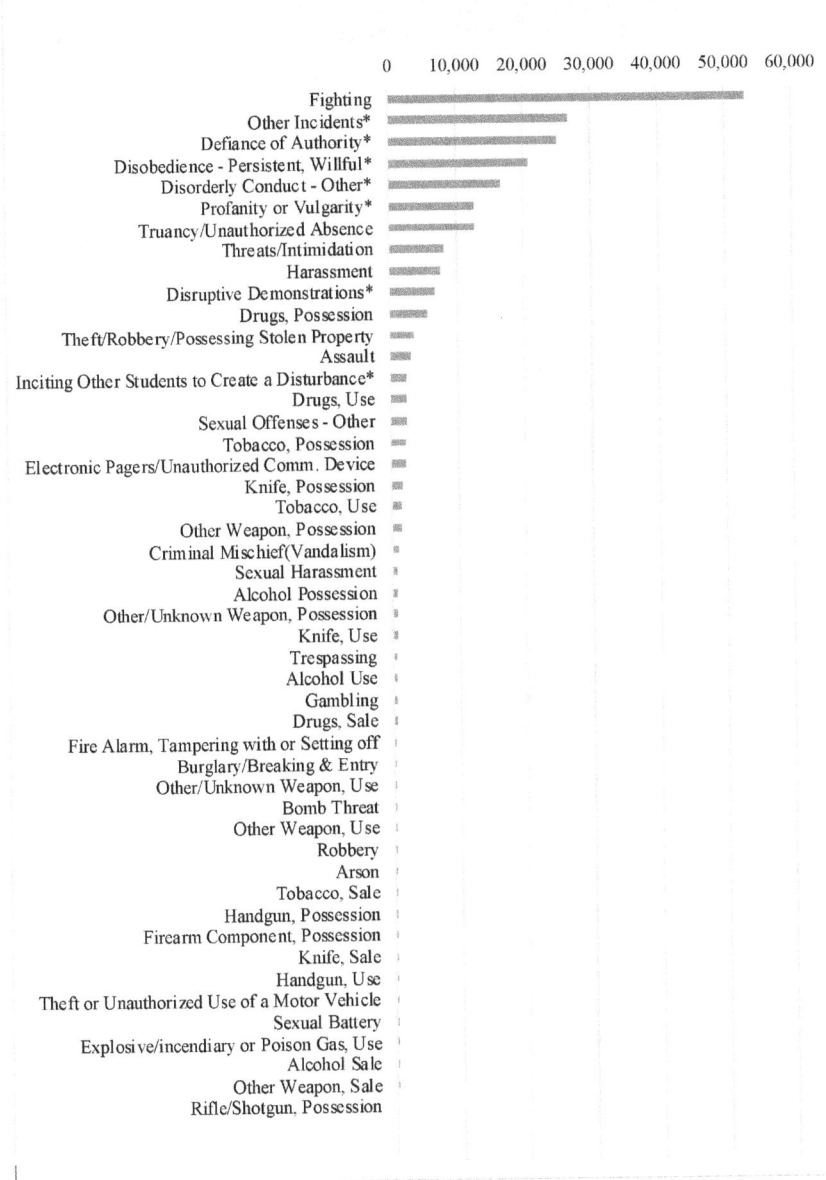

Figure 1.1   Number of Days of Suspension for Each State-Defined Incident in Alabama, 2015–2016. *Source:* Created by authors.

Alabama were for subjective incidents. Furthermore, five of the six most common incidents leading to suspensions were for incidents for which there are no zero tolerance policies; instead, they are incidents considered to be subjective. A challenge here is that, unlike the data available from the OCR, referenced above, which tell us which students are punished with in-school and out-of-school suspension, data provided to us or to the public from the ALSDE about incidents and suspensions in Alabama do not indicate which students are involved or any information about their identities. Instead, only days of suspensions are reported by incident. Days of in-school and out-of-school suspension are also combined, making us unable to determine how many and which students were consequenced in school or out of school for each type of incident. As previously stated, however, the extant literature is clear that removing students from classrooms and schools is detrimental, and educators' identification of subjective incidents is often bound up with negative stereotypes about Black youth. For example, Black students are often seen as defiant or disobedient (Skiba et al. 2002; Wentzel 2002) perhaps when exhibiting the same behaviors as their white peers such as talking back, critical thinking, questioning authority, or displaying skepticism in classroom settings. It is thus reasonable to infer that interpretations of comparable behaviors that differ because of students' race and then the disproportionate assignment of subjective incidents to Black students contribute to the discriminatory removal of Black students via suspension in Alabama.

EXPULSIONS

Though suspension and expulsion are often studied together, we draw a distinction here between these practices, defining expulsion as the removal from school for at least one semester. Expulsion from school often occurs in tandem with zero tolerance policies (Morrison and D'Incau 1997; Skiba and Rausch 2013); that is, students who commit certain incidents for which schools and school systems have zero tolerance are expelled. As earlier noted, legislation in the mid-1990s began to link mandatory expulsion for certain offenses, such as weapons on school grounds, to school funding. Many of the same detrimental effects from suspension occur—and are exacerbated by—expulsion as a disciplinary consequence, as it removes students from their classrooms and schools for even longer periods of time.

The 2015–2016 OCR report regarding school discipline in Alabama reveals that during that year, 3,677 students were expelled from school statewide. Data from the OCR do not shed light on what incidents were tied to these expulsions, but they do offer insight into who those students were. Of the 3,677 expelled students, 2,040 were Black, accounting for approximately

56 percent of the expulsions whereas Black students were only approximately 35 percent of total enrollment in the 89 school systems that used expulsion as a disciplinary consequence (594,567). Of those 89 systems, 69 had overrepresentation of Black students among those expelled, and in 23 school systems the rates of expulsion for Black students were disproportionate by a factor of two or more when compared to their share of the enrollment. In one system with 2,591 enrolled students, 832 (approximately 32 percent) of whom were Black, the system expelled 112 students, 80 (approximately 71 percent) of whom were Black.

The practice of expelling students for some incidents is troubling, raising questions, for instance, about whether students who are in possession of drugs at school should be denied a semester or more of instruction. In 2015–2016 in Alabama, according to the ALSDE, approximately 17 percent of all expulsions, the largest share for any single type of incident, were for drug possession. Similarly alarming is that some students were expelled for incidents related to perceptions about their behavior, considered subjective. During the 2015–2016 school year, 147 of the 485 expulsions (approximately 30 percent) in Alabama were for subjective incidents (see figure 1.2; subjective incidents are marked with an asterisk.). Each of the eight state-defined incidents we have characterized as subjective (see table 1.1) resulted in at least four, and as many as 43, expulsions that year. This rate of expulsion stemming from subjective incidents raises concerns similar to those we have already highlighted about suspensions, except that the negative consequences of expulsion are even more severe. The intersection of subjective incidents and expulsions points toward school-based practices that result in the removal of Black students in particular.

ALTERNATIVE SCHOOL PLACEMENTS

Alternative schools are often presented as options for students who experience difficulties in traditional K-12 school settings and who are labeled as at risk of dropping out (for a review of definitions of alternative education, see Porowski, O'Conner, and Luo 2014). Alternative education, however, also "mimics the traditional push-out mechanisms it was intended to react against: reinforcing inequality by promoting the control, exclusion, and imprisonment of marginalized youth" (Selman 2017, 214). Students across the country are increasingly referred to alternative schools (Lehr et al. 2009) in response to incidents for which they may have once been expelled under zero tolerance policies (Vanderhaar, Muñoz, and Petrosko 2014; Weissman 2015), such as drug possession, but also for being perceived as disruptive, disobedient, or deviant. Alternative education programming is also increasingly

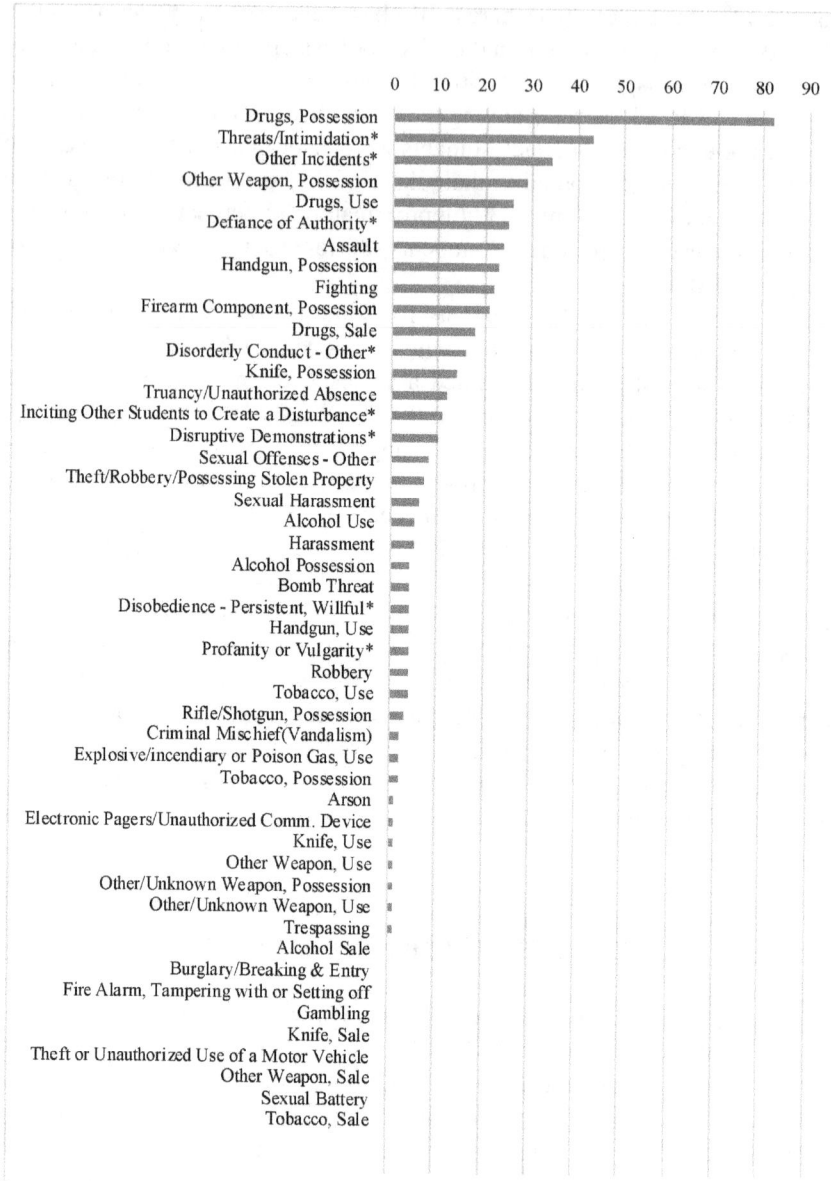

Figure 1.2   Number of Expulsions for Each State-Defined Incident in Alabama, 2015–2016. *Source*: Created by authors.

recommended for students who have been labeled as behaviorally and/or emotionally disabled (BED) (NCES 2002), though there is little evidence that these contexts better support students academically or behaviorally (Van Acker 2007) and the practice of diagnosing students in this way has been roundly critiqued.

Referrals to alternative schools and the development of new alternative schools have risen dramatically in the past two decades (Fedders 2017), and many alternative schools are composed almost exclusively of students of Color (Carver, Lewis, and Tice 2010; Vanderhaar et al. 2014). Increasingly, students are placed in alternative schools, where quality of instruction is often poor, because of the subjective determinations of teachers and school-based practitioners (Kennedy-Lewis, Whitaker, and Soutullo 2016). Students in alternative schools report that they feel stigmatized, that their teachers do not care about them, and that their ideas and perspectives are not valued (Baggett and Andrzejewski 2017); they often have difficulty returning to the schools from which they were removed (Kennedy et al. 2019).

National evidence of the prevalence of alternative school placements is mirrored in Alabama, where students were assigned 191,122 days of placement in alternative schools during the 2015–2016 academic year. Of those days, 87,007 (approximately 46 percent) were for incidents related to perceptions about student behavior, as opposed to drug or weapon possession, for example (see figure 1.3; subjective incidents are marked with an asterisk.). Note that even with the comprehensive list of state-defined incidents, the number of days of alternative school placement for "other" incidents was more than 28,000, the most days for any single incident, and every incident we have characterized as subjective resulted in thousands of days of alternative school placement statewide.

There are numeric data available from the OCR about which students were referred to alternative schools in Alabama in 2015–2016; however, many systems reported that no students were referred to alternative schools, even in systems for which we have firsthand knowledge of alternative school attendance. Even so, the federal OCR report indicates that 3,554 public school students were referred to alternative schools in Alabama during the 2015–2016 school year. Of those, 1,987 were Black (approximately 56 percent), but Black students constituted only approximately 37 percent of the total enrollment in school systems that reported using alternative school placements as a disciplinary consequence (61 systems with a total enrollment of 491,226). Of those 61 systems, 48 had overrepresentation of Black students among those sent to alternative schools; 19 systems had rates of referring Black students to alternative schools that more than doubled the rate of Black enrollment in the system. For example, in one Alabama system, where the enrollment was

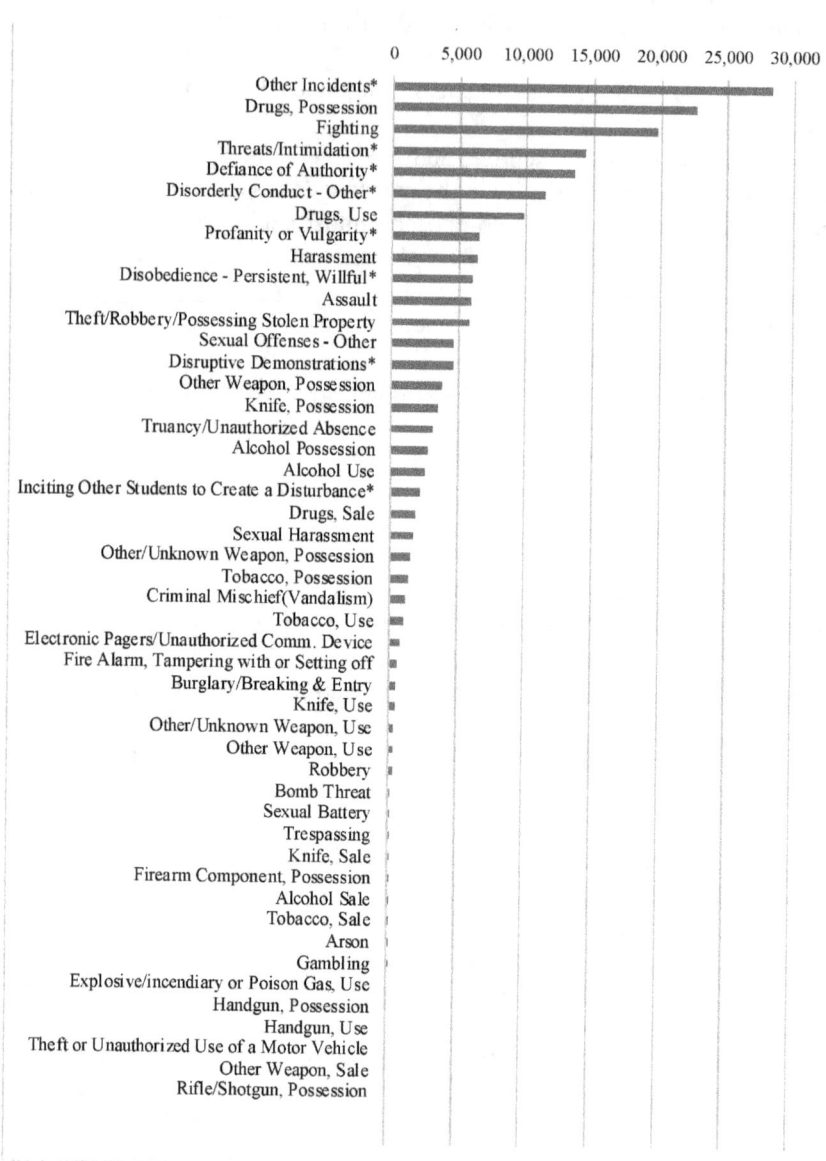

Figure 1.3 Number of Days of Alternative School Placement for Each State-Defined Incident in Alabama, 2015–2016. *Source*: Created by authors.

approximately 28 percent Black, approximately 66 percent of the students referred to alternative schools were Black.

The pairing of incidents related to perceptions about behavior (i.e., subjective incidents) with alternative school placement of students of Color, and particularly Black students, points toward an ethos of removal and relegation. Black students are removed, at rates that exceed their presence in the school population, from their traditional schools and relocated to inferior, alternative settings that are unlikely to offer rigorous and engaging instruction. Indeed, in our experience as teachers and researchers in alternative schools in Alabama, we see many more Black students than white students, even though the systems in which we work are predominantly white.

REFERRALS TO LAW ENFORCEMENT

As previously noted, the presence of police in U.S. public schools has steadily increased since the implementation of zero tolerance policies in the 1990s and the subsequent Columbine, Sandy Hook, and Parkland school shootings (Addington 2019; Beger 2002; Kupchik 2010; Vitale 2017). Large, urban school districts, often composed mostly of low-income students of Color, have invested millions of dollars since the early 2000s to implement technologies and personnel that function to surveil students, including cameras, metal detectors, and SROs. The anxiety driving this investment has also driven the implementation of harsh, and often life-long, consequences (e.g., felony terrorist charges) for students, even very young students, who are suspected of making threats, whether credible or not, toward their school; some have recently termed this "The Parkland Effect" (Alabama Appleseed 2019). This effect has led to increased cooperation between schools and law enforcement whereby school officials in some districts share student information with local police and SROs, prompting students to be targeted and surveilled inside and outside of schools (Robbins 2008). Some school districts, such as Clay County Schools in Florida, have established their own police forces (Keierleber 2019).

According to the National Association of School Resource Officers (NASRO), headquartered in Alabama, there are between 16,000 and 20,000 school-based police in U.S. public schools. That number has been questioned due to idiosyncratic reporting by state and local education agencies; some have estimated there are over 20,000 (Brown 2006) and up to 30,000 SROs (James and McCallion 2013) in schools today. According to the National Center for Education Statistics (NCES), there were SROs on site in 42 percent of public schools in the 2015–2016 school year, an increase of 10 percent from the decade prior (Sherfinski 2018). Alabama has seen similar increases in SROs, though it is difficult to estimate how many SROs are in schools statewide. Numbers of SROs are often only reported if they are stationed at a school full time; rural school systems, of which there are many in Alabama, often cannot afford SROs on site full time, and may share one or more officers across several schools each week. In 2018, the governor of Alabama instituted the Sentry Program, which provides "additional security measures for the schools without SROs," including administrators who can apply to carry a firearm on site and train to become sentries (Grotjahn and Brentzel 2018). In 2019, the governor approved the largest state education budget to date, with additional funds in the Advancement and Technology Fund which is disbursed to school systems based on enrollment. Historically, school security has come from this fund, with 28 percent of the $39 million in funds in 2018 spent on security; the fund for the 2019 fiscal year was almost $199 million, with large portions devoted to school security.

It is widely believed that, despite some public support for school-based police, the presence of SROs in public schools criminalizes student behavior (Hirschfield 2008; Kupchik 2010; Theriot 2009) and needlessly introduces students to the juvenile justice system or the criminal justice system, depending on age, judge, and prosecutor discretion (Advancement Project 2011; Brown 2006; Mallett 2016). Alabama, for example, permits trying defendants as young as 14 as adults for some offenses, even for those that occur at school (NJDC 2018). Many schools do not track student outcomes or trajectories once they have been referred to law enforcement for something happening on school grounds, and the ALSDE only reports how many incidents result in referral to law enforcement, not how many of those referrals result in arrest or adjudication. Research also suggests that the presence of SROs in schools increases the risk that students will be given exclusionary consequences (for a meta-analysis, see Javdani 2019). Student behavior that may have been at one time addressed by teachers and administrators may now be handled by SROs (Theriot 2009), including those incidents related to perceptions about student behavior (Na and Gottfredson 2013). Fisher and Hennessy (2016) explain:

> For example, unruly adolescent behavior might be considered "horseplay" by teachers and administrators, resulting in a visit to the principal's office or detention. Alternatively, an SRO might view the same behaviors as "disorderly conduct," potentially resulting in harsher school-based punishment and even involvement with the juvenile justice system. (218)

Thus, student behavior that was once viewed via developmental perspectives is now viewed via criminal and legal lenses. These effects are exacerbated when Black students are involved because of negative racial stereotypes.

That shift is readily evident in the numeric data from Alabama public schools for the 2015–2016 school year. In that year 199 of the 738 (approximately 27 percent) referrals to law enforcement in Alabama public schools were for incidents related to perceptions about student behavior for things like disobedience and defiance (see figure 1.4; subjective incidents are marked with an asterisk), which certainly would have been handled exclusively by school personnel in the past (Kupchik 2010; Na and Gottfredson 2013; Theriot 2009). For the 2016–2017, 2017–2018, and 2018–2019 school years, the ALSDE has publicly released reports indicating that referrals to law enforcement grew in number each year while the total public school enrollment statewide declined. Not only does it appear that more Alabama school children were referred to law enforcement each year, but also an increasing number of those referrals were for subjective incidents (see table 1.2).

In 2019, the Alabama Appleseed Center for Law and Justice published a report about the harmful effects of the growing presence of police in Alabama public schools. Drawing on numeric data from the OCR in conjunction with data gathered through public records request of the ALSDE, the Office of the Governor, and many school systems across the state, they found that the presence of SROs contributed to disproportionate referral to law enforcement of Black boys with disabilities (a ratio of 3.1 to 1, relative to the total school enrollment), Black boys (2.5 to 1), and Black children (1.5 to 1). The report also called for increased training for SROs and the educators who work with them, as well as increased transparency about the roles and guidelines for SROs and the outcomes related to their presence in schools.

The OCR data regarding disciplinary practices in Alabama during the 2015–2016 school year reveal that of the 592,870 students enrolled in the 85 school systems that referred to law enforcement officials 202,110 (approximately 34 percent) were Black. During that school year, the OCR reported that 2,183 Alabama students were referred to law enforcement; a disproportionate number of them were Black (1,171; ~54 percent), with 59 of the 85 school systems reporting disproportionate use of referral to law enforcement with Black students, 23 by a rate of at least double the rate of Black enrollment in the system. For one Alabama system, where the enrollment was approximately 14 percent Black, approximately 32 percent of the students referred to law enforcement officials were Black.

The disproportionate nature of school-based arrests was even starker: approximately 38 percent of the students enrolled in the 57 systems that reported arrests were Black (173,088 of 455,128); approximately 63 percent of the arrested students were Black (671 of 1,071). This results from the overrepresentation of Black students among those arrested at school in 39 of the 57 systems, 14 by a rate of more than double the rate of Black enrollment. In one particularly egregious case, the school system enrollment was approximately 27 percent Black, yet 100 percent of the students arrested for school-based incidents were Black.

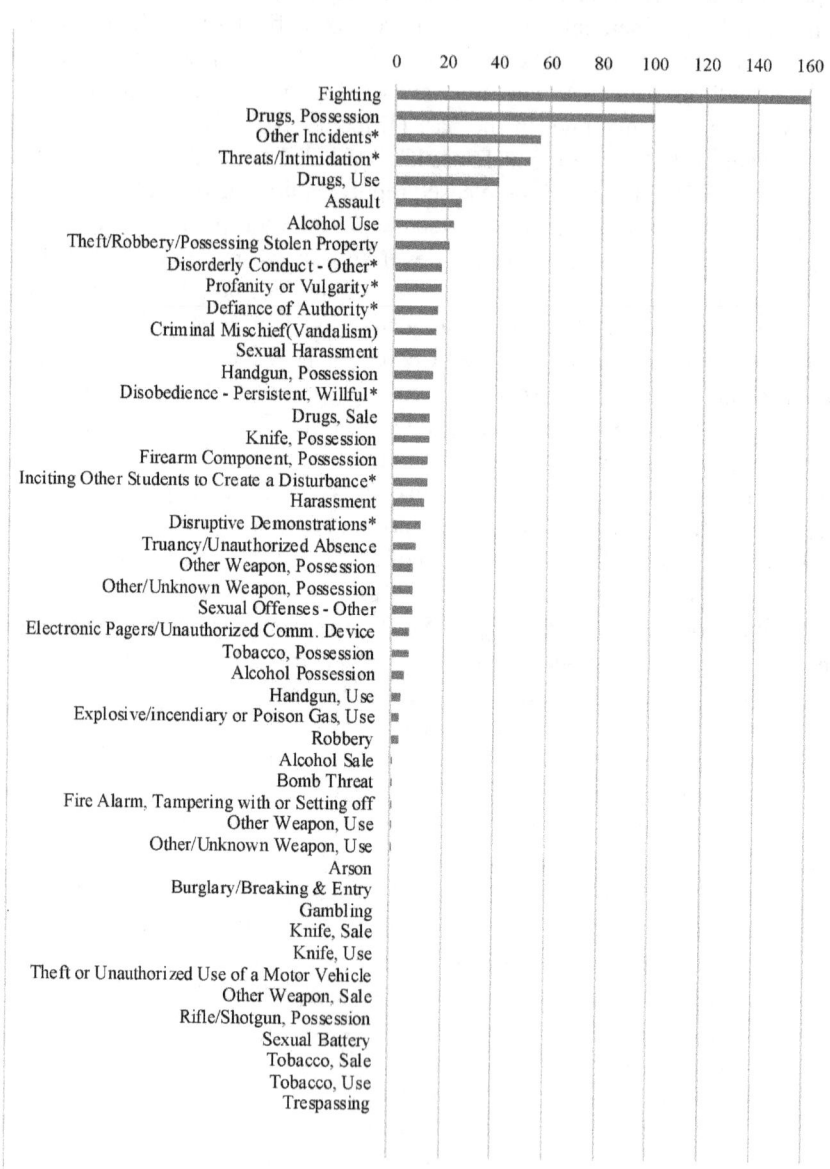

Figure 1.4   Referrals to Law Enforcement for Each State-Defined Incident in Alabama, 2015–2016. *Source*: Created by authors.

Table 1.2 Statewide Enrollments, Referrals to Law Enforcement, and Subjective Referrals

Year	Total Enrollment	Total Referrals to Law Enforcement	Subjective Referrals	Percent of Referrals for Subjective Incidents
2015–2016	730,563	738	199	~27
2016–2017	730,175	952	284	~30
2017–2018	726,924	1,152	375	~33
2018–2019	722,212	1,349	564	~42

CORPORAL PUNISHMENT

Corporal punishment, deemed a form of violence by the United Nations Committee on the Rights of the Child (2007), is still legal in 19 states in the United States, and it is applied to approximately 160,000 students per year across the country (Gershoff and Font 2016). Black and/or differently abled students receive corporal punishment at disproportionate rates to their white and abled peers (Gershoff and Font 2016; Gershoff, Purtell, and Holas 2015; Gregory 1995; Human Rights Watch and ACLU 2008). Corporal punishment often encompasses intentional "hitting, spanking, punching, shaking, paddling, shoving, and use of various objects, painful body postures, excessive exercise drills, and electric shock" (Society for Adolescent Medicine 2003) used to punish behavior (Dupper and Montgomery Dingus 2008, 243). Though many states have prohibited the practice over the last 30 years (Gershoff et al. 2015), corporal punishment continues to be used in schools in the Deep South, including in Alabama. Alabama is among the four states that account for 70 percent of the corporal punishment in U.S. public schools (the other three are Mississippi, Arkansas, and Texas; SPLC and CRP 2019). Alabama is also one of only three states, alongside Mississippi and Arkansas, in which more than half of the student population attends a district that uses corporal punishment (Gershoff and Font 2016). Whereas spanking by parents is often done with an open hand, school personnel are generally required to use provided instruments such as switches, belts, and wooden paddles. School-based corporal punishment has also been known to result in various injuries including "welts, blood blisters, severe bruising, skin discolorations, hematomas, blood clots, and broken veins (Hyman 1995)" (Dupper and Montgomery Dingus 2008, 243). However, legal proceedings have routinely favored school-based practitioners when their implementation of corporal punishment, or abuse masked as corporal punishment, is challenged (McCarthy 2005; Wasserman 2011), thus reinforcing the use of school-based corporal punishment in the states where it is used, including Alabama.

Figure 1.5 aligns state-defined disciplinary incidents with corporal punishment. According to the ALSDE, the six incidents most highly linked with

Figure 1.5 Instances of Corporal Punishment for Each State-Defined Incident in Alabama, 2015–2016. *Source*: Created by authors.

corporal punishment statewide in 2015–2016 were subjective, marked with an asterisk. Eight of the 30 kinds of incidents linked to corporal punishment and 18,214 of the 20,336 instances of corporal punishment (approximately 90 percent) were for subjective incidents. OCR data about corporal punishment in Alabama during the 2015–2016 school year reveal that 455,025 students attended schools in the 101 systems that used corporal punishment. Of those, 121,734 (approximately 27 percent) were Black. In the same year, 16,310 students were corporally punished. Of those, 5,334 (approximately 33 percent) were Black. Overrepresentation of Black students experiencing corporal punishment occurred in 87 of the 101 school systems that used corporal punishment. In 21 of those systems, Black students were overrepresented at rates that at least doubled the respective rates of Black enrollment, patterns that should be readily noticeable to school-based practitioners. For example, in one Alabama school system, 358 students were corporally punished. One hundred thirty-two (approximately 37 percent) of those students were Black whereas approximately 16 percent of the total system enrollment was Black.

CONSEQUENCES OF REMOVAL

On their face, the numeric data we have presented here are alarming. Schools are removing vast numbers of students across the state of Alabama from instruction and social interaction with their teachers and peers in the name of discipline, and many for incidents related to subjective perceptions about their behavior. We present these state data acknowledging that they obscure the identities of the affected students. We also present data from the OCR, which, although they do not map incidents onto consequences, do reveal some details about the identities of the affected students. These data indicate that every category of exclusionary discipline is used disproportionately against Black students in Alabama. At the same time as we highlight these state and federal data, we want to be sure to remind the reader, and ourselves, that these data are rooted in the experiences of real, identifiable students. These data are not merely abstractions. They point toward the ways that educational institutions, and the disciplinary policies and practices within them, are in the business of routinized removal of students and that the removal of students, particularly those who are Black, is part of the grammar of school discipline.

To restate, there is no evidence that Black students need to be disciplined more frequently and harshly. Black students do not misbehave more than other students. Decades of scholarship, by contrast, document the stark disproportionality in the application of discipline, a disproportionality that is racialized and discriminatory (Welsh and Little 2018). The devastating effects of removal on Black students are clear (Losen 2014; Losen and Gillespie

2012). We also note emerging scholarship about the ways that exclusionary discipline affects students who are in the same classrooms and schools as those students who are removed. For example, students in schools defined by a "culture of control" may experience impediments to success and achievement in these punitive environments (American Psychological Association Zero Tolerance Task Force 2008; Losen and Skiba 2010; Mitchell and Bradshaw 2013). A punitive school culture "destabilizes school communities and fosters anxiety and distrust (U.S. Department of Education 2014)" (Perry and Morris 2014, 1083). Thus, exclusionary discipline practices are not just detrimental to the students and families directly affected by them. They are also damaging to the broader school community, who may feel disconnected from school-based practitioners in contexts where harsh, exclusionary discipline is the norm. Students may also further stereotype and marginalize their punished peers; they may also laud those peers seemingly unaffected by punishment. In this way, school discipline practices are both a product *and* driver of ideas about race and students. We have often worked with students, teachers, and administrators in public schools who label and stereotype those students who are removed—those who are suspended, expelled, and referred to alternative schools and law enforcement, dubbing them "bad kids" and invoking a common colloquialism rooted in saviorism to describe the plight of students: "You can't save 'em all." These students are then juxtaposed to other students who are labeled "good" and who "want to learn."

In this chapter, we have focused largely on the intersection of exclusionary discipline practices and subjective incidents, and the devastating consequences those practices have for students of Color, and Black students in particular. We continue to focus on subjective incidents throughout the book as they account for a large amount of the removal of students via discipline in Alabama, and they are rooted in stereotypes and anti-Black racism. In a later part of the book, we position these behaviors in a frame of resistance to emphasize that even seemingly inappropriate behaviors are rooted in students' agentic responses to their contexts. Given what we know, however, about the ways that Black students are more likely to receive harsh punishments for minor (mis)behavior and the devastating effects of those punishments, the routine practices of exclusionary discipline and the removal of students from Alabama schools must be interrupted and rethought.

In the following chapter, we take up theory as a tool for making sense of the patterns we see in the numeric data provided by the state as well as the more narrative data we have accumulated working in schools. We explain removal and situate it within a historical, political, and racial context in the Deep South and in Alabama, exploring theoretical perspectives about the roles of white supremacy, whiteness, and anti-Black racism in conversations about, and enactments of, school discipline.

NOTE

1. We acknowledge the foundational work around colorblind racial ideology (i.e., Bonilla-Silva 2003; Gotanda 1991) and the expansion of that conceptualization to color-evasiveness (i.e., Annamma, Jackson, and Morrison 2017). We share their perspective that "educational practices that appropriate 'colorblind' ideologies are not color-blind at all—these strategies of erasure are simultaneous practices of whiteness" (de los Ríos, López, and Morrell 2015, 87).

Chapter 2

Motives for Removal

Public schools in the United States have long been critiqued as harsh, regimented, and oppressive institutions that fail to live up to their egalitarian ideals. Instead of presenting opportunities for social mobility and life opportunities for all, schools reify and reproduce social strata, attempt to correct incorrigible youth, and control the (future) working class (Anyon 1980; Bourdieu and Passeron 1977), especially those from marginalized and impoverished communities and communities of Color (Noguera 1995). The problem of school discipline for Black students, as it is bound up with these theories of social reproduction, has been conceptualized and theorized in myriad ways, including the prevailing discourse about a school-to-prison pipeline in mainstream educational research and policy circles (Heitzeg 2009; Skiba et al. 2003, 2014; Wald and Losen 2003), and, increasingly, schools as sites of pushout (Morris 2016) where "establishment of policies that integrate juvenile justice laws in school disciplinary code" (Meiners 2007, 3) is routine and taken-for-granted. School-to-prison pipeline literature has, for example, documented the rise of zero tolerance policies in schools, borne of an increasingly punitive political strategy in the late 1980s and early 1990s aimed at drug trafficking and border control and subsequently transferred to schooling policy, and implicated these policies in the increase of suspensions and expulsions of Black students. Likewise, the field of criminology has extended the school-to-prison pipeline discourse, detailing the criminalization of school discipline and asserting that a prison "track" is at work in public schools (Hirshfield 2008).

Rhetorically, the pipeline and track metaphors implicate schools as preparing Black students for a life of incarceration. Conceptualization of this phenomenon as a prison "track," however, renders schools separate and independent from broader carceral structures. Critics of school-to-prison pipeline discourse instead posit that the relationship between schools and prisons is not linear and that mechanisms present in educative systems have similarly shaped incarceration. As Sojoyner (2013), for example, explains, "Rather than a school-to-prison pipeline, the structure of public education is just as and maybe even more so culpable in the enclosure of Black freedom, which in turn has informed the development of prisons" (242). Further theorizing posits that public schools, as disciplinary institutions, are a manifestation of our prison nation (Richie 2012), as part of a carceral, surveillance state (Meiners 2016), an economy of incarceration (Gilmore 2007), a school/prison nexus (Annamma 2017; Meiners 2007; Stovall 2016), and as sites of manifestation of the War on Crime wherein schools are literally on the grounds of correctional institutions (Simmons 2016). Scholars also argue that schools are bound up with the prison industrial complex (Davis 2005) and its economic drivers in that "the policies by which we educate and police/punish are not only inextricably linked but . . . their joined-at-the-hip relationship is part of an economic imperative of free-market capitalism" (Fasching-Varner et al. 2014, 411). Thus, schools and the project of public education are thought to function as a means of upholding and maintaining a system of white racial and economic supremacy, situated in a sociohistorical and sociopolitical context of incarceration and racial capitalism, functioning as sorting mechanisms, and providing both capital and profit for the prison industrial complex. Schools and prisons also operate with parallel architecture, literally and figuratively, using similar structures, buildings, and mechanisms to control behavior, such as rewards and/or revocation of privileges, restraint, exclusion, and isolation. Thus, schools work to condition students to types of surveillance, isolation, and imprisonment, and then provide opportunities vis-à-vis disciplinary policies and processes to transition to formal systems of incarceration.

We certainly use these theoretical perspectives as a way to think through and explain what we see happening in our state with regard to school discipline, yet we extend these foundations by rooting school discipline and even incarceration in a particular socio-cultural-political context that is our home of Alabama. Angela Davis (2005) wrote that the prison industrial complex is "a way of disappearing people in the false hope of disappearing the underlying social problems they represent" (41). We see particular resonance with our work in studying school discipline processes that take for granted the removal of youth from classrooms and schools in Alabama. In this chapter, we identify a legacy of removal as the root of school discipline in Alabama. Here, we explore how this removal is situated in the Deep South, as well as the ways we see students removed, and what the motivations for that removal might be.

REMOVAL

Our U.S. context is predicated on the removal of some for the benefit, or maintenance of benefits, of others. Removal is perhaps most salient and relevant to our understanding of the erasure of Indigenous peoples. A historical investigation of removal, for example, reveals how European colonizers, and later, federal and state officials, removed Indigenous peoples from their lands and territories for financial and cultural gain. It also reveals the sordid history of colonizers and slavers' removal of Black Africans from homelands for enslaved labor and to build and fuel an economy, and the state-sponsored policies that formed the basis of modern systems of deportation and removal of racial and ethnic Others (for a tracing, see Kanstroom 2007). Contemporaneously, policy and legislation give rise to the removal of Indigenous people and people of Color from participation in U.S. society via enclosure on reservations, detention centers, incarceration, deportation, and acts of racial and ethnic terror and violence. They also prompt the removal of Indigenous people and people of Color from participation in the democratic project via voter disenfranchisement (see Anderson 2018); from economic opportunity via redlining (see Coates 2014), housing discrimination (see Taylor 2019), and employment discrimination (see Bertrand and Mullainathan 2004); and from access to human health, wellness, and reproductive justice (Roberts 1997).

The processes and language of removal are embedded in founding documents of the United States and are instantiated in education policy. Perhaps the most readily available historical examples of removal related to education are the state-sponsored removal of Indigenous children from their families via boarding school and adoption policies (see Jacobs 2009), or the removal of Black teachers and administrators from public schools in a post-*Brown* era (Ladson-Billings 2004; Tillman 2004), despite being more qualified than their white peers (Siddle Walker 2001). Now, at the macro level, segregated schools (see Hannah-Jones 2014, 2016, and 2017), academic tracking (see Tyson 2011), and school choice and charter movements (see Orfield and Frankenberg 2013) remove Black students from educational opportunity. Students are also removed in the name of school discipline—practices that lead to an embodied removal, or the literal physical removal or absence of Black students from the classroom via exclusionary discipline, which means removal from the opportunities that schools afford youth and the removal of students' experiences, cultural knowledges, and ways of knowing and being in classrooms, instruction, and curricula. Finally, the presence of school-based police and immigration and customs (ICE) officials threatens and removes undocumented, immigrant, and even U.S.-born students of Color.

REMOVAL AS AN ACT OF WHITE SUPREMACY

To further understand the legacy and practices of removal in the Deep South, particularly in the state of Alabama, we draw from several organizing principles and assumptions from critical theories about race and racism in the United States. Removal is an act tied to white supremacy: a ubiquitous, yet often unnamed, political system of racial hierarchy, globally enacting the domination of white Western bodies and culture (Mills 1997) that is bound up with settler colonialism, imperialism, and capitalism. The power system of white supremacy—always and everywhere—is an underlying assumption of our understanding of removal. This system of white supremacy "can and does morph and adapt as needed" (Matias and DiAngelo 2013, 5), even operating vis-à-vis seemingly contradictory strategies and tactics to justify removal (e.g., criminalization, infantilization, and adultification of students; surveillance and removal of bodies). Likewise, the concept of race itself has shifted over time to preserve white racial dominance (Haney López 2000). Racism, the enactment of white supremacy that adversely affects people of Color, shifts, morphs, and affects different racial groups in different ways. Anti-Black racism in the United States, for example, is rooted in a historical, political, economic, and cultural system of white profit contingent upon Black enslavement, degradation, incarceration, and dehumanization; it is "fluid, relentless, individual, and systemic" (Gillborn 2018). Contemporary ideologies such as color-evasiveness and deficit thinking about Black people operate in conjunction with ostensibly neutral policies and state-sponsored anti-Black violence and terror to inflict material, physical, psychological, and spiritual damage to Black people, upholding the racial hierarchy.

Whiteness is also a useful construct for understanding removal. Whiteness "acts as a symbolic structure around which values and meanings are organized, rather than a representation of how individual whites feel about their level of social empowerment" (Alcoff 2016, x; in the foreword to George Yancy's *Black Bodies, White Gazes: The Continuing Significance of Race in America*). That is, whiteness is part of the system of white supremacy within which we all operate; it is normal, untroubled, taken-for-granted, and manifests in various ways for white people and people of Color. White people inhabit whiteness when they evade race and racism; enact surveillance of people of Color; express entitlement to space and place; display emotions such as anger, disgust, and fear when prompted to consider race and racism (Matias 2016); and act as the ultimate authority in determining what is and is not racist. People of Color espouse and endorse whiteness in ways that may allow for protection from some aspects of racism, using the tools of whiteness to navigate oppressive contexts. Thus, whiteness and the ways of being associated with it act as a form of property (Harris 1993) for white people and that people of Color may work to try to obtain. Whiteness is always recentered, even in movements toward racial justice. As Yancy explained, "even where there is 'progress' for those of us whose lives don't matter, it is important to recognize that such alleged progress occurs within the framework of white interests" (Lim 2020, para. 19). These systems, and the inevitable recentering of whiteness, are at the root of well-intended but failed efforts toward reform.

This racist context and its socio-historical-cultural foundation, including racial stereotypes about all people, are manifest in schools. They are institutionalized in policy and internalized by policymakers, school-based practitioners, and stakeholders in education. In other words, the grammar of schooling is not immune from the conditions of white supremacy, shifting definitions of race, and different manifestations of racism; on the contrary, the grammar of schooling is part of the foundation of these conditions. Racist ideas, policies, and practices shift, move, and take new shapes, while continuing to serve their primary function: to preserve white racial dominance. For example, inasmuch as there is a history of removal connected to Black, Brown, and Indigenous people in the Deep South, white people also remove themselves and enact resistance to preserve the racial hierarchy. This was apparent, for example, with the rise of segregation academies after *Brown* v. *Board of Education* in 1954 wherein white families removed their students from public schools to private, all-white schools in lieu of sending students to newly desegregated schools (Ladson-Billings 2004).

The grammar of school discipline, the self-sustaining and internally consistent policies and systems comprised of removal, resistance, and reform, is problematic precisely because it was borne of, and perpetually enacts white supremacist ideas. It situates students who are deemed to be anything other than white as problems (Dumas 2016), and behaviors that are read to be anything other than white as in need of correction and/or removal. These policies and practices then produce racist ideas, which, in turn, further justify racist policies and practices (Kendi 2017). This grammar in Alabama is bound up with a history of white supremacist ideology and whiteness as normal, the colonization and removal of Indigeneity in the region, historical and contemporary anti-immigrant/Latinx sentiment, ableism, homophobia and cisheteronormativity, and the continued accumulation and concentration of social, cultural, and material capital among white people and those who inhabit whiteness. School discipline affects native/Indigenous students (in our state, for example, The Poarch Band of Creek Indians), Latinx students, disabled students, and queer students, and of course those students who exist at the intersection of these identities.

White students are also affected, as they too are removed from schools and classrooms in Alabama via school discipline policies and practices. Indeed, removal, as it is rooted in our context, has always caught up some majoritized people; but, this removal of some portion of majoritized students in schools also serves to legitimize the apparatus of removal, obscuring the racist and anti-Black nature of these policies and practices. Moreover, the grammar of school discipline also affects those large numbers of white students who are not removed, who witness the constant enactment of white supremacy on their peers of Color, and who may be unable to see whiteness at work in the power project of white supremacist institutions. These students might see the resistance on the part of students of Color, and particularly Black students, as in need of punishment and consequences, much as their teachers often do, thus reifying stereotypes about a racial Other in need of control and removal. Lastly, the grammar of school discipline also affects practitioners, as it asks us to take for granted the exclusion of some for the benefit of others, as it reifies dominant ways of knowing about who among us is deserving of space and time. It limits our ability to see and treat some students as fully human.

Though the grammar of school discipline affects us all, we choose to focus on anti-Black racism because of its legacy in our geographical, historical, and social consciousness and its perpetuity in spite of well-intentioned reforms. In addition to knowledge of the research literature about disparities in disciplinary practices for Black children (for a review, see Young, Young, and Butler 2018), we have witnessed firsthand, through our teaching and outreach work in public schools, deleterious effects on Black youth, teachers, and administrators in our area, and the ways anti-Black racism shapes the thinking and practices of school personnel. We also acknowledge the trepidation and fear with which many school-based practitioners approach (or rather, do not approach) conversations about race and racism, and how "despite evidence that racism contributes to disparities in referrals, suspensions, and expulsions, practitioners often do not factor racism into their disciplinary thinking or consider their roles in the reproduction of racial discipline disparities (DeMatthews et al. 2017; Gregory and Mosley 2004)" (Irby 2018, 696). Indeed, school-based practitioners actively avoid conversations about race and racism (Khalifa and Briscoe 2015). Thus, we bring this racism to the fore in our exploration of the ways that school discipline impacts Black students in Alabama "to identify how (but not if) racism is manifesting—morphing and adapting" (Matias and DiAngelo 2013, 5), with particular attention to the grammar of school discipline policy and practice: removal, resistance, and reform. In the remainder of this chapter, we further explore the idea of the removal of Black students in particular, and how that removal is bound up with and motivated by anti-Black racism in the Deep South.

WHAT MAKES REMOVAL POSSIBLE?

Criminalization

The United States and the Deep South are laden with a long history of removal related to social constructions of whiteness as juxtaposed to Blackness (Diamond and Lewis 2019; Dumas 2016; Gotanda 2004; Gutiérrez 2006; Kendi 2017; Muhammed 2010; Shedd 2015), presented in literature (Morrison 1992), mass media, propaganda, art, and theatre (Moriearty and Carson 2012). These constructions are rooted in enslavement and persist today, in the "afterlife of slavery" (Hartman 2007). Whiteness is constructed as natural, liberated, and normal, a symbol of purity and innocence, juxtaposed to blackness, constructed as evil, impure, criminal, fear-inducing and dangerous, even while discourse about race may be absent. White people, individually and collectively, benefit spatially, financially, culturally, and cognitively from these constructions.

In the Deep South, the slave trade, the cotton economy, debt peonage, slave codes, and Jim Crow laws were predicated on the dehumanization, degradation, and criminalization of Black people. The objectification, surveillance, restriction, and criminalization of Black bodies via the white gaze—both literal and figurative (Morrison 1992)—define the historical, cultural, and sociopolitical climate of the region (Leslie 1986; Muhammed 2010). Indeed, socialization in the Deep South (and across the United States) synonymizes innocence with whiteness (Yancy 2016), thereby positioning people of Color as "perpetrators against this presumed innocence" (Orozco and Diaz 2016, 132; see also Gotanda 2004; Gutiérrez 2006; Gutiérrez and Jaramillo 2006). In our contemporary context, this socialization comes via multimedia messaging about Blackness, wherein audiences are misled to view people of Color, especially Black people as criminal, violent (Farmer 2010; Moriearty and Carson 2012; Muhammed 2010; Smiley and Fakunle 2016; Welch 2007), and deserving of punishment (Coles and Powell 2020; Wun 2018) and removal from full participation in the United States.

Racial stereotypes and fear are bound up with one another (Frankenberg 1993; Lensmire 2010), with a particular white paranoia about Blackness and Black people (Butler 1993). Further, "white supremacist patriarchy requires the production of a normative white feminine subject that in the United States has been produced vis-à-vis the dangerous Black masculine subject" (Irby 2014, 786). The antebellum construction of white femininity as morally upright and defenseless was built alongside the persistent casting, via white owned and operated media, of Black men as a predacious, murderous, and sexually violent threat to white women (Davis 1981; Frankenberg 1993; Lensmire 2010; Leslie 1986). The perennial warnings about interracial sexual violence were indicative of the desire to protect white racial purity by rendering interracial intimacy, or even proximity, punishable. This is evidenced, for example, by the history of anti-miscegenation laws, manifested in resistance to desegregation efforts in public schools. Segregation, then, and by extension school discipline practices which remove Black bodies, alleviate this fear of proximity and intimacy. Irby (2014) points to the ways in which the social constructions of innocent white femininity and dangerous Black masculinity lead to justifications for the removal of Black students.

School-based practitioners, the majority of whom are white women, internalize these scripts about people of Color and therefore view Black bodies as threatening in classrooms and school spaces. Moreover, the condition of whiteness leads many educational practitioners to view schools as white spaces where students of Color, and Black students in particular, are seen as outsiders or trespassers. These conditions manifest in the surveillance, punishment, and removal of Black students for what school-based practitioners believe to be their (socially constructed) *potential* to be dangerous, in the absence of misbehavior (Casella 2003a; Emihovich 1983; Fenning and Rose 2007) or just by mere presence, interpreted to be disruptive to school norms rooted in whiteness (Jones and Powell 2020). When students of Color, and particularly Black students, are disproportionately disciplined, the presence of their bodies in locations such as in-school suspension or detention and the absence of their bodies in classrooms via out-of-school suspension, expulsion, or referral to law enforcement or alternative school settings, reinforce the idea that they are bad kids, troublemakers, and juvenile delinquents. That is, racist policies (i.e., the discriminatory removal of Black students) beget racist ideas (i.e., that Black students are bad and deserve to be removed), which reinforce racist policies, which uphold white supremacy.

Adultification

Descriptors of inherent violence and criminality are often focused on distortions of the literal bodies of Black people, including, for example, the ways that Black young people are adultified, like in the case of Timothy Loehmann's shooting of Tamir Rice, a twelve-year-old, and Darren Wilson's shooting of Michael Brown. In his testimony about the physique of Brown, Wilson asserted: "Holding on to him was like a five-year-old holding on to Hulk Hogan"; "he looked up at me, and had the most intense, aggressive face. The only way I can describe it—it looks like a demon. That's how angry he looked" (Sanburn 2014, paras. 5–6). This testimony is cruelly ironic given that Darren Wilson asserted that he was actually taller than Michael Brown, and, unlike the teenager that he shot, was armed. Wilson's characterization of Michael Brown's body is aligned with common stereotypes about the inherent violence and criminality of the Black male body, an indication of how adultification works in tandem with the dehumanization and demonization used to justify the murder and incarceration of Black men and boys in particular. These stereotypes become a self-fulfilling, and self-reinforcing, prophecy as the inference made about the disproportionate incarceration of Black people and the literal number of Black bodies in jail, or, in the case of schools, sitting in detention or suspension rooms, is that Black people must engage in violence and crime more than white people. This erroneous inference, of course, bolsters negative stereotypes about the criminality of Black people.

School-based practitioners often misinterpret Black students' "styles of dress, talk, and body language" to conclude that students are older and more mature than they are (Kupchik 2016, 49). As school-based practitioners surveil and adultify Black students, they interpret benign behavior—profanity, refusal to complete (meaningless) work, cell phone and social media use, dress code violations, or congregating in hallways (Irby 2018)—as in need of correction, punishment, and removal due to stereotypes about criminality and blackness and since some of those same behaviors may be seen as threatening when exhibited by a Black adult. Adultification, through both policy and practice, is intertwined with the legacy of dehumanization of Black people in the United States and is defined as:

> The treatment and consideration of Black youth in ways befitting adults ... Dehumanization also makes it permissible to treat Black children in ways that would otherwise be morally objectionable, making these children more vulnerable to severe treatment or adult-like punishment. In situations where they receive disciplinary sanctions, Black children are often treated as though they are at least four and a half years older than they actually are (Goff et al. 2014). (Kennedy et al. 2019, 133)

For example, white students in the hallway are often seen as hanging out, while Black students are often viewed as loitering, prompting educators to treat nonthreatening behaviors as though they threaten the safety of the school or the student body when they are enacted by Black bodies perceived as adult-like.

Much as anti-Black racism is socially and culturally constructed, so too are childhood, adulthood, and adolescence (see Lesko 2012). This includes, for example, ideas that associate innocence with childhood (Ladson-Billings 2011; Meiners 2016). Historically, however, Black youth have not been afforded the presumption of childhood innocence (for a tracing of this history, see Hinton 2015). High-profile shooting deaths of youth such as Trayvon Martin and Tamir Rice illustrate the adultification of Black boys and the ways that Black childhood is unimaginable (Dumas and Nelson 2016), particularly in educative contexts (Dancy 2014; Evans-Winters and Bethune 2014; Fasching-Varner et al. 2014) and policing contexts (Ellawalla 2016; Goff et al. 2014). Paradoxically, Black adulthood is also an impossibility as Black adults are punished harshly in dehumanizing and criminalizing ways while also being surveilled and controlled, like children. Black men, in particular, face "oppressive stereotypes that proclaim them as all body and no mind, bucks and beasts, monsters and demons" (Dancy 2014, 51). Once adultified, Black boys are subject to the same stereotypes and mistreatment as Black men. Further exacerbating this contested space of infantilization and adultification is:

> The "crisis" focus of the public discourse on Black males—in which young men and boys become constructed as "problems" in themselves—[which] prevents us from seeing Black boys outside of public fears and anxieties about their future lives as adults and locates crises within Black male bodies rather than the political economy and racial order that heavily determine the living conditions and life chances of Black males from boyhood on (Wilson 1996). (Dumas and Nelson 2016, 29)

This adultification is also predicated on sexualization (Meiners 2016), accentuating the intersections of race and gender. The historical rooting of Black bodies as overly sexual traces back to enslavement. In this history, gender maps on to race in ways that further criminalize Black bodies; one need only conjure the story of Emmett Till or jezebel stereotypes, for example.

Although the punishment of Black boys in schools is often the focus of much educational research and theorizing, Black girls experience school discipline at the intersection of racism and sexism (Blake et al. 2011; Wun 2018). For example, Black girls experience and endure racist and sexist stereotypes that are historically rooted:

> Loud, disruptive, confrontational, aggressive, unlady-like, ratchet, ghetto—these are all disparaging adjectives commonly used to describe the behavior of African American women and girls. These adjectives, rooted in race and gender stereotypes from the days of slavery, serve to reproduce social hierarchies and social constructions of race and gender. In the classroom, which itself is a reflection of social structures and systems, these stereotypes function to reflect and reinforce cultural beliefs. (George 2015, 101–102)

Likewise, Black girls face particular constructions of impossible childhoods, rendering them at once hypersurveilled and largely invisible, or as not mattering in national discourse that is often focused on Black boys (Annamma et al. 2019; Crenshaw, Ocen, and Nanda 2015; Evans-Winters 2005; Haynes, Stewart, and Allen 2016). Black girls are commonly perceived to be older, more mature, and less innocent than their white peers (Walker et al. 2017), beginning as early as preschool (Meadows-Fernandez, 2020). These misperceptions result in Black girls receiving harsher punishments and less support than their white peers (Blake and Epstein 2019; Epstein, Blake, and Gonzalez 2017). We need to only think of students like J'aiesha Scott, Salecia Johnson, Shakara, or Ashlynn Avery, who have been forcibly removed from school contexts (Hines-Datiri and Carter Andrews 2020) based on these perceptions. A school police officer in South Carolina violently dragged Shakara from her desk and subsequently arrested her, and a School Resource Officer (SRO) in Hoover, Alabama shoved Ashlynn Avery into a filing cabinet for falling asleep at her desk (Charles 2019).

Black trans, genderqueer, and nonbinary youth in schools also face overt discrimination along with more subtle forms of policing around gender norms (Chmielewski et al. 2016; Morris 2016) and Black queer youth often experience hostility and discipline (Truong et al. 2020) bound up with adultifying assumptions about their sexual identities and activities. Their removal from school lays bare how surveillance and stereotyping of Black bodies work in tandem to justify inhumane and unjust school discipline practices, mirroring unjust and inhumane treatment of Black people outside of school.

Surveillance

Although many school discipline procedures are premised on the infantilization of students, inasmuch as removal is akin to a time out that a parent might issue to a child who has misbehaved, many of the practices that occur under the guise of school safety (Skiba, Eckes, and Brown 2009) are distinctly adult in nature, regardless of the age of the students upon whom they are enacted. Passing through metal detectors on the way into school, being subject to searches by school-based and local police, often with K-9 units, and being maced or pepper sprayed for fighting, or for simply watching fights (Kupchik 2016, 6) on school grounds are but a few examples of routines that occur in buildings where students must attend to learn. As Kupchik (2016) explains, "In addition to individual students of color being at greater risk of punishment than white students, we also know that race matters at the school level, in shaping schoolwide practices. Schools with larger proportions of students of color tend to have different punishment and security practices" (42). To be sure, white students experience security routines; however, given the clear research on how Black students experience discipline, evidence suggests they are subjected to these practices in addition to bearing the burden of harsh exclusionary consequences. Ostensive efforts toward safety therefore rely on criminalization and adultification of Black students to benefit white students.

Further, rhetoric and subsequent policymaking around school safety affect Black students. Efforts to render schools safe include implementation of policies modeled after those in the criminal justice system, which increased dramatically with the rise of zero tolerance policies; the introduction of metal detectors, SROs and school-based police, including K-9 units (Kupchik 2016); and other surveillance technologies like cameras and radios. This modern, racialized, and racializing surveillance (Browne 2015) is rooted in anti-Black criminalization and stereotyping (Muhammed 2010). It is also rooted in history: "Slave codes enacted beginning in the 17th century made it illegal for slaves to congregate, marry, travel without their masters' permission, or even learn to read (Finkelman 1999). For Black slaves then, any attempt to engage in normal human activity made one a criminal" (Carter et al. 2017, 52). Racializing surveillance, then, functioned to determine who was allowed in which spaces and who had access to education. Now, this surveillance takes particular forms as it is intertwined with stereotypes about not just criminality and innocence, but also intelligence and expectations about who belongs in which academic spaces. These academic expectations are entrenched, persistent, and result in a phenomenon commonly known as "tracking" (Oakes 2005). Tracking, as a system that works across and within schools and classrooms, sorts students, along raced, classed, gendered, and abled identities into classes that differ in curricula, rigor, and the credit that a student can potentially earn in schools. For example, many schools attach higher weights or point values for courses that are labeled "Honors" or courses that are designed according to "Advanced Placement" (AP) or "International Baccalaureate" (IB) guidelines. Students enrolled in these courses have the opportunity to obtain higher Grade Point Averages (GPA) than their lower-tracked peers, making them more competitive for college admissions and scholarships. In public schools, Black students are systematically relegated to less rigorous classes, and even to lower tracks within classrooms, than white students, thus limiting opportunities for achievement and success (Irvine 1990; Perry, Steele, and Hilliard 2003). School segregation exacerbates this disparity, as Black students are more likely to attend schools where fewer advanced courses are offered (Baggett 2016; Tyson 2011) and where teachers are less qualified to teach advanced courses (Darling-Hammond 2010). Tracking as a barrier to academic achievement in tandem with exclusionary discipline practices that remove students from instruction have together been framed as the "education debt" (Ladson-Billings 2006) and "opportunity gap" (Milner 2012) that exist for Black students.

Discriminatory Legal Landscape

As we have described, nationally, students have experienced a "net-deepening" of disciplinary consequences (Irby 2013), whereby they are more harshly consequenced for disciplinary incidents than ever before. Black students are criminalized and surveilled, bearing the brunt of exclusionary policies and practices, thereby rendering schools unsafe for them. White students, by contrast, enjoy the benefits of "whiteness as a globally stretched-out norm, and a locally situated privilege" (Mattson 2009, 148) in schools and thus are the bodies intended to be kept safe from those who are perceived to be Other. As we have also described previously, there are a broad range of incidents for which students in Alabama public schools can be punished with exclusionary consequences, including those that are subject to practitioner interpretation. School discipline incident labels such as defiance, disobedience, and disorderly conduct are all dependent on the practitioner who observes student behavior, leaving room for idiosyncratic interpretation across and within schools and creating opportunities for racialized stereotypes to govern practitioner perspectives.

Further complicating and exacerbating the effects of exclusionary discipline, often imposed to punish subjective incidents, is the harsh, discriminatory legal landscape in Alabama. In 1975, the Supreme Court ruled on *Goss v. Lopez,* which held that students have a property interest in their public education and a liberty interest in their good name and reputation protected by the 14th Amendment, and that a school "may not withdraw that right on grounds of misconduct, absent fundamentally fair procedures to determine whether the misconduct has occurred." The decision further held that students were entitled to "some kind of notice and some kind of hearing" for school discipline proceedings. For suspensions of 10 days or fewer, students were to be provided with an oral or written notice of charges, an explanation of evidence, and an opportunity to share their side of the story. The court did not address out-of-school, long-term suspensions exceeding 10 days, only stating that "more formal procedures" may be required in longer suspensions/expulsions. After the *Goss* decision, individual states were left to fill in gaps for suspensions and expulsions more than 10 days. While other states, like neighboring Georgia, quickly defined what due process would mean and look like for students, Alabama did not. Thus, without statewide statutory protections, school systems in Alabama have wide latitude to create and enforce varying rules without consistency and are not required to enroll students who have been suspended or expelled from another system. This legal landscape means that, for students and families who do not have resources to access advocacy and representation on their behalf, there are idiosyncratic, local policies to navigate and no statewide statutes in place to protect them. Over the last two years, state legislators and legal advocates have worked to pass SB 189, which would create statutory due process protections, eliminate exclusionary discipline for truancy, and prohibit exclusionary discipline for students in Kindergarten through fifth grade, except in rare circumstances. Though it passed the state senate in early 2020, the legislative session was suspended due to Covid-19 concerns; it will be up again for a vote in the 2021 legislative session (Michael J. Tafelski, personal communication, September 11, 2020).

While legal remedies certainly do not solve the problems presented by systemic racism, we note that the absence of legal protections in the state reinforces the harsh, punitive context in which Black Alabamians live and go to school. In much of this section, we have focused on the social construction of Blackness and the ways that white supremacy and power shape these constructions; we acknowledge the cruel irony in policies and practices that are bound up with white fear of Black bodies (Baggett and Andrzejewski 2020b) in that there also exists Black fear—felt bodily, cognitively, emotionally—in connection with policies developed and enacted to protect whiteness and white bodies. Entering schools, where disciplinary policies are designed to prompt the removal and brutalization of Black students via interactions with school-based practitioners, corporal punishment, and law enforcement officers must be fear-inducing, yet it is unavoidable because school attendance is compulsory.

MOTIVATIONS FOR REMOVAL

Anti-Black racism and a system of privileging some at the expense of others have existed in the U.S. since enslavement (Thandeka 2001), working to divide and stratify poor and working-class whites from enslaved Africans and later, freed people, in order to preserve the material interests of the ruling class.[1] Anti-Black policies and practices work to secure and preserve material interests for the dominant class and to allay fears about the loss of access to and accumulation of those material interests—for example, property, wealth, employment, and education—that comprise and structure a way of life (Bell 1992). Those activists and advocates who work to dismantle anti-Black racism, organizing poor and working-class citizens across racial lines (e.g., Dr. King's Beloved Community), face hostility and state-sanctioned violence, demonstrating the power that is exerted when the status quo is threatened.

Sharing space and place is one way that threats to the material status quo come about, a sharing that is inherent in efforts toward integrated schooling. White families in the Deep South, for example, worked to protect space and place after *Brown* v. *Board of Education*. The prospect of attending schools (or sending children to attend schools) with Black children motivated white families to choose to enroll their students in newly formed, private "segregation academies." Anti-Black public discourse linking desegregation and integration with communism threatened an "American" way of life, and segregationists terrorized and murdered civil rights advocates and activists (Strunk, Locke, and Martin 2017). In Mississippi:

> Black people who were suspected of supporting the Civil Rights Movement were frequently fired from jobs, ran [sic] out of town, forced out of business, and evicted. White initiated violence was reported as Black initiated violence (as cover ups, set ups) and then connected back to communism and socialism. Such tactics supported white fear of "losing their way of life." By 1959, the white Citizens Council had more than 200 chapters and more than 80,000 members in the state (Bowers 2010). Moreover, many politicians won their seats in office by parroting the rhetoric of these groups, thus running their campaigns on the fear of change. They stirred up much white fear and opposition to seeing Black people as humans, through the portrayal of civil and human rights workers as "invaders" and "enemies" who were convincing "their negros" to become communists and socialists. (Strunk, Locke, and Martin 2017, 117)

School enrollment patterns and the public discourse and violence against proponents of desegregation were similar in Alabama.

Segregation in Alabama

Private, all-white schools had long existed before the Civil War in Alabama (Weeks 1915), where enslaved Black people were punished for seeking education (Cornelius 1983) and later, freed people were long denied education (for a historical treatment of Black schools in the Deep South pre-*Brown* v. *Board*, see, e.g., Siddle Walker 2000). After *Brown* v. *Board* in 1954, however, Alabama embarked on a series of efforts to resist the desegregation orders enshrined in the decision. For example, Amendment 111 to Alabama's long, heavily amended state constitution gave white families the "freedom of choice" about which public schools their children would attend (Bass 1993), and "pupil placement acts" granted authority to local school boards to circumvent desegregation orders. In 1967, a federal judge issued invalidations of many policies that gave white families the "choice" to opt out of desegregated schools, prompting increasing enrollment in segregation academies (Harvey 2018). After *Milliken* v. *Bradley* in 1974, federal courts had weakened authority to enforce desegregation (for a history, see Orfield and Lee 2007), and laws in Alabama allowed for the further creation of city and county systems, dividing tax revenues (Crain 2017). These legacies remain today in that, in 1990, for example, 52 percent of white students in Alabama's

Black Belt region, with the exception of students in Montgomery, attended private schools. By 2000, 15 percent of all white students in the state either attended private schools or were home-schooled (Flynt 2004). 2010 U.S. Census data revealed that the population in the largest city in the state was 73 percent Black, but 94 percent of the public school system was comprised of Black students during the 2013–2014 academic year (ALSDE). Put another way, there were only 254 white students of the total enrollment of 24,858 students in that school system. Since 2000, 10 additional school systems have been formed in Alabama, with wealthy, white communities seceding from larger systems, concentrating wealth and resources (Crain 2017). In the 2018–2019 school year, 43 of Alabama's reporting 142 school systems and charters were predominantly Black (i.e., 50 percent or more), and 143,791 of the state's 232,017 Black public school students (approximately 65 percent) attended those schools. For the same school year, 83 reporting school systems or charters had enrollments wherein Black students were underrepresented (i.e., fewer than 32 percent). Despite enrolling ~59 percent of the state's public school students, these 83 systems and charters only enrolled ~14 percent of the state's Black public school students (ALSDE). Unsurprisingly, some school systems in Alabama are still under federal desegregation orders (Larson, Hannah-Jones, and Tigas 2014), and other systems appear to be increasingly segregated (Hannah-Jones 2014).

Nationwide, public schools remain segregated, perhaps now more segregated than ever before (Frankenberg et al. 2017; Orfield and Lee 2007; Shyman 2018). The school choice movement may work to further segregate in some communities (Orfield and Frankenberg 2013; for a treatment of segregation in the United States, see Rothstein 2017), just as white families once chose to send their children to private segregation academies in the Deep South (and continue to do so). School segregation, under the guise of "choice" and its accompanying color-evasive rhetoric, affords white families opportunities to remove students from schools where they might be forced to share space and resources with Black students, while also managing to avoid conversations about structural racism or race (Rodriguez 2017).

Segregated schools are more likely to be underfunded, understaffed, and under resourced (Darling-Hammond 2004, 2007; Ladson-Billings 2006; Orfield and Lee 2005), preventing Black students from accessing important resources. Likewise, in schools that are more diverse, Black students are denied material and relational resources, such as Black teachers, equity-focused and anti-racist policies and curriculum, and extracurricular activities that are academic in nature (Irby 2014; Lewis-McCoy 2014). Desegregated, or more racially diverse schools, therefore also comprise dangerous contexts for Black students. Sociologists from the 1960s theorized that Black people posed a "power threat" both economically and politically, to the white majority, leading to the "imposition of punitive social controls in order to maintain dominance of the majority" (Welch and Payne 2010, 29). Contemporary sociologists and education researchers have taken up these ideas that a "racial threat" exists in schools (for a review, see Butler and Triplett 2019), whereby discipline policies and practices are harsher and more punitive in schools comprised of more Black students (Irwin, Davidson, and Hall-Sanchez 2013), much as there is concentrated policing, surveillance, and incarceration in Black communities. However, there may be a "racial tipping point" with regard to place-based composition in schools, wherein Black students in diverse schools may be seen as a threat, thus triggering harsh disciplinary mechanisms (Welch and Payne 2012).

Exclusionary discipline—the removal of students via in-school and out-of-school suspension, expulsion, alternative school placements, and referrals to law enforcement—further shapes public school classrooms and access to resources. Across all schools, exclusionary discipline serves to segregate by criminalizing Black students, removing them from what are perceived to be the white spaces of schools. Fewer Black students in class ensures that more resources are available for white students. Thus, segregation and exclusionary discipline function as tactics to homogenize, reinforcing and preserving the status quo of classroom space, materials, and relationships, while enacting anti-Black removal and violence (Coles and Powell 2020).

REMOVED FROM DATA

As we noted in the first chapter, it is difficult to explore school discipline incident data in Alabama because of the ways those reports are shared by state offices. Thus, here, we take up the removal of student demographic information, including racial identity, from those reports. In early 2016, we began to request ostensibly publicly available data from the Alabama State Department of Education. Officials responded that they were working to disaggregate data by students' ethnoracial and gender identities for school discipline reports for the current academic year (2015–2016). These data would enable us to determine which students are specifically affected by exclusionary discipline in the state and for which incidents. When the ALSDE issued discipline data for that school year, they did not include information about students' identities, indicating also that no disaggregated data would be made available for any previous academic year. These data are, however, reported to the Office of Civil Rights (OCR) every other year and are routinely collected by schools and systems. Moreover, state policy documents have also acknowledged the need for disaggregated data.

In 2020, the Public Affairs Research Council of Alabama (PARCA) issued a report of their analysis of disaggregated discipline data. PARCA offers "independent, objective, nonpartisan research," and while their analysis of the state-provided data offers results very similar to the ones we present here in terms of racial disparities in school discipline, they offer little interpretation of these results and make no mention of racism. Our interpretation of ALSDE's selections about when and to whom to provide data is that they are politically motivated and expedient, affording the appearance of transparency without the need to confront the systemic anti-Black racism that is the ideological foundation of the grammar of school discipline in the state. That is, these data were shared with PARCA, and illegally withheld from us, because PARCA could make no mention of *why* the patterns are what they are. PARCA would not challenge racist interpretations that attribute disparities to deficits in Black children and their families.

What people choose to reveal about race and racism is just as important as what they do not (Leonardo 2013). Socializing discourses and understandings about race, racism, whiteness, and Blackness posit that focusing on race is "racist," a misconception that is revealed when people are challenged to reject color-evasive approaches and to name structural and interpersonal racism. Put another way, a rejection of race-evasiveness is equated with racism (Milner 2012). Many people fear being labeled "racist" (Stevenson 2014), which is often equated with being an inherently bad or immoral person (DiAngelo 2011). This anxiety or neurosis around race and racism (Matias and DiAngelo 2013) means that many white people are both unprepared to engage in and averse to discourse about race and racism (Winans 2005). By extension, this aversion to race and racism also prevents disclosure of institutionalized racism in that people who are employed by and benefit from social institutions, such as education, may be unmotivated and unwilling to explore and disclose racialized disparities. Moreover, they may be unwilling to analyze the anti-Black, racist roots of those disparities, since acknowledging that systemic racism exists also means acknowledging that one is complicit in and benefits from it (Trepagnier 2006).

Here, we have focused on the removal of Black students from schools in Alabama as part of the prevailing and pervasive grammar of school discipline, highlighting the relationships between anti-Black racism, and removal of Black students via the mechanisms of criminalization, adultification, surveillance, and exclusionary policies and practices. We have also articulated that a rejection of threats to status quo and a desire for protection of resources motivates this removal. These motives and methods are present not only in the conduct of school discipline but also in the reporting, or lack of reporting, thereof; students are removed from their schools and then largely removed from the data about their schools' disciplinary practices, a doubled removal.

Our intent, in pointing out this removal, and the racist foundations of it, is not to vilify practitioners at the local or state levels. Rather, we aim to reveal the anti-Black racism that is at the roots of removal, even while discourse about race and racism may be absent: "racism without racists" (Bonilla-Silva 2003). For example, the language in Alabama Code 16-1-14 regarding "Removal, isolation, or separation of pupils creating disciplinary problems; state approval necessary for rules implementing such measures; deprivation of right to equal and adequate education may not result" might serve as a touchstone in considering how students' rights are violated when they are removed from schools and classrooms in our state, but this language also does not account for the racial inequities already present in schooling and the deep-rooted stereotypes that exist about Black students.

In the next chapter, in an effort to further contextualize the role of removal via exclusionary practices in the grammar of school discipline and to identify those students most affected by it, we hone in on Cotton County Schools in Alabama. Removal of students, particularly Black students, is commonplace in Cotton County, even though this school system enjoys a positive reputation. Here, student interactions with SROs, sometimes leading to arrests, are not only common but also valorized in the media and public policy, thus demonstrating how surveillance, criminalization, and disciplinary practices of removal are related.

NOTE

1. Many of the ideas presented here also appear in Baggett and Andrzejewksi (2020b).

Chapter 3

A Portrait of Removal

Cotton County Schools (with Jasmine S. Betties and Sangah Lee)

A visit to the Cotton County Schools website shows the usual information about upcoming events in the system, Twitter and Facebook feeds on the left-hand side of the screen, and an image of the Alabama state seal. A closer look reveals a gradient background landscape image of a cotton field, an explicit nod to the county's agrarian past, and a reminder of the enslavement that drove the cotton economy in this county in the northern part of the state. A look at historical maps suggests that Cotton County has long been and continues to be a high cotton producer (NCC 2018), had more than 14,000 enslaved people in 1860 (Blake 2003), and a higher average farm value relative to other counties in the region in 1850 (Barnard and Jones 1987). The image of a cotton field on the school system's website appears in lieu of images referencing the contemporary economic driver of the area: the county seat and its suburbs are sites of major aerospace engineering. Like many school system websites, Cotton County School's site has tabs for the school board, athletics, resources, employment, as well as images of smiling students and staff. There is, however, scant mention of school disciplinary practices, with the exception of the Student Code of Conduct, which is three clicks from the homepage. Although not often present in public school system websites, the omission and concealment of discipline practices in Cotton County Schools is glaring because this system accounts for a disproportionately large amount of the exclusionary discipline in Alabama. That is, the system's reports to the Alabama State Department of Education (ALSDE) indicate that student removal by way of exclusionary discipline is a prominent feature of school life in Cotton County Schools, yet it is hardly featured at all in the public-facing image constructed by the school system.

    In this chapter, we focus on Cotton County Schools in Alabama because this system is emblematic of the fallacy of "good" schools. That is, Cotton

County has a reputation for offering high-quality education. Test scores are high relative to the rest of the state, a high percentage of their students graduate and attend institutions of higher education, and they boast about the qualifications of their teachers. Yet, despite positioning equity as one of their four pillars of educational practice, this school system accounts for a disproportionate amount of the exclusionary discipline practices in the state of Alabama and has faced media criticism for using exclusionary practices almost exclusively with Black students.

THE FALLACY OF "GOOD" SCHOOLS

As previously mentioned, Cotton County Schools enjoy a reputable status among Alabama public school systems. Schools there are often considered to be among the best schools in the state and are graded well by the ALSDE (2017; B for 2016–2017 school year when 73 systems across the state earned a C or D). In a Niche (2020) ranking of the systems in Alabama, Cotton County Schools arrive at number 29, the second highest ranking for a county system. Similarly, SchoolDigger (2018) rankings of Alabama systems based on 2016–2017 test scores position Cotton County Schools at 19, the highest county system, up two positions from the previous year. Though the system is still under federal desegregation orders from the Department of Justice, Cotton County Schools match some of the most demographically diverse schools in the state with respect to students' races and ethnicities, in many ways mirroring the population of the state. Finally, according to the U.S. Census Data from 2010, Cotton County Schools are also more affluent than nearly all of the other county systems in Alabama, boasting a wide range of well-resourced curricular and extracurricular programming.

The Cotton County School system also holds an egregious disciplinary record, representing the ways in which school officials can remove students by employing some of the most exclusionary consequences possible for school-based disciplinary incidents. The system, which consistently enrolls approximately 19,000 students, approximately 19 percent of whom identify as Black, doled out 22,609 total days of suspension and 18,670 total days of alternative school placement as consequences for school discipline incidents over the course of the academic years from 2010 to 2016. Also, during those years, school officials meted out 2,562 instances of corporal punishment, expelled 54 students, and made 606 referrals to law enforcement for disciplinary incidents that occurred at school.

The earliest school year for which data about referrals to law enforcement in Cotton County Schools are available is 2008–2009; in that academic year, officials referred just one school-based incident to law enforcement. Over the next five years, those numbers increased dramatically and peaked during 2014–2015 (see table 3.1 for more information about law enforcement referrals from 2008 to 2016). Cotton County Schools alone often accounted for a huge percentage of all statewide referrals to law enforcement for school-based disciplinary incidents during this time period. In the 2013–2014 academic year, for example, approximately 45 percent of all school-based referrals to law enforcement in the state of Alabama came from Cotton County Schools, despite the fact that they enrolled less than three percent of the public K-12 students statewide. That year, according to data reported to the Office of Civil Rights (OCR), they referred 179 disciplinary incidents involving 148 students to law enforcement; 43 (approximately 29 percent) of those students were Black. Of those referrals, 33 resulted in students being arrested; 10 (approximately 30 percent) of the arrested students were Black. During the 2014–2015 academic year, school leaders in Cotton County referred 186 incidents to law enforcement, accounting for more than 36 percent of all referrals statewide. This year marked the highest number of referrals from 2008 to 2016. In Cotton County Schools, those incidents that school-based practitioners are mandated to report to law enforcement officials involve student possession of a firearm, a weapon (explosives, incendiary devices, or poison cases), or a knife (SCC, 28–30); alcohol and drug possession; and some types of theft and physical harm. Yet, during 2014–2015, only four of those 186 incidents referred to law enforcement involved the possession of a weapon; the remainder included: five criminal mischief (vandalism), 67 drug-related offenses, 11 sexual offenses, 20 tobacco offenses, two for truancy, 11 alcohol-related offenses, 26 instances of fighting, five of harassment, three larcenies, and two assaults. Thirty of the 186 referrals that school year were for discipline incidents such as defiance, disobedience, and disorderly conduct, which are subject to practitioner interpretation. The following year 2015–2016, 23 of the 98 instances reported to the state that resulted in a referral to law enforcement were also for subjective infractions. For the same year the OCR reported that approximately 40 percent of the students referred to law enforcement were Black, whereas the system's enrollment was approximately 19 percent Black. OCR data also reveal 30 school-based arrests that year, 12 (40 percent) of which were Black students.

Given that school system and state policies did not change during the years when referrals to law enforcement peaked, what could account for this shift in discipline practice? Recent efforts in Alabama have resulted in increased scrutiny and pressure for school systems to invest in accurate and consistent reporting. Also, in the early 2010s, around the time that the School Resource Officer (SRO) program started in Cotton County Schools, the local district attorney's office met with school principals and the leadership committee.

Table 3.1 Referrals to Law Enforcement in Cotton County Schools for Subjective Incidents

Year	Total Law Enforcement Referrals	Defiance	Disobedience	Disorderly Conduct	Disruption	Inciting Others to Create a Disturbance	Profanity	Threats	Other	Total Subjective Referrals
2008–2009	1	0	0	0	0	0	0	0	1	1
2009–2010	1	0	0	0	0	0	0	0	0	0
2010–2011	0	0	0	0	0	0	0	0	0	0
2011–2012	2	0	0	0	0	0	0	0	0	0
2012–2013	141	1	0	4	0	4	0	9	1	19
2013–2014	179	5	0	2	2	3	0	3	10	25
2014–2015	186	4	5	1	0	2	1	4	13	30
2015–2016	98	2	2	2	0	1	0	9	7	23
Total	608	12	7	9	2	10	1	25	32	98

In this meeting, the district attorney expressed concerns that school officials needed to be more consistent in reporting incidents that required intervention by law enforcement, thus establishing an explicit link between the school system and the local prosecutors. SROs in Cotton County Schools have also received two national awards. Though the SRO program in Cotton County Schools is premised upon building relationships with students and families and SROs are to serve as a "counselor, role model, and advocate for students, families, faculty, and staff, while bringing personalized policing to an important segment of Cotton County," these awards were bestowed upon the SRO team during the same time period that referrals to law enforcement spiked.

Though not in Cotton County, the National Association for School Resource Officers (NASRO) headquarters are in Hoover, Alabama. Given the conservative aims of the organization, and the conservative, right-wing political climate in the state, it is unsurprising that the organization lauds its members in Alabama and beyond while denying the connection between school-based police and the introduction of youth to the juvenile justice system. A statement on the organization's website (n.d.), for example, under the FAQs link reads:

> Do school resource officers contribute to a school-to-prison pipeline? No. Carefully selected, specially trained school resource officers who follow NASRO's best practices do not arrest students for disciplinary issues that would be handled by teachers and/or administrators if the SROs were not there. On the contrary, SROs help troubled students avoid involvement with the juvenile justice system. In fact, wide acceptance of NASRO best practices is one reason that the rates of juvenile arrests throughout the U.S. *fell* during a period when the proliferation of SROs increased. (see *To Protect and Educate: The School Resource Officer and the Prevention of Violence in Schools*)

This argument is also fallacious since, even if juvenile arrests overall decreased, it is still possible that SROs arrested more students at school than before. Further, the Alabama criminal justice system tries many youth offenders as adults, so even if juvenile arrests decrease, those young people might be accounted for in number of adult arrests. These claims are also counter to the overwhelming research asserting how SROs in schools do actually handle many more issues that were once handled by teachers and administrators and that they are not obligated to comply with the wishes of school leaders (Alabama Appleseed 2019). The Alabama Juvenile Justice Task Force reported in 2017 that, as of 2016:

> The offense profile of youth entering the juvenile justice system on complaints has grown less serious. . . . Nearly one-third of complaints come from schools,

up from one-fifth in 2006. In some counties, up to three-quarters of complaints come from schools. . . . In stakeholder roundtables, judges, JPOs, and prosecutors reported that minor misbehaviors in schools, such as fighting, are sent to juvenile court more readily than in the past. . . . And despite a 27 percent drop in juvenile crime over the previous five years, Alabama nevertheless managed to increase the number of youth held in detention facilities, largely through the detention of juveniles for low-level crimes like shoplifting, fighting in school and truancy. (5)

In 2014, a Cotton County Schools SRO interviewed by a local online news magazine asserted, "We're a big deterrent. If students see an SRO, they know what will happen if they get caught. It's also good because students can be familiar with SROs and have a better feeling toward them instead of all the negative that comes out." Given the data around school discipline policy and practice in Cotton County Schools, the presence of SROs in their schools did not deter student misbehavior at all. Instead, the presence of SROs in Cotton County and elsewhere in Alabama contributes to the removal of students from their classrooms. SRO presence supplants and removes the work in which administrators and teachers must engage to build learning spaces that are safe and inclusive. SRO presence also removes scrutiny of police and policing, directing attention toward "a few bad apples" in the student body rather than toward systemic mistreatment of Black students. They uphold a system of exclusionary practice and embody the most drastic consequences available to school leaders that criminalize students (Hirschfield 2008), practices which, in Alabama and nationwide, remove Black students (PARCA 2020), students with disabilities (Alabama Appleseed 2019), and LGBTQ students (Lambda Legal 2012). That is, SROs, in addition to school-based practitioners, participate in the surveillance and control of student behavior; that surveillance leads to the removal of students via exclusionary sanctions (Fisher and Hennessy 2016).

EXCLUSIONARY DISCIPLINE

From 2010 to 2016, leaders in Cotton County Schools routinely engaged in the removal of students from instruction and the business-as-usual social contexts of schooling for disciplinary incidents via exclusionary consequences. School leaders also used corporal punishment as a consequence (Corporal punishment is still allowed in Alabama, as well as 18 other states, and the majority of Alabama school systems still permit the use of corporal punishment despite recommendations by the Alabama Association of School Boards and the Alabama Education Association that all systems prohibit paddling and other forms of corporal punishment.). Cotton County Schools system leaders also suspended students (both inschool and out-of-school), sent them to alternative schools, and expelled them for disciplinary incidents (see table 3.2 for total exclusionary practices from 2010 to 2016). As previously mentioned, they also referred students to law enforcement at alarming rates.

These exclusionary discipline practices are troubling for a number of reasons. First, the practice of referring school discipline incidents to law enforcement potentially facilitates increasingly punitive consequences for students since those referrals often result in formal charges (petitions) and arrests at school. This practice expedites the introduction of public school students to arrest, adjudication, and broader penal contexts such as the juvenile justice and the criminal justice systems for incidents that happen in school. (In Alabama, defendants as young as 14 can be treated as adults [Ala. Code § 12-15-203], and "Once an Adult, Always an Adult Ala. Code § 12-15-204(b)" [NJDC 2018].) Put another way, referring students to law enforcement for school-based incidents narrows and flattens the figurative and literal distance between schools and prisons. At school, law enforcement referrals potentially take the place of more relational, restorative practices between and among students, teachers, and administrators. Students who are referred to law enforcement may also be further excluded from instruction and the social aspects of schooling since students subsequently must often miss class for court hearings and meetings with probation officers.

Students who are excluded from instruction via in- and out-of-school suspensions, expulsions, alternative school assignments, and law enforcement referrals are likely to underperform their peers on measures of achievement and matriculation. For Black students in particular (for a review, see Young, Young, and Butler 2018), exclusionary discipline is a contributor to achievement (i.e., opportunity) gaps (Gregory et al. 2010; Milner 2012; Morris and Perry 2016), and the education debt (Ladson-Billings 2006). Students who are removed from classrooms, teachers, and peers are also denied opportunities for exposure to culturally relevant and meaningful instruction and engagement in the socioemotional learning that comes with school interactions. Removal also denies students opportunities to access education for liberation and school-based empowerment. Further, there is evidence that high rates of exclusionary discipline have a deleterious effect on the academic achievement of all students in a school, even those who are not themselves excluded (Perry and Morris 2014).

SUBJECTIVE DISCIPLINE IN COTTON COUNTY

In Cotton County Schools, officials often use removal as a consequence for discipline incidents that are labeled as subjective; that is, these incidents are

Table 3.2 Exclusionary Discipline Practices in Cotton County Schools

Year	Total Number of School Discipline Incidents	Suspended Days	Alternative School Days	Corporal Punishment	Expulsions	Referrals to Law Enforcement
2010–2011	1,704	3,669	5,148	307	15	0
2011–2012	2,207	4,241	4,400	620	5	2
2012–2013	2,289	4,452	2,328	612	13	141
2013–2014	1,825	3,436	2,287	462	11	179
2014–2015	1,667	3,220	2,067	246	6	186
2015–2016	1,720	3,591	2,440	315	4	98
Total	11,412	22,609	18,670	2,562	54	606

open to practitioner interpretation and their definitions allow for ambiguity and idiosyncratic assignment to student behavior. For example, from 2010 to 2016, Cotton County Schools expelled eight students for disciplinary incidents that were subject to practitioner interpretation, such as threats/intimidation (3), harassment (2), disorderly conduct (1), and defiance (1). The eighth student was expelled for an incident described simply as "other" (see table 1.1 for a list of all disciplinary incident types defined by the ALSDE, including those which are considered subjective). These eight expulsions comprised approximately 15 percent of all of the expulsions in the system over those six school years.

During that same time period (2010–2016), the system placed students in alternative school, where the quality of instruction is often poor and students are isolated from most of their peers and school resources such as extracurricular activities (Losen and Edley 2001), for 5,747 days for these types of subjective incidents. According to data from the OCR, in 2015–2016, approximately 34 percent of the students sent to alternative schools in Cotton County were Black, a rate double to their white peers. Also, during that time period, students spent 11,148 days in suspension for subjective incidents, including both in-school and out-of-school suspension contexts where they may have received little, if any, education services (Green, Maynard, and Stegenga 2017). In 2015–2016, approximately 30 percent of those students were Black, again making the rate at which Black students experienced suspension double the rate to their white peers. From 2010 to 2016, there were a total of 2,562 instances of corporal punishment in Cotton County Schools. Of those instances, the majority (approximately 88 percent) were for subjective offenses such as defiance, disobedience, disorderly conduct, disruptions, and profanity. In 2015–2016, the OCR report indicates that approximately 23 percent of the corporal punishment in Cotton County was administered to Black students, also an overrepresentation as Black students comprised approximately 19 percent of the total enrollment. Finally, a total of 97 incidents subject to practitioner interpretation were referred to law enforcement over the course of 2010–2016 (see figure 3.1 for information regarding how much of the exclusionary practices in Cotton County were tied to subjective incidents in 2010–2016). In 2015–2016, the OCR report indicates approximately 40 percent of those referred to law enforcement were Black, indicating again that the rate at which Black students were referred was double that of their white classmates. The report also indicates that approximately one in every 10 of these referrals results in arrest. In 2015–2016, 30 students were arrested for school-based offenses in Cotton County. Of those, 12 (40 percent) were Black, making Black students, again, arrested at school at more than double the rate of their white peers.

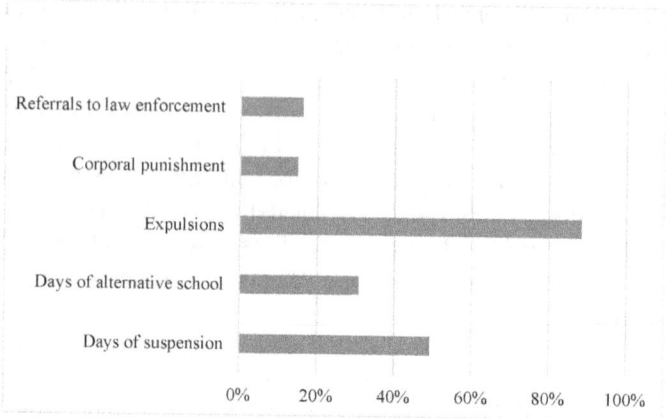

Figure 3.1 Percentage of Exclusionary Practices Issued for Subjective Incidents in Cotton County, 2010–2016. *Source:* Created by authors.

DISCIPLINING TOWARD REMOVAL

As previously noted, no state-level discipline data are made available from the ALSDE that are disaggregated by students' ethnoracial status, gender, disability status, and/or LGBTQ status. Although some demographic data are routinely collected and compiled by schools and school systems and required to be reported to the ALSDE (2010), publicly available state databases do not provide data pertaining to discipline incidents, exclusionary discipline, referrals to law enforcement, or corporal punishment by student demographics. But, data from the OCR indicate that Black students in Cotton County Schools were disproportionately suspended (in-school and outof-school), expelled, referred to law enforcement, arrested, and corporally punished as compared to school system demographics for each year that these data were reported (every other academic year, including 2009–2010; 2011–2012; 2013–2014; and 2015–2016). Black students in Cotton County have been overrepresented with regard to every disciplinary consequence reported by the OCR in every cycle of their reporting. These data do not, however, indicate the incidents for which students were consequenced via exclusionary measures.

Topical analyses of school discipline policies in Cotton County Schools specifically, as well as in Alabama generally, reveal a picture of the ideal school environment as one where students do not express themselves and are punished when they do so. For example, students are silenced and pushed toward removal when they are labeled disobedient, defiant, and disorderly, frequent occurrences in Cotton County Schools (686 incidents in 2013–2014 alone). Next, when students are consequenced via exclusionary practices, including suspensions and expulsions, they are spatially, academically, and socioemotionally distanced from their classrooms and peers. That is, they can no longer object to the events in that classroom. Their voices and bodies are literally removed even from the potential of relational or curricular discourse. Referring students to alternative schools for disciplinary incidents also excludes and removes them from their regular school context. Structures that guide many alternative school settings function to promote conformity in behavior ahead of student learning and engagement. Likewise, when schools use corporal punishment, which is widely employed in Cotton County Schools (see table 3.2), students are both physically harmed and removed from the opportunity of a relational interaction. Corporal punishment thus takes the place of any discussion or mediation about a classroom conflict. Corporal punishment occurs behind closed doors, removing this practice from public comment or critique.

Looking at the data that are available thus reveals a tension: that of the espoused ethos of inclusion in Alabama public schools, evidenced in pervasive rhetoric about educating "all students," and the removal of students via punitive policies, exclusionary practices, and data reporting. This tension is especially salient around the use of exclusionary discipline for incidents that are subject to practitioner interpretation, interpretations which are bound up with stereotypes about Black students and anti-Black racism. Many subjective incidents are directly tied to student resistance. Patterns indicate that when students are resistant to or critical of their schooling experiences, which we take up in the next part of the book, they are often removed.

OPPORTUNITIES FOR REFLECTION AND ACTION REGARDING REMOVAL

Our aim in this text is to present portraits of school discipline in Alabama as heuristics for practitioners to support efforts to make sense of the grammar of school discipline in their own work environments. More specifically, we urge school-based practitioners to consider the ways in which the systems, schools, and classrooms in which they work are like Cotton County Schools and classrooms. What are the racial achievement/opportunity gaps in their schools, and in what ways might discriminatory discipline account for them (Gregory et al. 2010)? How frequently are students excluded from instruction or arrested at school, and what is the role of subjective disciplinary infractions in exclusionary consequences? What is the function of SROs in their schools? How might that presence escalate and exacerbate school discipline practices and lead to the loss of instructional opportunities for students? Given that the OCR and many state agencies require that discipline data be recorded to document affected students' identity markers, how might those data be used, even if they are not reported publicly, to conduct an equity audit? Equity audits are practical tools for exploring the ways that race (as well as ethnicity, gender, ability, and other identity markers) matters in schools, the ways they shape the experiences students (are able to) have.[1] They are designed to explore disproportionality in many school practices (e.g., referral to special education services, enrollment in advanced and honors classes, access to leadership positions) including discipline. A comprehensive school- or system-based equity audit can support efforts to address the questions provided above. We encourage school-based practitioners to advocate for their use. Finally, we encourage practitioners to begin to consider what types of exclusionary discipline are routine in their school contexts and what types of disciplinary incidents often result in these consequences. How might teachers and administrators push back on the routine practices of discipline in their schools, reconsidering that perhaps student (mis)behavior should not result in removal?

NOTE

1. See, for example, the tools made available by the Mid-Atlantic Equity Consortium, recommended by *Teaching Tolerance,* now known as *Learning for Justice,* available at https://maec.org/res/tools/.

Part II

RESISTANCE

Chapter 4

Removed for Resistance

The officer came into the classroom behind Hannah, who was sitting with Ethan, DeVon, and Zavion looking at handouts about Muscogee food practices and rituals in the region of East Alabama.

Police: Is this Rachel's stuff? He pointed to Rachel's backpack and lunchbox.
Hannah: Yes, sir.
Police: Thank you.

Rachel had just walked up to the front of the school to use the restroom. Hannah noticed that she had been gone for a little while, but thought maybe she had gotten into a conversation with the alternative school principal, Mr. Owlson, whose office is adjacent to the restrooms, and who often sat at a table in the hallway in front of his office.

Hannah looked at the other students. Their faces looked as confused as she felt.

Hannah: Did I miss something?
Zavion: I saw her eating some candy out of her lunchbox. Maybe it was drugs?
Ethan: I of all people would have noticed if she were eating drugs right next to me. Giggles from his classmates. Ethan, who was 18 and a senior, had a history of drug experimentation, though that wasn't the reason he'd been sent to the alternative school.
Hannah: I don't think so. That was just . . . weird.
DeVon: Uhhhh . . . yeah. Cops just bustin' up in our classroom and took all her stuff.
Hannah: I'll check in with Mr. Owlson later and see what's up.

After school, Hannah spoke to the principal, who shared that Rachel had in fact been engaged in conversation with him on her way to the bathroom. He recounted that she had "used profanity" in her response to his request about how she was doing that day. He told her to go back to class, after which she told him that she needed to use the restroom. He gave her the option to either "go back to class" or he could call the officer to take her home. She chose the officer, who retrieved her belongings, picked her up, and took her to her mother's house. She remained at her mother's house, suspended for the next five school days.

We assume that Rachel, in our opening portrait, was removed for the incident of defiance, disobedience, disruptive behavior, or even just using profanity, all commonly reported incidents in Alabama school discipline data that are consequenced with exclusionary discipline (collectively nearly 71,000 instances in 2015–2016 alone). What happened to Rachel is emblematic of the ways in which the removal of students from schools, particularly Black students, can be capricious and multilayered. Rachel had been removed, via exclusionary discipline policies and practices, from her traditional high school and placed in an alternative school, where she was a student in Hannah's class. At the school, she faced enhanced surveillance, a controlling environment, and a lack of access to engaging with classmates and teachers for most of her school day. Rachel was then excluded from the alternative school for five full days for her choice of words. Those five days, as well as the days of her sentence in the alternative school, are measurable. So are some of the consequences thereof, such as declining grades and a potential loss of course credit. Other consequences are less tangible: the loss of affiliation with school, a further breach of trust with adults who had been entrusted to care for her at school, and the impact her punishment had on her relationship with her family. These are the consequences of removal.

In the first part of the book, we focused on the removal of students, like Rachel, via the use of exclusionary discipline policies and practices. We situated this removal, one part of the grammar of school discipline in Alabama, in a historical, political, and racial context. We focused on the removal of Black students from schools and classrooms in Alabama by way of surveillance, adultification, and racist stereotypes about deviance and criminality. We underscored the research showing that educators' identification of subjective incidents is often bound up with negative stereotypes about Black youth, and how Black students are often seen as defiant or disobedient when they enact behaviors like talking back to school-based practitioners, engaging in critical thinking, questioning curricula and instruction, or expressing discontent with or cynicism about the taken-for-granted processes of schooling. In many ways, we positioned Black students and families as victims of racism and unfair, discriminatory treatment.

But, these students are not just victims; they are agentic, and they exhibit resistance to the structures and practices that victimize them, as do their families and the educational stakeholders who feel responsible for them.

Removed for Resistance 73

Thus, in this part of the book, we focus on resistance, the second part of the grammar of school discipline. In the remainder of this chapter, we define resistance as always happening, though it may manifest differently across contexts and depending on who is enacting it. We suggest that student behavior that practitioners often label as rude, apathetic, or defiant (i.e., subjective incidents) might be reframed as resistance (Raby 2005). This reframing affords opportunities to ask about *what* students might be resisting in their schools and classrooms. We next present portraits of Black students at an alternative school, amplifying their voices as they engaged in play, authentic learning, and relationship building in an effort to prompt readers to engage in their own resistance to dominant narratives about "bad kids." We end this part of the book with portraits of resistance enacted by Black school leaders as they identified and countered taken-for-granted school discipline policies and practices in their own buildings, at times at professional cost.

UNDERSTANDING THE "SUBJECTIVE" LABEL

As we have written elsewhere, the extant research about school discipline often characterizes certain incidents as subjective, while others are labeled as objective. Subjective incidents include student behaviors like willful defiance, disruption, disorderly conduct, and threats/intimidation (see table 1.1 for reference). When we first became interested in looking at school discipline data in Alabama, we were struck by how those incidents accounted for a large share of the exclusionary consequences resulting in the removal of students. For example, during the 2015–2016 school year, approximately 60 percent of all reported incidents were subjective. Of the 225,573 days of suspension that students received, approximately 48 percent of them were for subjective incidents, and approximately 27 percent of the 485 expulsions that year were for subjective incidents. Of the 191,122 days of alternative school placement, approximately 34 percent were for subjective incidents. Of the 738 incidents referred to law enforcement statewide, approximately 22 percent were subjective. Subjective incidents also accounted for the majority of the corporal punishment in Alabama that year; of the 20,336 instances of corporal punishment, approximately 75 percent were for subjective incidents.

Alabama State Department of Education (ALSDE) glossary entries for these subjective incidents often reference the order of schools and classrooms; behaviors considered to be problematic are viewed to disrupt or defy that order. For example, "defiance of authority," which comprised approximately 16 percent of all reported disciplinary incidents in 2015–2016, is defined as:

willful disobedience of a direct order of instruction from a school board employee or others having legal authority. A contemptuous opposition or disregard of an order of instruction from a school board employee or others having legal authority (policeman, fireman) openly expressed in words or actions. This conduct substantially disrupts the orderly conduct of a school function or is behavior that substantially disrupts the orderly learning environment or poses a threat to the health, safety, and/or welfare of students, staff, or others.

"Disorderly conduct," which comprised approximately 8 percent of incidents in 2015–2016 is defined as:

any act which substantially disrupts the orderly conduct of a school function or which substantially disrupts the orderly learning environment or poses a threat to the health, safety, and/or welfare of students, staff, or others. If the action results in a more serious incident, report in the more serious incident category. This category does not include fights. This category includes an individual who: makes unreasonable noise; in a public place uses abusive or obscene language or makes an obscene gesture; without lawful authority, disturbs any lawful assembly or meeting of persons; obstructs vehicular or pedestrian traffic or a transportation facility; congregates with other persons in a public place and refuses to comply with a lawful order.

These definitions beg certain questions: what constitutes order in schools? Order for and from whom, and, in what ways are prevailing notions of order premised on white entitlement—indeed responsibility—to surveillance of Black bodies (Muhammed 2010), rigid racial hierarchy, and anti-Black racial stereotypes? The order of schools cannot serve Black students while simultaneously accommodating stereotypes about them as defiant, deviant, and criminal, and as long as they are viewed as threatening or disruptive when merely congregating. Given the power of these stereotypes, Black students' very presence might be seen as defying or disrupting the order of schooling, an order premised on whiteness as natural and normal. Black students are removed, over and over again, from schools under these pretenses and in the name of order.

Thus, instead of viewing patterns of disciplinary incidents as rooted in deviant behavior by Black students, we suggest that many of the incidents labeled as subjective might first and foremost be misinterpretations of student behavior. Those misinterpretations are deeply rooted in stereotypes and internalized messages about blackness as disruptive to a normal (read white) order of things. For example, the congregation of Black students in a hallway—once an illegal act in the Deep South—remains punishable in schools because the congregation itself defies the order of school. Instead of insisting on conformity to the order of whiteness and relying on stereotypes of Black students as threatening to justify removing congregating students, practitioners could refrain from reporting or punishing students and instead engage with them. Doing so may position school-based practitioners to learn about, and rectify, the sources of their misinterpretations of students' behaviors, exploring and reflecting about why a group of Black students simply being together violates the order of schools. Doing so may also make it possible for practitioners to learn about their students and their experiences, positioning them to make meaningful connections with their students.

Similarly, scholars have argued that what is often considered to be "deviant" behavior might also be:

> an extension of, and a special case of, the cultural repertoire or tool kit of cultural practices. They are produced out of cultural communities and the only distinction between cultural practices that are successfully labeled as deviant versus those that are not is that they are labeled and defined in relation to the symbolic order of respectability. Thus, labeled practices of deviance are cultural practices. (Dixon-Romàn 2014, 15)

"Deviant" behavior is hence constructed in juxtaposition to "respectful behavior." Dominant ways of knowing respect and being respectful in school, though, are rooted in whiteness and the affordances that come with it. The labeling of what may be better understood as cultural practices as deviant is, at best, arbitrary and, at worst, discriminatory. Such labeling highlights the expectation that Black students should conform to dominant ways of expressing and recognizing respect in schools—an assimilationist perspective (Kendi 2017) rooted in white supremacy. Relationships between students and school-based practitioners become increasingly complex given dominant narratives about Black students as criminal and deviant—perhaps inherently disrespectful—especially when considered in tandem with common tropes about adolescents as disorderly or rebellious. This way of pathologizing certain behaviors as deviant, and then punishing that deviance allows for this racialization to occur while also affording those who punish the opportunity to avoid scrutiny for punishing a particular group. Given this racialization, studying what is commonly understood as deviant behavior is a worthy endeavor:

> Through a focus on "deviant" practice we are witness to the power of those at the bottom, whose everyday life decisions challenge, or at least counter, the basic normative assumptions of a society intent on protecting structural and social inequalities under the guise of some normal and natural order to life. However, not only do these individuals daily act in opposition to dominant

norms, but they also contradict members of Black communities who are committed to mirroring perceived respectable behaviors and hierarchical structures. (Cohen 2004, 33)

Put another way, what is considered deviant behavior in school discipline data is inherently racialized; studying what is understood to be deviance uncovers the racialized narratives that are so often told and internalized. Reports published by the Office of Civil Rights (OCR) in conjunction with state-level numeric data and national trends reveal that practitioners disproportionately punish Black students via all exclusionary methods of discipline (i.e., suspension, expulsion, referral to law enforcement and alternative schools, and school-based arrest) in Alabama. Much of the exclusionary discipline in Alabama is used as a consequence for subjective incidents, and subjective incidents are disproportionately assigned to Black students nationwide. Thus, we suggest that students' enactment of behaviors that are commonly, if subjectively, understood to be problematic, such as Rachel's profanity in the opening portrait, might also be students' enactment of "dangerous dignity . . . in response to and in anticipation of . . . ongoing humiliation and hypocrisy" (Tuck 2011, 819). That is, Rachel's profanity and other behaviors that are labeled as defiance, disruption, inciting others to create a disturbance, and so on might be viewed as her resistance to everyday indignities (Tuck 2011) experienced at school. Such indignities occur as by-products of school policies—both explicit and implicit—and practices that are rooted in stereotypes about Black students and in racist notions of order. Reframing such behaviors as resistance to oppressive school environments provides an opportunity for reflection: what might students be attempting to communicate; what might they be trying to teach practitioners about the systems of schooling and their experiences within those systems?

Rachel's profanity in our opening portrait was understood by the school principal to be disrespectful, disruptive, and defiant, deviant from some normal, desired behavior; this profanity triggered a mechanism for punishment as evidenced by her subsequent removal via a week-long suspension. Rather than assuming that youth like Rachel are deviant, or impulsive, immature, and out of control, practitioners might instead give them the benefit of the doubt. Youth, perhaps especially Black youth, might be readily able to identify hypocrisy and inequity in systems like schools, and to then implement strategies to confront the problems they face within them. Those behaviors that are often characterized as deviant, defiant, and disrupting a natural order to the running of schools and classrooms might be reframed as resistance, a resistance that serves agentic and communicative purposes.

UNDERSTANDING RESISTANCE

Within oppressive contexts and taken-for-granted processes, people enact resistance. Just as removal is sociopolitically, culturally, and historically rooted in the Deep South, there are long-standing traditions here of resistance to anti-Black racism via spiritual and faith practices, congregating, ceremony, nonviolent direct action, social and political agitation, joy, and love (Dillard 2016). Resistance, as it is broadly studied, is usually set in opposition to theories of reproduction (Dimitriadis 2011), emphasizing the ways that individuals have agency and become empowered in the midst of oppression. Resistance, scholars argue, might be understood as an essential feature of institutions or as an expression of individual agency with implications for identity development (for brief reviews of the ways that different fields approach the study of resistance, see Kim 2010 or Raider-Roth, Stieha, and Hensley 2012). Youth resistance in particular has been studied across student identity groups including work about, for example, white working-class boys (Willis 1977), Latinx youth (Villenas and Deyhle 1999), Chicanx students (Solorzano and Bernal 2001), Indigenous youth (Brayboy 2005), Asian American youth (Kwon 2006, 2013), and African American youth (Noguera 2009; Noguera, Tuck, and Yang 2013).

Resistance began to be studied formally in education as scholars critiqued many of the social reproduction theories they viewed as deterministic, static, and inadequate at capturing contested educational contexts wherein agency is exerted. As Giroux (1983) asserts, for example, "there are complex and creative fields of resistance through which class-, race-, and gender-mediated practices often refuse, reject, and dismiss the central messages of the schools" (260).

Certain behaviors enacted by youth in schools may perpetuate their own oppression: those behaviors labeled as "self-defeating," but which also may be rooted in critiques of institutions and ways of being and knowing that create hostile and oppressive contexts (Fine 1991; Foley 1990; Nolan 2011; Solorzano and Bernal 2001; Valenzuela 1999). There might also be a "conformist" resistance wherein youth do not necessarily agree with the norms and workings of schooling as an institution, but work the system for individual advancement. A "transformational resistance" has been conceptualized, rooted in critical theories of race and racism, which includes ideas about how "oppositional behavior may be an impetus toward social justice" (Solorzano and Bernal 2001, 310).

Models of youth resistance predicated on Westernized notions of social justice projects may aim for marginalized groups simply to be more fully included in a capitalist system (for review, see Tuck and Yang 2013). Resistance, these scholars argue, might instead be understood as everyday and as underscoring the limits of systems of oppression (Tuck and Yang 2011, 527). Youth disrupt and exploit fractures in oppressive policies, by, for example, dropping out of school as a form of biopolitical resistance to the effects of oppressive and hostile policies and practices on the body (Ruglis 2011). Youth might enact a form of "racial wisdom" (Paperson 2011) that functions "in response to those who represent, or serve as agents of systemic injustice" (Sosa and Latta 2019, 109).

Resistance as Strategy

To restate, rather than pathologizing behaviors deemed to be deviant (Cohen 2004) and treating them as cause for removal, we call on practitioners to reframe those behaviors as a productive resistance, a cause for reflective work. School-based practitioners might reinterpret student resistance—for example, to following instructions, to complying with rules, to engaging in learning tasks, those behaviors that might be otherwise understood as deviant—as communicative (Grahame and Jardine 1990; Kim 2010). This resistance may function as a self-defense mechanism so as to avoid failure in learning contexts; as a demand for meaningful, relevant instruction; or as a way to empower. Students who are disruptive or defiant may be engaged in strategies designed to instruct their teachers about their work as practitioners and about the overall systems of schooling. These pedagogical moves by students may be meant to communicate resentment about expectations of conforming, or they may be meant to call attention to the irrelevance of the curriculum and the pedagogies of the teacher. In these moments, students are engaging in acts of communication about their state of being within controlling and constraining contexts; they are perhaps engaged in resistance to everyday indignities (Tuck 2011). When students are removed for these behaviors, teachers miss an opportunity to explore what is communicated by them. Practitioners might instead understand resistance as historically, politically, and socially rooted; even if it initially creates a disruption of or interruption in a relationship, resistance might also be a path toward understanding and repair (Raider-Roth et al. 2012). As Noguera, Tuck, and Yang (2013) explain: "Resistance is important because it affirms our humanity, and it reminds us that we can be more than simply victims of oppression or observers of a particular historical moment" (71).

Reframing Rachel's use of profanity to respond to a school principal that day as resistance that is meant to communicate (Kim 2010), we might consider that she could have been reflecting how her experiences and ways of knowing and being (and those of students like her in the school) had been removed from existence by way of omission from formal curricula and instruction. She could have been responding to the ways her school experiences were not respectful or inclusive of her. She may have been demanding more relevant, rigorous instruction, given that she often complained to us about how boring her classes were and how tired she was of filling out worksheet packets. She may have been communicating that her previous demands for meaningful instruction and content from teachers had been refused. She may have been expressing her cynicism about school, curriculum, pedagogy, or discipline. Or, she may have been actively attempting to trigger her removal from a context that she perceived to be hostile and uncaring, enacting a "dangerous dignity" (Tuck 2011) to preserve and affirm her core humanity. She may have been indicating that she, herself, felt disrespected.

Indeed, in our work in alternative schools in Alabama, we have heard countless stories from Black students about feeling disrespected, unheard, and unseen by teachers and school leaders. Students often described frustration and a sense of unfairness about authority figures who exhibited favoritism and preferential treatment in alternative schools, echoing the experiences that led to their removal from their previous schools. Students described what they called "disrespectful" behavior from teachers and other school personnel who "don't even know" them and who made assumptions about who they were based on the fact that they were students at an alternative school; they were "bad kids", treated like they were misbehaving before any actual behavior had occurred. School personnel often justified their punishments with explanations such as "I'm older" and "I've already got my degree"; students further described feeling like "they don't care about us." Sometimes, students voiced these concerns in the middle of, or even at the expense of, our planned instruction for the day. We suspect that, for some teachers, the voicing of those concerns may have been viewed as interruptions, disruptions, or even as defying the natural order of a classroom, and that those students may have been punished for voicing those concerns. Instead, though, we tried to keep these types of moments in context, working to keep our reactions reflective and humanizing rather than punitive, and keeping in mind that resistance is an everyday, macro-level practice that may be rooted in racial knowledge, cultural repertoire, and the savvy identification of fractures in oppressive systems. For our part, we resisted systemic expectations about how school-based practitioners should engage in the grammar of schooling as it is bound up with whiteness and anti-Black racism as well as expectations that prioritize efficiency, covering the standards, and upholding unjust discipline policies.

In the next chapter, we delve into the daily experiences of teaching Rachel and her classmates at the alternative school; we position humanizing, often joyous portraits of them to counter dominant narratives in the community about who they were as students and people. Following these portraits, we explore how two different school leaders engaged in resistance to school discipline policies and practices in their respective school contexts.

Chapter 5

Who Are the "Bad Kids"?

Portraits of Alternative School Students (with Sean A. Forbes)

DeVon: Man, those adults over there, they're crazy. Coach A sends us to ISS [in-school suspension] when our shirts are untucked.
Levi: Yeah, and if he don't like you and your shirt *is* tucked in, he'll come up behind you and untuck it.
DeVon: Yeah he told Coach B [the head football coach] that I shouldn't play 'cause he said I walk around with my shirt untucked.
Hannah: So when you got sent to ISS for that stuff . . . about your shirt, do you know what they put on the form? Like, what the write-up was for?
DeVon: Defiance.
Levi: Yeah, defiance. And they do stupid stuff like suspend people for talkin' in the hallway. Once I got suspended in cooking because I didn't feel like chopping tomatoes.
Hannah: What was the write-up for that time?
Levi: Disobedience.

One morning toward the end of the school year, DeVon and Levi appeared to want to let it all out: their stories about authority figures at their high school who were "disrespectful" to them, who made "trouble out of nothing," and the ways they had been treated as "bad kids" before being sent to the alternative school. They recounted the ways that the coaches at Muscogee High School chastised and harassed them, fabricating their defiance, before sending them to in-school suspension. They also recounted the rampant favoritism shown to some athletes, and especially football players, at their home high school: "They can show up smellin' like weed and still get a four-year scholarship to Georgia or Alabama or somewhere." They listed the types of things they had been written up and suspended for before coming to the alternative school: "disrespectful," "not following directions," "talking in class," and "disturbing other students."

In previous chapters, we have addressed the ways that Black students are routinely removed from their classrooms, teachers, and peers by way of exclusionary discipline practices, including being placed at alternative schools, and particularly for subjective incidents such as being labeled disrespectful, defiant, or otherwise enacting deviant behavior. In this chapter, we again take up the intersection of exclusionary and subjective discipline to emphasize the ways that students were removed from their home school to an alternative school in a particular school system. We then describe our work at the school, a context that was hostile and oppressive, offering portraits of Black students as a form of resistance to dominant narratives both about their identities as students and how they should be treated.

DEFINING ALTERNATIVE EDUCATION

Our work at the alternative school began as part of a university-funded outreach project. Drawing on our experience as former public school teachers, our work as instructors of research methods at our institution, and our desire to spend time with high schoolers, we worked with students to study food systems, engage in research projects, and contribute to efforts housed at an established community garden. The community garden space included a greenhouse; outdoor garden with animals like goats, ducks, and chickens; and a carpentry shop. We hosted two student markets each semester, where students presented findings from their research projects and sold things they had grown or otherwise made (birdhouses, vegetable starts, flower bouquets, and wood carvings of popular phrases like "Live, Laugh, Love," "Faith," "War Eagle," and "Roll Tide"). On paper, we taught agriscience; the curriculum we developed included topics around food systems, food security, community food production, and environmental justice. We also incorporated lessons that prompted students to consider things like sense of purpose, imagined futures, and collective action to systemic injustice, topics that were not included in any formal standards for our particular course.

In many ways, though, our teaching in the alternative school was well aligned with the stated goals of alternative education in Alabama. Disciplinary alternative education programs, known as DAEP in some states, ostensibly provide highly structured learning experiences for those students who are perceived to need targeted instruction and support services in order to be academically and socially successful, as defined by school policy and leadership (Kennedy-Lewis, Whitaker, and Soutullo 2016; Kim and Taylor 2008). Programming in these schools is wide ranging, and may include, in addition to core courses like Language Arts, Math, Science, and Social Studies, curricula such as career and technical training, socio-emotional learning, teen parenting and teen pregnancy programming, dropout prevention, and high-stakes test preparation (for a review of definitions of alternative education, see Porowski et al. 2014). Some alternative school models are positioned as contexts where students can opt in when they struggle with attendance, overwhelming social environments, or academics, in addition to those alternative programs aimed at students who have dropped out or aged out of traditional school models (Ruzzi and Kraemer 2006). Indeed, "second chance schools" may provide disconnected youth with vital support and resources, drawing on experienced teachers and community organizers to do so (Flennaugh, Cooper Stein, and Carter Andrews 2018).

Alternative schools in Alabama are just as wide ranging, where "programs and models designed to meet the needs of students at risk of school failure are as diverse as the students themselves" (ALSDE 2011). Most alternative schools in Alabama, however, function as exclusionary, carceral contexts to which students are removed for disciplinary incidents, even if they also allow students to opt in. Much like incarcerated youth who exist in a "betwixt and betweenness" that is "neither here nor there" as they work to navigate an oppressive, marginalizing school/prison nexus (Winn 2010, 2011), students in alternative schools exist in a contested space wherein students are housed, in between their home school contexts and their actual homes, at the literal and figurative last stop before being pushed out (Morris 2016) of public schools altogether. Students are removed from their home schools via disciplinary policies and practices and into an alternative school designed to "scare students straight" with even more strict policies and routines that resemble carceral contexts (Selman 2017) and where they are subjected to punishment as pedagogy (Selman 2018).

Alternative schools in Alabama might, for example, serve in place of expulsion for incidents such as possession of weapons or drugs, fights at school, or other objective offenses for which system policies specify zero tolerance (Kennedy et al. 2019). Increasingly, alternative school placements are also seen as viable options for students who have been disciplined for subjective incidents, those students like Levi and DeVon who were viewed as defiant, disruptive, or disobedient. These students are removed from traditional school environments in order to be corrected via the carceral climate of alternative schools. In Alabama, a majority of students in alternative schools are Black, mirroring nationwide trends in the employment of alternative education (Kennedy et al. 2019; Vanderhaar et al. 2014), though it is often positioned as a reform, an "alternative" to exclusionary discipline. In 2015–2016, data from the Office of Civil Rights (OCR) revealed that approximately 33 percent of enrolled students statewide were Black, while approximately 56 percent of students placed in alternative schools were Black. In that same year, of the 61 school systems in the state that year that referred students to alternative schools, 48 of those disproportionately referred Black students. In other words, students, particularly Black students, are ostracized and confined to alternative education programming at high rates in Alabama, and often for misperceptions about behavior that are rooted in racist stereotypes.

ALTERNATIVE EDUCATION IN MUSCOGEE CITY SCHOOLS

Figure 5.1 describes the incidents, including those that are subjective (marked with an asterisk), that accounted for days of alternative school placement in Levi and DeVon's school system, Muscogee City Schools. Subjective incidents accounted for 11,050 of the total 21,356 days (approximately 52 percent) over the space of six academic years. As reported in figure 5.1, the incident leading to the most days of student placement in the alternative school in Muscogee City Schools was fighting, which we characterize as an objective offense (4,633 days). However, defiance of authority, an incident that is subject to practitioner interpretation, and also bound up with stereotypes about Black students, accounted for only three fewer days of alternative school placement (4,630 days) than fighting. Defiance of authority as an incident resulted in the most days of alternative school placement in four of the six school years reported (2012–2013, 2013–2014, 2014–2015, and 2015–2016). Of the next five incidents accounting for large numbers of days of alternative school placement across all years—drug possession, willful disobedience, disruptive demonstrations, other incidents resulting in state-defined disciplinary action, and profanity/vulgarity—four were subjective, accounting for 5,562 days collectively. Given this pattern, it is unsurprising that subjective incidents, which we linked to anti-Black stereotypes in chapter 2, accounted for more than half of the days of placement in the alternative school in this system.

We also note that the latest data available from the OCR indicated that there were twenty-one School Resource Officers (SROs) employed in the school system, a system with only twelve school counselors, comprised of 4,258 students, approximately 60 percent of whom were Black. In this system, Black students were underrepresented in Calculus, Chemistry, and Physics enrollment. They were also underrepresented in public preschool attendance, while they were overrepresented in all of the disciplinary categories the system reported using (i.e., in-school suspension, out-of-school suspension, and referral to law enforcement). 2015–2016 OCR data also indicated that the

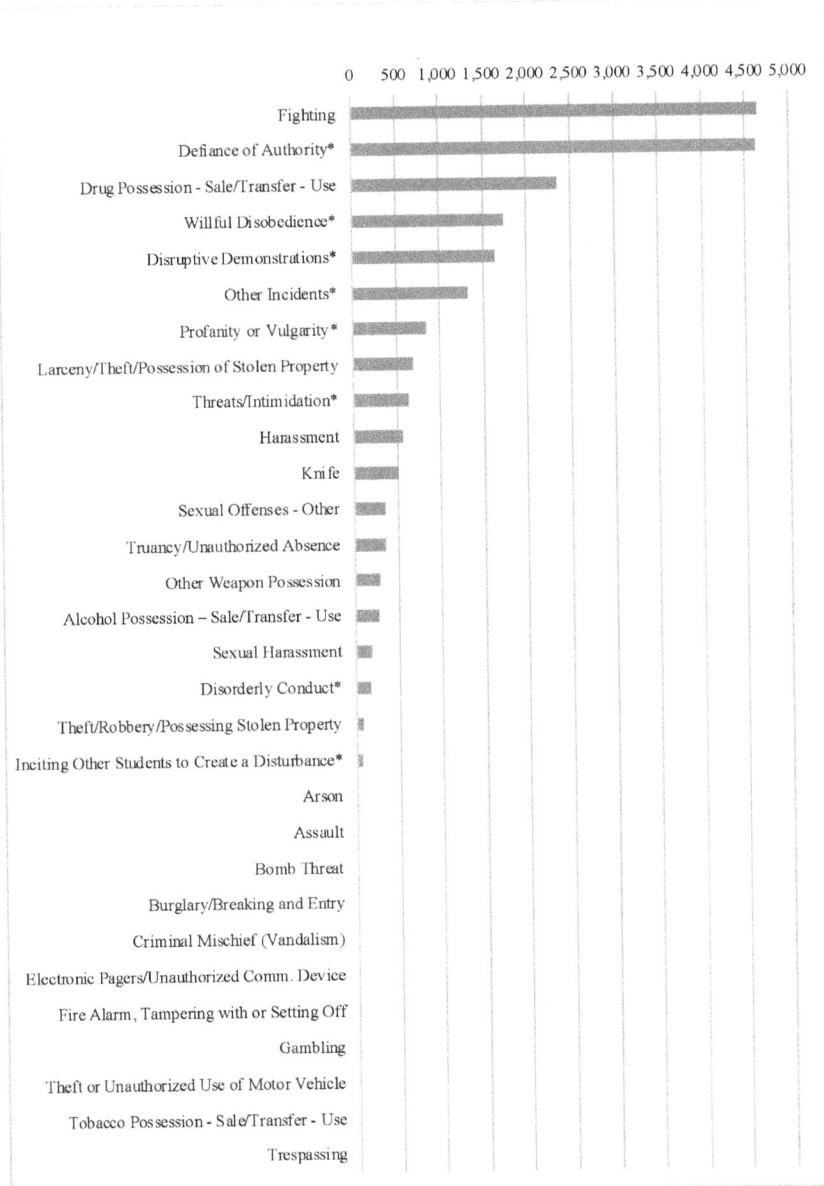

Figure 5.1 Days of Alternative School in Muscogee City Schools for Each State-Defined Incident, 2010–2016. *Source*: Created by authors.

system reported that no students had been referred to alternative schools, a discrepancy which we take up in the last chapter of the book.

"BAD KIDS"

Daniel: I miss people there [at the high school], but I really just don't like any of the teachers or principals there. They're fast to jump to conclusions. About anything really.

Carey: What kind of conclusions do you think they reach?

Daniel: A lot of people know I skateboard and stuff, and there's a little prejudice against that. They judge me just 'cause I ride a piece of plywood with wheels on it. [They assume] I'm a bad kid; I'm a troubled kid. I used to be, but I've kinda straightened out now.

Samuel: That I'm sneaky. 'Cause I'm quiet. And, I don't talk to a lot of people because I feel like I just get in trouble. I don't wanna be in trouble. I just don't got time for it. So I just . . . be quiet. But when it's time to talk, I'll talk.

Carey: So, what do you wish teachers knew about you?

Samuel: That I'm a good kid. I'm a funny kid. I'm quiet, but at times, when it comes to it, I'll have a little fun. Then, when I'm older, I want them to know that I'm doing good. That I made it. I did a lot more than they thought I would probably do. Some people just didn't like me. I don't know why. They probably think I'll end up being locked up or somethin'.

These were, ostensibly, the "bad kids"; they were deviant and criminal, to be feared. Students at the alternative school in Muscogee City were often treated like criminals, made to participate, for example, in a morning routine of being searched on their way into school, akin to that which people experience at the hands of police. Indeed, there was often a police officer on site. Though students felt "disrespected" by this search, they also said they knew "it was for safety purposes," and they had to participate in the daily routine of being searched without talking. All students with whom we worked, across all the semesters we spent at the school, perpetually lamented the fact that they could not speak to one another during the school day or at lunch without being penalized or punished. We had also seen school leaders call police to school (if they were not already in the building) in instances where students talked back or went to the bathroom without teachers' explicit permission, in the name of keeping the environment safe. Students chalked these routines up to the idea that authority figures in the building saw them as criminal and expected them to misbehave; they were being targeted, searched, and silenced because they were "bad kids," in their words. To be clear, these procedures of surveillance, control, and criminalization are certainly not unique to alternative schools; they occur across schools in Alabama. What sets this context apart, however, was that students at the alternative school had internalized messages about who they were as kids and students in ways that we had not seen in other schools, often justifying these routines with claims that they were deserving of them.

Their punishment, and thus their exclusion, was often explained by assertions about how they were not serious about school, and "didn't care about learning" or education, tropes that are commonly invoked when students, across all schooling contexts, do not conform and comply. Instead, we observed students at the school engage in learning, play, relationship building, and philanthropic intentions, student behaviors that were not at all in keeping with what we had been told about them or what they had been told about themselves. Daniel and Samuel, above, harken to the tension of having been stereotyped and of wanting people to know that they were good kids. They articulated how they hoped authority figures would see them and how they believed they deserved to be viewed. Yet, it was clear they had not been afforded opportunities to talk about these desires in the teachers' classrooms at the school from which they'd been sent to the alternative school, or at the alternative school itself, absent our conversations with them in our class. Instead, they were surveilled based on teachers' and administrators' presumptions and simultaneously never truly seen by authority figures.

Isaac decided early in the semester that he was going to spend his time in the woodshop. He measured and cut carefully, painstakingly crafting an array of lettered signs scrolled from 2 × 4s that he then hand sanded, painted, and sealed.

Sean: These look great!
Isaac: I guess . . . this one came out good. We'll see if anyone'll buy one.
He pointed to one of the "love" pieces painted black with red dripping from the top of the letters.
Sean: I bet Mr. Taylor [the Muscogee City Schools truancy officer] would like these.
Isaac: I hope he doesn't come by. He'll just yell at me for being off campus!

The day of the market, Isaac was early. He helped set up the tents, put out road signs, and carefully arranged his products for sale, rivaling the most experienced merchandiser. Isaac confidently explained to potential customers how each item was made. In the flurry of activity, he didn't notice Mr. Taylor's arrival.

Mr. Taylor: You made these?
Isaac, without much enthusiasm: Yeah.

Mr. Taylor, seemingly impressed: I didn't know you could do this.
Isaac: There's a lot you don't know about me.
Mr. Taylor: Apparently.

Students, like Isaac, often talked about the ways teachers mischaracterized them or generalized their identities, not affording them opportunities to refute assumptions. They felt both stuck in old assumptions about them and misunderstood by their teachers and school administrators. The alternative school was a contested space where students were punished for prior wrongdoing, unsure about when they would be determined eligible to return to their home schools, feared and misunderstood by both teachers and other students. Thus, this context produced the students within the alternative school building as problems in need of correction. Students at the school were further ostracized from the school community in that they were prohibited from participating in extracurricular events in the system, including theatre, dance, academic clubs, sports; nor were they allowed to attend any athletic or celebratory events, such as football games and proms. Students could, however, attend their own graduations. Students also lived in small, fairly tight-knit communities in the area where attendance at the alternative school was well known. That is, many Black community members knew about the school, knew people who went there at some point, or may have even attended themselves; its existence, and the reasons for its existence, were taken as a given. It was, though, a school meant to house and correct students who were deemed unfit for the traditional school setting because they were disruptive, frightening, and threatening. To be clear, this characterization of alternative school students was constructed from assumptions, stereotypes, rumor, partial truths, and snippets of decontextualized stories that nevertheless confirmed this dominant narrative of deviance.

Narratives about students are racialized, given, for example, the robust literature pointing to how much more likely teachers are to ascribe descriptors like 'sneaky', 'lazy', and 'aggressive' to Black students (Cooper 2003; James 2012; Marsh and Noguera 2018) and given the ways that Black students are removed from instruction and schools by way of these stereotypes. Before working there and meeting the students at this particular school, we heard the stories in the community, and it was easy to imagine that the behaviors students enacted to warrant their placement in alternative education must have been violent and egregious. Data regarding incidents that result in alternative school referral in Alabama, however, and at this particular school, do not bear that out. What we found was that only their placement in the building and the stories told about them made them frightening. We met people who were serious students concerned with challenges that plague communities, like food insecurity, and who were willing to work to address them. We met people who were goofy kids who wanted to play, build relationships with one another, and explore. Thus, the paradox of this school was that, although it was ostensibly built to house frightening students who must have had done things to warrant being sent to an alternative school, it instead created the illusion of scary students. That is, alternative schools create and reinforce the constructed narrative about the students housed in them.

In the data collection phase of our semester-long research project, students prepared to explore food rituals and practices with some of the elementary students at the school, using collages of food pictures to elicit conversation. Students practiced a round of interviewing first with peers in their class, and then went down the hallway to an elementary classroom for the interviews. After some brief introductions, the teenagers in our class had all the little kids engaged in conversation, with their cutest smiles and most accessible tones. Wallace and a little girl leaned toward one another, holding a steady conversation. DeVon and a little boy talked in low voices, and the little boy was pointing at something on the wall as they talked. They looked up and Hannah winked at DeVon. He replied with a big smile. Javier and Ray were at a table with three little boys, all eager to participate. One of the boys pointed at Javier's collage of food pictures and, jabbing his finger rapidly to each food on the page, said, "I like this and this and this and this and THIS." Javier looked up at us, his eyes wide, full of amusement. Later he said that his student was much more interested in talking about the pictures than answering questions. Similarly, Ray and two little boys chitchatted about his collage.

Tessa worked with another very little boy in some chairs on the other side of the room.

Tessa: Hey, I'm Tessa. What's your name?
Little boy: Roman!
Tessa: How old are you, Roman?
Roman: Five!
Tessa: Five, huh? What's your favorite food?
Roman: Pizza!
Tessa: What about snacks . . . what kind of snacks do you like?
Roman: Pizza!
　　　Tessa giggled. Roman did too.
Tessa: What's your favorite vegetable?
Roman: Apples!
Tessa: That's a fruit.
Roman: Oranges?
Tessa: That's a fruit, too. You like green beans, or corn?
Roman: Yeah, I like corn.

After about five minutes, the elementary teacher worked to get the students' attention: "Touch your head if you can hear me. Touch your nose," and so on. All of us "big kids" followed her requests until she had all of the students' attention.

As previously mentioned, school personnel and the broader community criminalized students at the alternative school, positioning them as troublemakers, expecting them to misbehave. They also expected them to forego opportunities to engage in learning, but this was in direct conflict to what we observed when working with students. During our agriscience course, students exhibited interest and concern about food systems and food security, both in their local community and in broader contexts. This interest manifested in community-based research and activism to better understand food systems. Students gathered online resources, collected surveys, conducted interviews with community members and fellow students at the alternative school, and made print and audiovisual materials.

Rachel: What's most exciting about graduating?

Jenny: Hmm . . . the most exciting thing about graduating is that you don't have to come to school every morning. You don't have to wake up at five o'clock every morning to come to this place. And then, I can work freely, I don't have to have a work permit. I'm officially an adult basically, ready to explore the world. Stuff like that.

Rachel: Okay, what is most scary about graduating?

Jenny: Hmm. College. I'm very scared about college. I don't know what college life is going to offer. What it's going to be like. And stuff of that nature.

Rachel: Okay. What is your best memory from your time as a high school student?

Jenny: Umm. When I went to Orange High School, I was on the track team for three years. Being part of a sport and being part of a team, it makes you feel good. And it makes you feel like you're a part of something.

Rachel: What is your worst time from being a high school student?

Jenny: Um. When I got pregnant. I got bullied really bad. And when I say really bad, I mean really, really bad. So. Yeah, being bullied. I wouldn't say the being pregnant part was really bad. But getting bullied . . . kids pick. They're not nice, they were kind of evil.

Rachel: What do you know now that you wish you had known as a freshman, sophomore, and junior?

Jenny: Come to school. Come to school. And if you ain't got an excused absence, just don't even bother. Make up your work when you come to school the next time. Ask for your make up work. You'll just be looking crazy at the end of the 9 weeks, I promise. Grades count. They really do.

Students' interests in the class had also manifested in relationship building, peer mentoring, and support about how to navigate their present circumstances while pursuing more desirable futures. Rachel and Jenny had been particularly interested in documenting one another's stories, conducting interviews toward the end of one semester. Rachel looked for wisdom that Jenny might bestow as a graduating senior, wisdom that might support her efforts to navigate a contested school environment. Jenny's status as an adult, with a child of her own, was clear; she was expected to come to school and advocate for herself after any absence, even those connected to her child's health and well-being. Yet, her status as a child was also clear; subjected to the constraints of childhood, including limitations on the number of hours she could work each week and compulsory schooling, she was frustrated and resentful. To be clear, we are not arguing that students should work long hours each week while also attending school; though, we know of many teenagers whose work situations require them to work well past legal limits in Alabama, which include working no more than 18 hours per week and having to finish shifts by 7 o'clock. Rather, we highlight this exchange between Jenny and Rachel to demonstrate the ways that Jenny was treated as both child and adult and how she worked to navigate and resist this tension.

This in-betweenness resembled a more heightened and multilayered version of what we've often seen in our work with adolescents in other settings, the ways in which high schoolers are both emerging adults and children. In earlier chapters, we wrote about the impossibility of Black childhood in that Black children are often adultified and viewed to be older than their actual ages, leading to adult consequences and punishments; simultaneously, Black youth are treated as children in need of correction and strict rules. The alternative school students with whom we worked faced the layered complexities of Black racial identity and narratives about them as problems and troublemakers who "didn't want to learn." They were expected to both embody the identity of the obedient, compliant child and bear the weight of adult consequences. This rendering simultaneously denied them the luxuries of both childhood *and* adulthood. That is, they were saddled with the burdens of both life stages in the forms of lack of autonomy and exposure to harsh consequences while still navigating an oppressive educational system and school climate. Students had assumed adult responsibilities, such as paying bills, acting as primary caregivers for their own children and younger siblings in the after-school hours, and having been punished as adults with parole officers. Yet, they still very much cared about school, their grades, and perceptions about them in the community related to school completion. Our students repeatedly asserted that they were planning to attend college, even as some of them carried the baggage of having to navigate the justice system and even had criminal records.

Kevin and Kendall had been chasing each other around the building, which stood, looming and brown, in front of the community garden. They whooped, giggled, laughed. It was hot, not summertime-in-Alabama-hot yet, but hot enough that we exchanged knowing glances as soon as the students started to run around and get sweaty: we'd be riding back to school in a bus filled with the weird smells of adolescence. We were just wrapping up our day at the garden, spent watering and tending our ornamentals and vegetables, and had a couple of minutes to spare before we had to head back to the alternative school. This was the precious time that students relished in their moments of being able to talk to one another, play with one another, and, on the occasional bad day, get ornery with one another.

As they rounded the building, Kevin leading and Kendall narrowly behind, Kevin leaped over a length of chain at the top of a small incline. He seemed to hang for a moment, that thing that Michael Jordan could do when he really got "air," which Hannah referenced to the group standing there watching them. A couple of students rolled their eyes, smirked, since MJ had been eclipsed as a sports figure by Kobe, LeBron, Kyrie, other greats of later times than her 80s childhood. Hannah remarked on their smirks, reminding them that almost everyone in the group was wearing Jordans. Kevin landed next to the group without breaking stride, using one hand to hold his belt and his pants up, using the other to signal victory in whatever race he and Kendall had been running. Two girls laughed, twinkles in their eyes, those two who had been competing for Kevin's attention all semester; Jenny rolled her eyes. Sean gave a little motion toward the bus. "Alright y'all, let's go!"

When we got back to school, we had some transition time. Kevin sat at his "favorite" computer station, pulling up the flier he had been working on to advertise for our upcoming market. He entered some text into an HTML frame on the side of the screen, coding which images he wanted to appear on the flier and where. Kendall got his binder from the shelf and pulled out the paper he'd been working on about deforestation and its effects on ecosystems. Jenny measured her growing tomato plant, recording both centimeters and inches into her binder as she tracked its time from germination to bloom.

Play was an experience not often afforded to the students with whom we worked. Although adultified and infantilized, they were not generally permitted to actually behave like children. Instead, they were surveilled and silenced, burdened with assumptions about criminality, and confined in spaces removed from their traditional schools and the peers and opportunities therein. But, despite already occupying many adult roles and some being punished as adults via the criminal justice system, students also asserted their desire to "just be kids." In addition to community-based research, students worked to grow and harvest nutritious foods for donation to the local food bank, and it was in the context of their agricultural work that we often had the most opportunities to see them engage in play and silliness. We saw them play tag in the green space next to the community garden, brag to one another about whose beets were fatter or whose tomatoes were taller, and search for worms in the garden dirt (Baggett 2021). Despite often facing adult consequences for school-based disciplinary incidents, and facing the impossibility of childhood, these students who had been labeled as so dangerous and disruptive that they deserved exclusion from broader school contexts actually embodied childlike wonder, playfulness, and silliness.

In addition, by being treated as individuals with interests of their own, including academic and social interests, they demonstrated that they could be trusted to manage their own time, play when it was time to play and work when it was time to work. We had no need for infantilizing tactics, such as control and coercion, or adultifying tactics, such as the threat or implementation of harsh consequences, though school personnel would have had us believe that, without them, "who knows what they might do?" Without these threats and without the customary confinement of the school, we saw students engage in self-directed learning and relationship building in the context of inquiry-based projects that were important to them, demonstrating their commitment to their work in our class.

In this chapter, we have presented portraits of the students with whom we worked at an alternative school in an effort to resist and counter dominant narratives about them in the community. Black students face stigmas by virtue of racist stereotypes that equate blackness and criminality; those stigmas and stereotypes are further reified when practitioners remove Black students from many of their classmates and teachers by way of exclusionary discipline policies and practices. It is dehumanizing to remove students from their intended educative environments, surveilling them without seeing them as complex individuals, and allowing their potential for play, intellectualism, and activism to be overshadowed by presumptions of criminality or guilt. In presenting the portraits in this chapter, we hope to have humanized students, demonstrating that they are smart, engaged, resilient, funny, and capable of teaching us so much, and warded off the stigma of "bad kids." We encourage readers, especially practitioners, to use the portraits we have presented here as models by which to engage in honest and careful thinking about all students, and especially the "bad kids" in their lives.

In the previous chapter, we asked readers to think carefully about what might be learned from student behaviors that can be understood as resistance to oppressive contexts and practices. Here, we have highlighted the ways that readers can position students and their work in schools to resist dominant, damaging narratives about them. It is important to remember that resistance is contextually and temporally bound (Tuck and Yang 2013) and always operating within changing conditions. For example, youth enact shifting, varied, and contested forms of resistance—to teachers, administrators, ideologies, assimilation, and conformity—as a way to preserve and keep intact a core of being and to communicate about the conditions they must navigate. Likewise, school-based practitioners navigate contexts that change and morph over time. Thus, "resistance is always in context, in a place, between real people—even when some of those people embody the state" (Tuck and Yang 2013, 8), such as school-based practitioners enacting disciplinary policies and practices. In the next chapter, we highlight the resistance enacted by two leaders in a school system, providing parallel portraits of how these leaders worked to resist on behalf of the students and communities to whom they felt beholden.

Chapter 6

Resistance and School-Based Practitioners

School-based practitioners operate in pockets of resistance across the country and across the schooling contexts. In the context of school leadership, for example, scholars have explored how school leaders should enact culturally responsive leadership (Khalifa 2018) and community-based leadership for justice (DeMatthews 2018) and have detailed the social justice identities of school leaders (Carpenter et al. 2017) and the ways that leaders face resistance in enacting social justice in their schools (Theoharis 2007). Cultivating resistance among school-based practitioners is often difficult, however, because, rather than being positioned as agents for change, school leaders and administrators are made to operate as middle managers in increasingly marketized/business models of education (Bartlett et al. 2002). They are often held responsible for implementing top-down rather than locally driven policy, while also avoiding conversations about race and racism (Khalifa and Briscoe 2015). Moreover, school-based practitioners, including leaders and teachers, are racially socialized as we all are in a white supremacist system and thus draw on harmful stereotypes and enact racist policies and practices (Toure and Dorsey 2018). Teachers are often conditioned to be and think of themselves as passive (for a review, see Furman 2020), making works like hooks' (2014) *Teaching as an Act of Resistance* and Love's (2019) *Abolitionist Teaching* so important. Finally, many school-based practitioners are socialized to espouse ideas of neutrality in teaching (Dunn, Sondel, and Baggett 2019) rather than working toward racial justice and activism in and outside of the classroom, despite an increased focus on social justice and equity in many educator and leader preparation programs. What might it look like if more school-based practitioners worked to resist policies and practices that perpetuate inequity? For example, how might the school principal in our portrait of Rachel in chapter 4 have engaged in an act of resistance? Would

Rachel have been removed if he had reframed her behavior not as an act of deviance but as an act of youth resistance and communication about her schooling context?

In this chapter, we highlight portraits of two Black school leaders—Leonard and Marcus—who were tasked with being disciplinarians in their schools. We explore how they worked to resist policies and practices that were bound up with stereotypes about race, academics, and space. We also emphasize the ways that they worked to reframe student behavior as agentic, resistant, and communicative. We note that the system in which they worked was one where Black administrators were strategically dispersed and tokenized; that is, it was rare for a single school building to have more than one Black administrator. We highlight how their experiences were similar but not shared; Leonard and Marcus processed their experiences with us, as researchers, not with each other. We bring their portraits together here to highlight the potential of subverting intentional separation and tokenism to form communities of practice and support for doing racial justice work across school buildings.

Leonard: In the mornings, students are allowed to go into the buildings for inclement weather or just to wait until school officially begins. However, this particular morning the administration was summoned to one of the buildings on campus because a group of students was causing a disruption. I immediately ran to the building that housed mostly higher level courses. When I arrived, the hallways were very normal. There were no loud outbursts or anything. I radioed that front office to ask who called for an administrator. I went up to this [white] teacher and asked her who was causing the disruption.

"This group right over there. They have no reason to be in this building. They do not take any classes over here."

I took a pause to survey the group of students and discovered that all the students were Black. "What were they doing? Were they being loud? Were they being disrespectful?"

"No. Do they have to be in this building?"

"All buildings on campus are available for all students to hang out before school starts."

If students were not causing a disruption, then there was no reason for the teacher to alert the office. As a Black administrator, I was disgusted with the idea that a public school teacher in the 21st century would have reacted in this way. How do I address this situation in a professional manner without accusing this teacher of racial profiling in the school? Not just as a professional, but as a Black man. After this encounter, I thought about "white flight": when Blacks started moving into white neighborhoods, whites moved to other areas of the city or other towns. There was a fear the teacher felt because she did not teach Black students. I assumed she felt threatened having Black students in the hallway before school. Fear is very real. "I do not want you in my neighborhood . . . I mean . . . near my classroom."

Here, we sketch a portrait of Leonard, a Black school leader and the context in which he worked where he was charged with being *the* disciplinarian for Black students, and particularly Black boys. Formally, public school administrators are often assigned the tasks of disciplining students based on grade levels, content areas, parts of the alphabet (i.e., the first letters of students' last names), or hallways or wings of school buildings. In many schools, however, school leaders are implicitly expected to deal with certain groups of students, often based on similarities in racial and/or gender identity. For example, Black men educators in schools face particular challenges as a default of their racial identities wherein their colleagues and administrators often expect them to supervise, surveil, and control Black boys (Brown 2012). Those committed to racial justice face additional burdens in that "public discourse and broader conversations embrace and promote heroified Black school principals that are harsh, deficit-based, and often abusive toward minoritized students. Such Black savior-principals are seen as cleaning up the problems associated with Black, Brown, and low-income students" (Khalifa 2015, 259–260). Thus, Black men in schools, including administrators, are assigned the dual tasks of both punishing and saving Black boys (Brockenbrough 2015), perhaps emulating the Joe Clark character in *Lean on Me* (Avildsen 1989) in the removal of students who have "taken up space . . . disrupted the school . . . harassed [the] teachers and intimidated [students]" to ostensibly create a space for the remaining students "to learn, to work for what [they] want." This version of school leadership is rooted in race-evasive, individualistic, and bootstraps mentalities: help students pull themselves up by their bootstraps while reminding them that their futures are their responsibilities, while punishing and eliminating students who have not demonstrated the ability to do so, or who are not perceived as able to do so. This positioning, of course, ignores systemic barriers to students' success. It also dismisses students' resistance to those systemic barriers.

Likewise, Black women educators, and administrators in particular (Peters 2012; Reed 2012; Tillman 2004), are expected to both discipline and save Black girls who are often perceived according to "Sapphire" and "Jezebel" tropes and stereotypes; tensions they must navigate with the additional roles of being "othermothers" and working as change agents in broader school communities (Loder 2005; for a review, see Newcomb and Niemeyer 2015). Black women school leaders may draw on and work within community contexts outside the immediate school in their "lifelong responsibility" (Dillard 1995, 552) for caring for Black children in schools.[1]

Thus, Black administrators writ large are "constantly trying to locate their own negotiated places in a hierarchically racialized terrain (Anyon 1997; Evans 2007; Reed and Evans 2008)" (Khalifa 2015, 259–260). They are charged with the burden of disciplining and punishing Black students and are also beholden to broader racial communities wherein they are expected to be culturally responsive and sustaining, practice antiracist leadership, and work toward justice and equity in schools (for a review, see Khalifa, Gooden, and Davis 2016). Black administrators must also balance these burdens and responsibilities with the expectations of school cultures that are steeped in whiteness, race-evasive discourse, and racism, school cultures that task them with enacting surveillance, particularly of students of Color.

As illustrated in the opening portrait of Leonard, "principals often witness racist encounters in their daily work and intercede in cases of harassment and interpersonal conflicts that may be based in subtle stereotyping, taken-for-granted understandings and practices, and curricular and organizational decisions (Ryan 2003)" (DeMatthews et al. 2017, 523). In this context, Leonard was expected to enact an extension of surveillance by restricting Black students' access to a space understood to be "white": white, advanced classes, a white, segregated space, where Black students did not belong. The teacher with whom Leonard interacted that morning asserted that the students near her classroom had no right to be in the school building, enacting "surveillance patterns across time and space that share a goal of marginalizing racialized others and reinforcing intersecting, race, class, and gender hierarchies" (Dunning-Lazano 2018, 335). In addition to viewing the students as out of place, the teacher's assertion was rooted in an assumption that because they were Black, they were not likely to be in advanced classes at the school and were therefore unlikely to need to be on her hall, in her building.

To be clear, this teacher's assumptions were reinforced by system-wide enrollment patterns, evidence that racial hierarchies inform the thinking and behavior of individuals precisely because they are systemic and woven into the fabric of institutions. According to data from the Office of Civil Rights (OCR), Black students comprised approximately 26 percent of the system enrollment in 2015–2016, but were underrepresented in eighth grade algebra (approximately 7 percent), calculus (approximately 5 percent), physics (approximately 11 percent), chemistry (approximately 8 percent), International Baccalaureate curriculum (approximately 8 percent), and Advanced Placement classes (approximately 8 percent). Black students were also overrepresented among those retained, determined to be incapable of advancing to the next grade level with their same age peers; of the 186 students retained during the 2015–2016 school year, 111 (approximately 60 percent) were Black.

These consistently reinforced stereotypes about Black students' intelligence and where and how they should be allowed to congregate manifested in a desire for those students to be punished, removed, banished: "They have no reason to be in this building. They do not take any classes over here." Their very presence threatened the racial academic and behavioral hierarchy in the building. Only white students were normal there, a manifestation of how whiteness and stereotyping distort the ability to see all students as capable and deserving of belonging. Leonard had to navigate this tension while also having to navigate the fragility of his white colleague (DiAngelo 2018).

DISCIPLINE IN CREEK CITY SCHOOLS

The school system where Marcus and Leonard worked, Creek City Schools, was one in which Black students were consistently overrepresented in all disciplinary consequences (in-school suspension, out-of-school suspension, expulsion, referral to law enforcement, and school-based arrest) for all the years about which the OCR reports data (2009–2010, 2011–2012, 2013–2014, and 2015–2016). In these same reporting years, Black students were consistently underrepresented in advanced and college preparatory courses, at the same time they were overrepresented among students retained.

In this professional environment, Marcus and Leonard's efforts were both informed and constrained by the tension between acknowledging and ignoring race and racism. They worked within and against not just racialized and exclusionary school discipline policies but also the tensions and expectations of white principals at the schools, a primarily white leadership team in the school system, and a broader white school community that clung firmly to both race-evasive and racist ideas about Black students as troublemakers. For example, the superintendent of the school system did "not believe there's a bias" regarding the ways in which students of Color were disproportionately suspended, expelled, and referred to alternative placements and law enforcement in public schools across the country, or in Creek City. Despite this superficial focus on race-neutral discourse and practice, racial stereotypes, historically constructed and rooted in fears about Black bodies and potential Black access to resources, operated with material and psychological consequences for students of Color in the school system.

Marcus: "Well, we've had enough of you." That can't be a justification for removing kids from school, especially students of Color. I've worked really hard to be careful and clear about that. There are times when a referral comes in, probably for disrespecting a teacher and I'll think, that shouldn't have come to me in the first place.

For example, we had a [Black] kid who became pretty defiant, refusing to leave the classroom to speak with the teacher in the hallway. But, I just told the teacher, "he has a lot of extenuating circumstances, and sometimes if you just walk away, it won't escalate." It didn't escalate to anything bad, he just didn't want to leave the room to talk.

The teacher focused on how the other kids were looking at her, because she's telling him to go into the hallway and he was telling her "no" and wouldn't respond to her otherwise. Writing that referral was to show the other kids that she was doing something, that she wasn't just going to take it so they wouldn't think they could do the same thing, so they wouldn't think they could get away with defiance. There's a case to be made that she'd just had enough.

But that was a battle that she should not have gotten into. I've told her that we could have disciplined him after the fact, after we'd taken care of his other needs. Just let it sit for a bit and go on about your day. Because he wasn't really doing anything. He just wouldn't respond. His behavior may not have seemed respectful or kind, but perhaps he was in a headspace in that particular moment where the best choice he felt he could make was to do nothing; perhaps he felt he could either escalate the situation or stay out of it altogether. I understand why that's frustrating as a teacher, but it is possible his defiance was actually a sign of restraint. I want to help teachers calibrate those kinds of reactions, honor kids' experiences, emphasize the relationship, and send fewer referrals to the office. I want teachers to hold themselves to a higher standard with regard to what they handle themselves and what they pass off to me as the assistant principal.

As Marcus indicates in this portrait, discipline referrals to school administration are most likely made by classroom teachers (Anyon et al. 2018; Gregory and Thompson 2010; Skiba et al. 2002). Despite this location of the root of most disciplinary action within classrooms and between teachers and students, public school administrators, including principals and assistant principals, are often charged with enacting school discipline policies as part of their roles and responsibilities as school leaders (Butler and Triplett 2019). Like Leonard, Marcus was charged with enacting school discipline policy; he was *the* disciplinarian at the school. He took that charge to mean that much of what he had to do was reeducate teachers about what incidents were serious enough to refer to the administrative office, generally those that compromised students' safety or those that had become chronic, and which should really be handled in the classroom, including those that were subjective and low-level. He also acknowledged that some student behavior is really quite innocuous and might also be reframed to be viewed as agentic and communicative, a resistance to an oppressive context.

Marcus indicated that discipline comprised more than half, 55 to 65 percent, of his workload. Accordingly, school administrators bear some of the responsibility for racial disparities in discipline. Although discipline is a strategy often ostensibly used to achieve the goals of maintaining positive learning environments and safe schools, school administrators are likely to readily accept cultural norms that position Black students as problems and then lean, unquestioningly, on policy that permits their exclusion and places them at risk for school failure (DeMatthews et al. 2017, 520). That is, teachers may be the primary mechanisms by which students receive referrals (e.g., when they are sent to the office or "written up"), but school administrators are largely responsible for making decisions about which students will face what consequences, including those that are exclusionary. In this case, Marcus opted to confront the teacher's behavior rather than the student's, disrupting a seemingly foregone conclusion to the teacher that the student should be removed.

Importan in Creek City Schools, and in the buildings where Marcus and Leonard were both tasked with disciplinary responsibilities, is the intersection of subjective incidents and exclusionary consequences. Table 6.1 describes the context of Creek City Schools, a system that consistently has a Black enrollment of approximately 26 percent, in terms of their use of exclusionary practices for all incidents, drawing on numeric data provided by the Alabama State Department of Education (ALSDE). Aligning the figures in the table with the biennial OCR reports gives some indication of the racialized nature of these practices. For the 2011–2012 school year, approximately 60 percent of the students suspended in school, approximately 68 percent of students suspended out of school, and 50 percent of the students expelled were Black; no data were reported to the OCR regarding the referrals to law enforcement or alternative schools indicated in the state-level reporting. (We take up broader data discrepancies in chapter 11.) In 2013–2014, approximately 64 percent of students suspended in school, approximately 71 percent of those suspended out of school, 80 percent of those expelled, and 100 percent of those referred to law enforcement and arrested for school-based offenses were Black; no data were reported to the OCR regarding the referrals to law enforcement indicated in the state-level reporting. For 2015–2016, approximately 61 percent and approximately 71 percent of suspensions, in-school

Table 6.1 Exclusionary Discipline Practices for All Incidents in Creek City Schools

Year	Total Number of School Discipline Incidents	Suspended Days	Alternative School Days	Expulsions	Referrals to Law Enforcement
2010–2011	274	961	478	4	0
2011–2012	339	1,379	536	4	1
2012–2013	352	858	1,815	2	0
2013–2014	305	837	441	2	0
2014–2015	251	646	266	0	0
2015–2016	352	978	1,318	0	0
Total	1,873	5,659	4,854	12	1

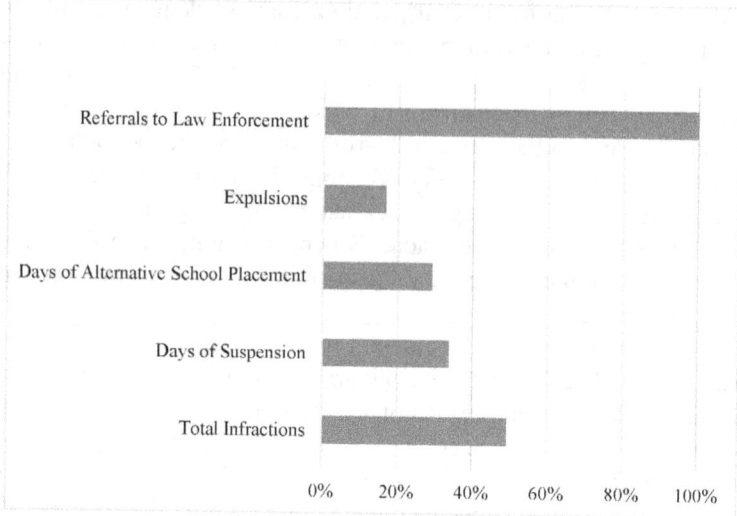

Figure 6.1 Percent of Exclusionary Discipline for Subjective Incidents in Creek City Schools, 2010–2016. *Source*: Created by authors.

and out-of-school, respectively, were assigned to Black students; no data were reported to the OCR regarding the referrals to alternative schools indicated in the state-level reporting.

Figure 6.1 unpacks the data in table 6.1 further, indicating how much of that exclusionary discipline was assigned for subjective incidents. Although the data used to generate this table and figure are not disaggregated by race, Leonard and Marcus' interviews, as well as the national and local trends explicated in the extant literature and the OCR report, suggest that many of the subjective incidents (e.g., defiance, disobedience, and profanity) would have been assigned to students of Color. Over the six years for which we have ALSDE-provided numeric data, more than half (approximately 51 percent) of all incidents reported in Creek City were subjective. Moreover, as indicated in figure 6.1, much of the use of exclusionary discipline, particularly suspensions, was for incidents subject to teacher and administrator interpretation, which, as we have noted elsewhere, are bound up with anti-Black stereotypes and misconceptions.

"LOUD" AND BLACK IN CREEK CITY

Leonard: A teacher ran to my office to tell me that two students were arguing and almost started fighting in the stairway. She told me that one of the male faculty members tried to escort the student to the office, but he broke away and ran. I immediately left my office to investigate the situation. I came upon two male faculty members that were in the area. I asked them what happened.

"Two students were talking loud between classes and we told them to move along and they did."

"Were they arguing?"

"Oh no. They were just talking loud, but they went to class when we told them."

"Hmm." Why would this teacher tell me one thing when nothing happened?

I went back to my office and the teacher comes in and asks, "Did you get them?"

"You told me they were arguing and getting ready to fight. The [other] teacher confirmed that they were just talking loud, but they went to class when asked."

By this time, another assistant principal entered my office. The teacher continued to tell us that when other assistant principals were at the school, students were removed when a teacher called the office. I asked, "Where did the students go?"

"I don't know. I think they were suspended from school."

"They never talked to the teacher to get an explanation of what happened in the class?"

"No. They removed them and the student did not return for a while."

She continued to express her displeasure of having this particular Black student disrupt the campus and nothing was being done. She asked, "What do I need to do to get him out of here?" My facial expression was all the other assistant principal needed to see; she immediately walked the teacher out of my office before I gave her some choice words about removing a kid from obtaining an education, probably saving my career.

As a Black administrator, I struggle with the boundaries of being a school administrator and how to address blatant racism. I do not want to be labeled as an administrator just for Black students or as an administrator who is an "Uncle Tom." I just want to be an administrator who is fair, consistent, and who wants to do what is best for ALL students.

In the portrait above, Leonard describes the ways that processes in the day-to-day running of schools, like discipline practices, are routinized (Diamond and Lewis 2019). This routinization intersects with the ways that school-based practitioners internalize racialized messages about students, including ideas about inherent criminality, guilt, innocence, or intelligence, for example, in addition to stereotypes about Black students in particular. The organizational routine of discipline creates multiple dangerous timepoints for students of Color as they move through discipline processes and are issued consequences (Diamond and Lewis 2019; Gregory et al. 2010). In this case, Black students in the hallway were hypersurveilled, already suspected of wrongdoing; in this space, talking loudly was interpreted as an offense. Here, we take up Carabello's (2019) arguments about what it means to be loud: "Loud in comparison with what or whom? Like other qualifiers, 'loudness' is arguably relative, and therefore, 'being loud,' does not mean much as a term on its own, although it takes on a host of meanings when we consider with whom the loud person is being compared" (1293–1294). The teacher mistook this Black loudness as arguing, a precursor to fighting, or some other criminal behavior. This mistake is historically rooted and also wrapped up with interpretations of loudness as "incompatible with 'being smart'" (Carabello 2019, 1281), an instance of Black students being relegated by white discourses of achievement. This teacher, like the teacher in Leonard's first portrait, was asserting the whiteness of school space, and deemed anyone who threatened that whiteness as worthy of removal via a call to an administrator. This action mirrors that which often occurs in the public sphere, like in the instance of "Barbeque Becky" (Zhao 2018) wherein white people often call police for the mere presence of Black people (for a treatment of "Beckyism," see Matias 2019).

Leonard's portrait also displays the differences in routines in schools; here, between ostensive organizational practices—those that assert how things *should* be done, and performative practices—how a practice is implemented or *actually* done (Diamond and Lewis 2019). It is in delineating these practices that, in addition to the ways that Black students are hypersurveilled, illuminates the ways that racialized stereotypes inform the process of disciplining students. In other words, all parts of the discipline routine are racialized, from:

> differential selection (institutional practices that might lead Black students to get picked out for wrongdoing more often despite episodes of misbehavior similar to those of white students) to differential processing (institutional practices that might lead Black students, once picked out for wrongdoing, to get different sanctions despite transgressions similar to those committed by white students; Gregory et al. 2010; Piquero 2008; Skiba et al. 2011). (Diamond and Lewis 2019, 838)

The ostensive practice, in this case, is that students should be disciplined for fighting, according to the zero tolerance policy at the school. But the teacher, by calling attention to students' hallway talk, performed a practice that racially profiled and stereotyped Black students; she misinterpreted their conversation, whether loud or not, as arguing or a precursor to fighting, thereby treating these students as "inherently suspect" (Diamond and Lewis 2019, 837). Leonard worked to disrupt this performative organizational process by investigating the teacher's claim that students were arguing rather than disciplining them for a behavior that had not actually occurred. He protected students' rights to be in conversation in a hallway at their school rather than also enacting some kind of performative practice that is discriminatory.

Leonard also reported that at the school where he was an administrator, students were most frequently referred to law enforcement for possession of weapons or drugs, and for starting fights, though data provided by the ALSDE indicate that only one student was referred to law enforcement in the school system and that the student was referred for a subjective incident. As already mentioned, we take up this data reporting discrepancy later; here, we note the ways that Leonard described how race played a role even in these seemingly objective incidents. For example, policies around possession of drugs at school were applied in discrepant ways, such as the way a Black student who had a very small amount of marijuana—"small enough to fit in a gum wrapper"—was arrested at school, while a white student who had a large amount of marijuana and multiple knives in her possession was able to be "picked up from school by a parent." Leonard often faced pressure from administrators in the district office to "get tough" on students; for his part, he tried to push back on those messages by involving School Resource Officers (SROs) only when he felt there was no other choice but to do so. Leonard also described being pressured to collaborate with police and to facilitate police presence at the school beyond students' day-to-day interactions with SROs. For example, he recounted, "Police have come to school before with a warrant and demanded to get students—one student was arrested on the field during football practice for robbery. Another student was lured outside by two administrators so that police could arrest him." Similarly, he described leaders in the district who wanted to use law enforcement to "send a message" about fighting at school: "If you fight, we will file a petition" (i.e., the student will be charged).

This idea of "sending a message" or "setting an example" is not unique to Leonard and Marcus's school system. Indeed, many school leaders nationwide have faced pressure to set an example with students; this was no more apparent than during the rise of zero tolerance policies around fighting. While there is no evidence to support the idea that zero tolerance policies dissuade student behavior (Skiba 2000; Welch and Payne 2018), there is overwhelming evidence that these policies disproportionately affect students of Color, introducing them to arresting officers and potentially the juvenile justice system (Nicholson-Crotty et al. 2009). Despite reform efforts in some areas to abandon zero tolerance policies, these policies are still in place in many districts around the country, including in Creek City Schools where Leonard and Marcus worked.

In this context where Leonard was expected to be the disciplinarian for Black students at the school, he worked in various ways to resist the bleak process of discipline, a process in which he felt very much complicit. For example, one summer, he implemented programming for students who had been disciplined repeatedly at the school by other administrators, and by himself, inviting those students' families to the school in an effort to get to know them better. He led these families on a tour of the school, providing lunch, building relationships with them, and engaging them in conversations about what was happening in the students' lives. Leonard also worked to mediate recommended consequences when students were disciplined. For example, he recounted that, while a white teacher might recommend that a student be suspended out of school for some classroom-based incident, he often worked to reduce the severity of those recommendations to assign a student for in-school suspension instead. Despite his resistance, however, the expectation that Leonard act as disciplinarian for a group of students on the basis of racial identity devalued the potential for him to advocate for students in other ways, a desire for advocacy rooted in a long history of Black educators working for justice and equity for Black students (Siddle Walker 2019).

The professional experiences of these two administrators—Marcus and Leonard—are therefore emblematic of the tension present in this context, and others, around school discipline. Namely, there is a tension between a race-evasiveness in the discourse about school discipline and the discriminatory enactment of school discipline. That is, Black students are routinely and disproportionately excluded from classrooms and schools via discipline; at the same time they are absent from prevailing discourses or data about school discipline. Marcus and Leonard adopted various strategies to name the raced aspects of discipline processes at their schools, while also navigating a space governed by whiteness. Both administrators were charged with disciplining Black students while also navigating repercussions with colleagues and other school leaders, made especially difficult by those who were unable or unwilling to acknowledge the ways in which school discipline processes in their context were racialized and discriminatory.

As we have written elsewhere, institutional policies, in addition to internalized messages and stereotypes and fears about people, drive and shape disciplinary practices. At certain points, practices become so routinized that their underlying drivers go unquestioned and unexamined, even when the routine practices are misaligned with ostensive practices. For example, school personnel, ostensibly, want to educate all students. That desire and a belief in its possibility are expectations of teachers and administrators enshrined in state and national standards. Yet, explicit policy, which allows for the exclusion of students under some conditions, creates the school contexts in which Black students are routinely excluded from educational opportunity. In this chapter, we have presented portraits of the work that Leonard and Marcus undertook in their context—some of which appear in their own words—in an effort to illuminate how anti-Black racism operates at a very granular level. These portraits of resistance display not only the burdens these administrators faced but also what is possible when administrators make choices to disrupt the taken-for-granted processes of school discipline.

So routinized and taken-for-granted are some discipline processes in Alabama that they often do not even merit attention or debate from many school or stakeholder communities. One such practice in Alabama school is corporal punishment. Marcus, however, was an administrator who was willing to make professional sacrifices in order to disrupt and resist the practice of corporal punishment, the practice we focus on the next chapter.

NOTE

1. We acknowledge in reviewing this literature that we have reinforced a gender binary; we face a tension here in wanting to acknowledge critical race and black feminist scholarship while also not wanting to reinforce a binary that contributes to the erasure of nonbinary and genderqueer people.

Chapter 7

Hitting Kids "Just Doesn't Sit Well"
Resistance to Corporal Punishment (with Benjamin Arnberg)

Marcus: "We've just had enough of you" also can't become the justification for corporal punishment, but it may be used that way. I can see kids not wanting to come to school if they get paddled all the time, especially if it's because a teacher said they were being disrespectful. I can imagine a student actually not wanting to come to school, that they might become more truant because of corporal punishment, and I can imagine schools using corporal punishment to motivate kids to stay home.

I've never been willing to engage in corporal punishment, even when it meant I wasn't considered for an assistant principal position. Once, I applied to a district. They were looking for a new assistant principal and it became clear they were looking for someone who would be willing to implement corporal punishment. In an interview, they asked me how did I feel about it? I told them that I felt it was antiquated. I didn't think that corporal punishment was a good option to have and that I would not be comfortable with paddling students. If you have to hit a kid . . . , that just doesn't sit well with me. There are other ways that you can deal with students. I do it every day. I don't have to raise my voice, stand up and hover over kids to intimidate them, or anything like that. Developing good relationships with students and being visible, I think that helps a whole lot more than trying to walk around and be an intimidating figure. By that time, I had been in the classroom for more than 10 years, knowing what I've done in the classroom with kids and what I've seen other administrators do: build good relationships with the kids. Be consistent; kids need to know that you mean what you say and you'll follow through. Hitting a child with a paddle, that just isn't a good thing. School is supposed to be a safe place.

Administrators like Marcus must be unusual in Alabama given just how often corporal punishment occurs and what that must mean about the numbers of administrators who are willing to enact it. There are many systems in Alabama where it is simply a requirement of the job, as evidenced by the questions posed during Marcus's interview for an administrative position. Marcus's concerns about corporal punishment are well founded as there is clear and robust evidence that corporal punishment is ineffective and harmful. His reflection also points to the troubling intersection of corporal punishment and subjective incidents, like disrespect, as well as the potential relationship between corporal punishment and students disappearing from school via truancy.

In this chapter, we first examine the history of corporal punishment and provide an account of contemporary corporal punishment policy and practices in Alabama. Then, we draw from data provided by the Alabama State Department of Education (ALSDE) from 2011 to 2016 and the Office of Civil Rights (OCR) to focus in one area of the state where corporal punishment is very common, highlighting how implementation of this practice has remained fairly static in the state, despite reforms and movements to abolish it elsewhere.

OVERVIEW OF CORPORAL PUNISHMENT

In the United States, corporal punishment began in colonial households (Garrison 2007; Ryan 1994), as a practice imported from Europe. Indeed, parents and schoolteachers of the era often relied on biblical and religious justifications for its use on children (Strauss 1994) in that their "'misbehaviour' was viewed as reflecting their innate depravity, and . . . harsh or even brutal punishments were necessary to control depravity and that God mandated such chastisement (Glenn 1984; Greven 1990)" (Holden, Wright, and Sendek 2018, 294). Grounded in conservative, Puritan and Protestant beliefs, the use of corporal punishment relies on the notion that "subservience, even through physical pain, is in the ultimate interest of a 'wayward' person (Dupper and Dingus 2008; Kafka 2011)" (Kennedy, Murphy, and Jordan 2017, 241). Also imported from Puritan ideology in Europe were ideas about not just the innate depravity of man, but an Aristotelian philosophy of human racial hierarchy which rationalized the superiority of white/light-skinned people over other groups (Kendi 2017, 17). Thus, while intended to correct (mis) behavior, corporal punishment is rooted in contexts historically and socially defined by ideas about strict religious piety, race, and enslavement, perhaps particularly so in Alabama. As enslavement, justified by religious and philosophical arguments about race as a new construct and white racial superiority, ballooned across the Deep South, so did the practice of corporal punishment. Enslaved African (American)s transferred the practice from white enslavers, as a manifestation of fear for their children: "Slaves as parents were under tremendous pressure to shape their children into docile field workers and to teach them proper deference and demeanor in front of whites" (Patton 2017, para. 9) lest their children be brutalized by slave owners.

Efforts toward both reforming the practice and abolition of corporal punishment also date back to its colonial inception, with critics arguing it was barbaric and inhumane (Glenn 1984; for a history of opposition to corporal punishment in the United States, including opposition to school-based corporal punishment, see Holden et al. 2018). Despite these critiques, household corporal punishment has persisted through the 20th century and into the 21st and has functioned as an invisible or taken-for-granted practice because "everyone does it" (Strauss 1994). Contemporary use of corporal punishment by parents, including spanking, is a contentious, often studied, and hotly debated issue, though a majority of U.S. Americans still appear to endorse the practice (Child Trends 2014). Children whose parents use corporal punishment, including spanking, face negative cognitive, emotional, and behavioral outcomes; spanking is often conflated with other, more abusive practices (for a meta-analysis, see Gershoff and Grogan-Kaylor 2016).

The use of corporal punishment by parents is complex. Research suggests, for example, that some Black parents support its use (Owen and Wagner 2006). Black mothers, for example, have reported using corporal punishment in ways that are rooted in both religious beliefs and in love and protection of children, noting: "I would rather me discipline them than [the police] discipline them. They gonna kill them without love" (Taylor, Hamvas, and Paris 2011, 65). Ta-Nehisi Coates (2015) recalled similar messages from his father in *Between the World and Me*: "Either I can beat him, or the police" (16). Indeed, some Black families may employ and justify the use of corporal punishment as a "form of protection from threats in . . . distinctively hostile environments" characterized by the legacy of racial violence, such as the geographic regions of the Southeast and the Deep South (Ward et al. 2019, 6).

This broader parental support of corporal punishment translates to support for its use in public schools, though the practice of corporal punishment in schools is related to a variety of negative outcomes for students of all racial identities (for a review, see Gershoff 2010). Students who experience corporal punishment may feel alienated and exhibit misbehavior (Hyman and Perone 1998) and may be more likely to engage in bullying behaviors (Espelage and Swearer 2004). There is also evidence that just one instance of corporal punishment is traumatizing (Hyman 1995). For example, the student at the center of *Wells* v. *Ayers* was diagnosed with PTSD, anxiety, and depression after an assistant principal at his school paddled him for making an "obscene" gesture at school in 2016.

Scholars have linked the use of corporal punishment in schools, and its contentious nature to fundamental differences in philosophies and purposes of education and the place of discipline in schooling to those ends (Cuban 1993; Kafka 2011; Tyack 1974). Contemporary connections to corporal punishment in schools are often explained by region, political affiliation, and religiosity. Specifically, corporal punishment is concentrated in Southeastern states, where it is more concentrated in Deep Southern states especially in Alabama, Arkansas, and Mississippi (Ward et al. 2019). It is more common in rural areas marked by political conservatism and Evangelical Protestantism (Font and Gershoff 2017; Owen and Wagner 2006) and less common in urban areas (Ward et al. 2019). In these regions, Black students are often more likely to receive corporal punishment in schools (Gershoff and Font 2016; Gregory 1995), though in some schools with high numbers of Black students, the practice is less common (Ward et al. 2019). Font and Gershoff (2017) explain that "while the broader population of voters and parents in a district may influence whether [corporal punishment] is allowed at all, where it is allowed, schools may be reacting primarily to their own student population in deciding how frequently it is applied" (13).

More recent research connects the practice of corporal punishment in schools with the legacy of anti-Black racial violence. Corporal punishment is more prevalent in schools located in counties where white people whipped and lynched Black people between 1865 and 1950 ("confirmed lynchings," Ward et al. 2019). In these schools, practitioners are more likely to administer corporal punishment to all students, though researchers found that "each additional lynching is associated with a 7.5 percent increase in the rate of black corporal punishment incidence compared to a 4.8 percent increase in the rate of white corporal punishment incidence." These researchers conclude that "Not only are the lynching effects larger for black students, but they are also statistically stronger" (10).

CORPORAL PUNISHMENT IN ALABAMA

As previously stated, corporal punishment is concentrated in the Deep South, and racial differences in its use are most pronounced in Alabama and Mississippi (Ward et al. 2019). Here, we focus on Alabama's disciplinary data from the Alabama State Department of Education (ALSDE) from 2015 to 2016. During that year, more than 100 districts (104/138) employed corporal punishment at least once. The most common incidents leading to corporal punishment in the 2015–2016 school year were: willful disobedience (5,748) and defiance of authority (3,995) (see figure 1.5; subjective incidents are marked with an asterisk.). Indeed, 18,214 of the 20,336 applications of corporal punishment (approximately 90 percent) were for these and other subjective incidents. As previously noted, nationwide, Black and differently abled students are more likely to be corporally punished even though more white students, nationally, live in districts that use corporal punishment (Gershoff and Font 2016). Alabama is no exception to these national trends. According to data from the OCR for the 2015–2016 school year, approximately 74 percent of Alabama school systems used corporal punishment, and these systems enroll approximately 61 percent of the students in Alabama. Within these schools, Black students comprised approximately 27 percent of the enrollment and approximately 33 percent of the students corporally punished, with 87 systems using corporal punishment in ways that disproportionately affected Black students. Data from the ALSDE during that same time period indicate that 68 of the 104 systems that used corporal punishment were comprised of Black students at rates above the state average of 26 percent; many of these districts corporally punished primarily for incidents that are subject to practitioner interpretation. By contrast, several white, affluent districts banned, or never used, corporal punishment over the period from 2011 to 2016.

Patterns in the national data are clear that Black students are recipients of corporal punishment practices more than their white peers in schools, regardless of the racial identities of practitioners in school buildings (Gregory 1995). Although some research suggests that Black students are more likely to receive corporal punishment regardless of school composition (Gershoff and Font 2016), 68 of the 104 school systems that used corporal punishment in Alabama in 2015–2016 had disproportionately larger enrollments of Black students. Twenty-four of those systems had Black enrollment of greater than 50 percent, and eight had Black enrollment of greater than 90 percent. The state's most disproportionately white and affluent districts ban corporal punishment altogether. Thus, these patterns suggest that corporal punishment remains a practice in schools comprised of predominately and sometimes exclusively Black students. In response to these conditions, we focus on Black Belt school systems, which account for a disproportionate share of corporal punishment use in the state. Collectively, these systems also account for large enrollments of Black students, who comprised approximately 73 percent of the total enrollment across the Black Belt in 2015–2016.

CORPORAL PUNISHMENT IN THE BLACK BELT

In Alabama, there are 18 counties that are considered the "core" of the Black Belt. The Black Belt was named for the rich, dark soil there, but this moniker took on an additional meaning when landowners developed cotton plantations in the early 1800s. With the rise of plantations in the region came increased numbers of enslaved Black laborers. Today, Black Alabamians still comprise the majority of the population in the region. Of the counties in the Black Belt, only one had banned corporal punishment by the 2015–2016 school year, the year for which the most recent numeric data were available. Three others have come close to a de facto ban, since each system reported fewer than five instances of corporal punishment on fewer than five occasions that year. The remaining 14 counties accounted for 2,808 out of Alabama's 20,336 instances of corporal punishment in the 2015–2016 school year, meaning 14 counties accounted for approximately 14 percent of all corporal punishments in the state that year despite only enrolling approximately four percent of the state's public school students. We focus here on seven of the Black Belt counties, where school systems are predominately comprised of Black students.

In 2015–2016, school systems in these seven counties used corporal punishment across a variety of disciplinary incidents; figure 7.1 provides a full account of all disciplinary incidents that led to corporal punishment in those seven counties for the year, and subjective incidents are marked with an asterisk. As evidenced in the figure, the majority of corporal punishment (approximately 88 percent) administered in these seven county school systems was in response to incidents that are subject to practitioner interpretation. As noted previously, subjective incidents are more likely to

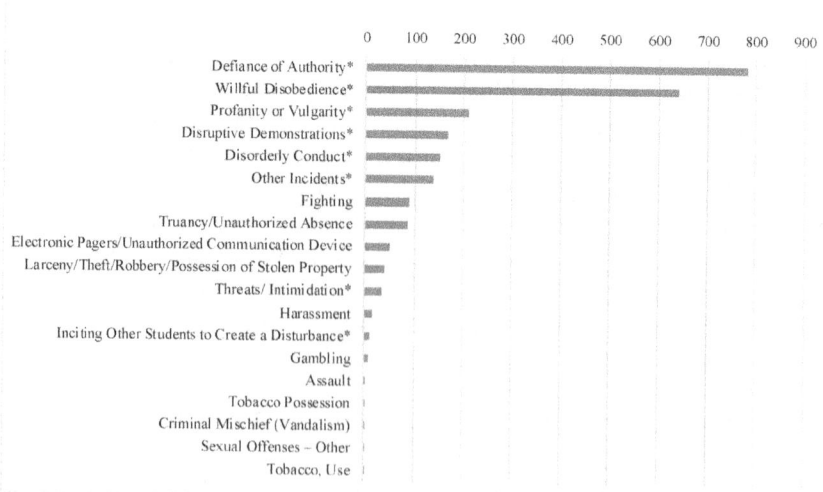

Figure 7.1 **Incidents for Which Students Were Corporally Punished in Seven Alabama Black Belt Counties, 2015–2016.** *Source*: Created by authors.

be attributed to Black students than their white peers, and assigning subjective incidents is bound up with racist stereotypes about Black students as defiant, disobedient, or disruptive. These patterns in the use of corporal punishment are consistent with other research suggesting that it is often a practice used to punish subjective, minor offenses (Human Rights Watch and the ACLU 2008; Gershoff and Font 2016; Mitchell 2010; Shaw and Braden 1990).

Elsewhere, we have described the role of white supremacy and practitioners' stereotypes about Black students' as deviant and criminal as part of anti-Black racism. We further note the role of anti-Black narratives when practitioners interpret and label Black students' behaviors as disobedient, disorderly, or as harassment, and when the "threats" of students, even elementary aged students, are deemed sufficiently serious to warrant corporal punishment. When everyday behavior of Black students is interpreted as deserving of physical violence, school-based corporal punishment thus operates as a blanket excuse to physically harm Black students for what could otherwise be seen as minor incidents. Paddling for incidents like these, therefore, underlines how systems justify and even encourage treating Black students as inherently deviant, criminal, and in need of swift and painful correction. Finally, we take note of the 138 applications of corporal punishment in the Black Belt under the label "other," which is not clearly defined and offers practitioners latitude to engage in corporal punishment without even the pretense of cause.

Given just how common corporal punishment is, then, in the Black Belt, Marcus's decision not to work in Alabama schools where corporal punishment is practiced removed him from the running for many jobs, and potentially all jobs in one large region of the state. Marcus's reluctance to embrace corporal punishment as a legitimate strategy for maintaining school discipline diminished his qualifications in the eyes of the system superintendent; his unwillingness to injure students hurt his job prospects, and he was not ultimately offered the job. Thus, his efforts to resist the implementation of corporal punishment came at a professional cost.

In the fall of 2016, more than 80 national organizations, including the National Women's Law Center (NWLC), the ACLU, the American Academy of Pediatrics, the NAACP, and the National Education Association, signed an open letter to educational agencies and lawmakers calling for the end of corporal punishment in schools. Approximately two weeks later, former Secretary of Education John B. King issued guidance for schools to stop using corporal punishment as a disciplinary procedure, becoming the only U.S. senior government official to release a public statement about the practice in the past decade (King 2016). However, the practice of corporal punishment remains commonplace, unquestioned, and unexamined by a vast majority of practitioners, stakeholders, and policymakers in Alabama. Public indifference to corporal punishment persists in Alabama even as it is used disproportionately with Black students and students with disabilities. For the 2013–2014 school year, statewide summaries from the OCR indicate that 2,260 of the 18,066 students in Alabama who received corporal punishment had disabilities. While the use of corporal punishment with students with disabilities has been outlawed in other states such as Mississippi and Arkansas, where corporal punishment is also common, policymakers in Alabama have expressed that they are unconcerned with the practice and that addressing it is "not a policy priority" (Whites-Koditchek 2019).

In this chapter, we positioned corporal punishment as an often unquestioned practice protected by law and policymakers and rooted in norms and mores that are racial, regional, historical, and religious. This practice brutalizes students, particularly Black students, in educational contexts where they should feel safe, as Marcus indicated in his account. We encourage practitioners to question and investigate the use of corporal punishment in their schools and to engage parents and other stakeholders about the ways in which this taken-for-granted practice is harmful to students and school climates. Collaborating with colleagues to articulate a philosophy of discipline for the school or system, or working toward clarity about a philosophy of discipline in individual classrooms, may reveal that corporal punishment is not well aligned with what school-based practitioners hope to accomplish. Doing so may point toward more humanizing disciplinary practices, perhaps even more humanizing practices in all facets of school life. In addition to engaging the topic of discipline philosophically, we encourage practitioners to engage in legal and historical analysis of the commonplace discipline practices in their contexts. Knowing and understanding the history of a practice, its justifications and impacts can benefit advocacy efforts toward racial justice and humanizing schools.

Policymakers and practitioners should also note that statewide efforts often have little impact on corporal punishment use. That is, most statewide bans are implemented after substantial local efforts to reduce these practices. Efforts to ban corporal punishment may also have unintended consequences: research suggests that a decrease in corporal punishment in some racially diverse schools may also mean an increase in suspensions for students of Color (Curran and Kitchin 2018), indicating how reforms might fall short in their intended impacts for Black students. In the next part of the book, we focus on the ways that disciplinary issues are being taken up around the state as we define the third part of the grammar of school discipline: reform. We highlight the pockets of reform happening in several areas of the state, in addition to the unintended consequences and limitations of school discipline reform.

OPPORTUNITIES FOR REFLECTION AND ACTION REGARDING RESISTANCE

School-based practitioners' reactions to what they perceive as misbehavior from students are often rooted in ideas about respect, and we know that teachers and administrators often take students' behaviors personally. Indeed, it is hard not to take challenges personally in a profession where the personal and professional are so closely intertwined and when our emotions are so intensely engaged (Zembylas 2007). We ask, however, that practitioners begin to do some emotional work before, and perhaps in lieu of punishing students, approaching the study of patterned behaviors with curiosity rather than value judgments. For example, how might practitioners, like Leonard and Marcus, engage in critical self-reflection (Khalifa 2018) as they work to be responsive to their contexts, confronting how stereotypes and preconceived notions about students guide interpretations of their behavior? Where do "bad" behaviors (and labeled incidents) occur, and to whom are these behaviors ascribed? How might behaviors likely to be labeled as "bad" (i.e., defiant or disruptive) be reframed as resistance, and what might the pedagogical purposes of that resistance be? What are the costs of further disenfranchising students who may already feel disconnected from their peers and teachers? How might practitioners engage others in meaningful conversations about discipline that include an explicit acknowledgement of how race and anti-Black racism shape our interactions in schools? How might they build, analyze, and discuss datasets that are not race-evasive? What might they do when they witness colleagues whose practices and perspectives are clearly rooted in anti-Black racism? How might they position their work as justice-oriented activism, and how might they locate likeminded teachers and leaders who are clear about goals to develop a community of practice to address inequity?

Part III

REFORM

Chapter 8

Efforts toward Reform

Alabama is no doubt home to notoriously conservative, fundamentalist, oppressive policies and policymakers; egregious poverty and institutional, interpersonal, and environmental racism; and private, for-profit prisons in a state that incarcerates many of its residents, year after year. It's also the home of the Lowndes County Freedom Organization; the Montgomery bus boycott and Selma marches; high profile centers working toward civil rights and justice, such as the Southern Poverty Law Center and the Equal Justice Initiative; and wide grassroots organizing around voting rights, prison abolition, and environmental justice. In many ways, Alabama serves as ground zero in some of the toughest, longest running fights for civil rights, justice, and legal reform in the United States.

In the first two parts of the book, we detailed removal and resistance as parts of the grammar of school discipline in Alabama. We first explored the ways in which large numbers of students in Alabama, and particularly Black students, are removed from public schools in the name of school discipline. We then highlighted the ways that we have seen alternative school students and school-based practitioners, including administrators, resist these policies and practices. In this next part of the book, we take up a third aspect of the grammar of school discipline: reform. We position reform as part of the grammar of school discipline because it is taken-for-granted and oft-engaged even as discipline outcomes remain largely unchanged. Reform takes place in institutions that are inherently anti-Black. Educational (or indeed legal, justice, social services, etc.) systems are designed to benefit some at the expense of others. These same systems determine the (inadequate and ineffective) strategies available to reformers. Thus, although education reformers make heroic efforts to better their schools, communities, and lives, their efforts are intentionally constrained so that they do not result in significant shifts in educational policy or practice. That is, the tools available to reformers are designed to fail in the name of preserving and sustaining the racial hierarchy.

As we have highlighted previously, research detailing the effects of exclusionary discipline is robust, drawing attention to the dropout/pushout of Black students and the school-to-prison pipeline in the past decade and entering the mainstream consciousness of many school-based practitioners around the United States. Racial disparities in school discipline have prompted many schools and school systems to think about reform. Trends in reform represent a:

> swinging of the pendulum from the 1990s, when school leaders hurriedly implemented strict no-nonsense discipline policies, to the 2000s, when some feared the policies had gone too far, to today, when school districts and school leaders across the nation are implementing policies limiting school personnel's ability to exclude students for certain offenses. (Ritter 2018, 134–135)

Reform efforts nationwide are varying and rooted in different approaches, including school-based professional development for educators to shift philosophies around the ethos of discipline; models that emphasize racial and restorative justice; training to implement positive behavior interventions and supports (PBIS or PBS) that prompts teachers and administrators to focus on individualized, tiered plans for students who exhibit (mis)behavior; bias training to prompt school-based practitioners to examine the misconceptions they hold about those who are racially different from them; policy revisions with subsequent professional development to alert school-based practitioners to the content and application of the shift; and community-based coalition approaches (see, e.g., the Dignity in Schools campaign, https://dignityinschools.org).

We continue this chapter by giving an overview of reform efforts, nationwide, that have aimed to shift discipline policy and practice at the intersection of exclusionary discipline (those consequences that remove students from instruction, their teachers, and their peers) and subjective incidents, such as defiance, disobedience, disorderly conduct, and disruption (descriptors of behavior that are subject to practitioner interpretation and bound up with anti-Black racism). Then, we zoom in again to Creek City schools, where Leonard and Marcus worked, to explore the reforms they saw implemented and the data about discipline in their school district. We close this part with a chapter about the reforms that another school system in Alabama undertook in collaboration with a legal advocacy group and a group of community stakeholders.

AN OVERVIEW OF REFORM

Many schools and systems across the country have focused on reforms to disrupt the troubling intersection between subjective incidents and exclusionary consequences. Some, locating the source of the problem in students, have focused on collective and individual interventions, such as programming around PBIS for students, tiered responses to disciplinary incidents, and alternative placements and programs (Childs et al. 2016; Crone, Hawken, and Horner 2015). Other school systems have devoted increased budgetary and personnel resources to implement "school-justice partnerships," such as the one created in Clayton County schools in Georgia, and expanded to include other local education agencies in the Southeast. Here, students participate in mediated sessions with adult facilitators who guide them in examining the antecedents and consequences of their actions, holding them accountable while also acknowledging how institutionalized and contextual factors, such as racism, poverty, and gun violence in broader communities, manifest in schools. Reforms like these locate the problem of school discipline both in the students and in the institutions that surround them, as they mirror those more progressive practices in the criminal justice system (for a review of restorative justice practices, see Anfara, Evans, and Lester 2013). That said, we have observed schools that implement restorative justice practices emphasize personal responsibility and gloss over or ignore contextual and institutionalized factors. Still other reforms aim to teach students social and emotional skills (SEL), which have also been critiqued as these approaches are often implemented in a race-evasive way, absent discussions about broader racial (and gender) inequity, focusing solely on students' socio-emotional learning even though students and teachers exist in an "ecology," and implicitly teaching students that they should endure racist interactions (Gregory and Fergus 2017, 118). A final popular reform works to address the systemic nature of discriminatory discipline in school with policy revisions and professional development for school-based practitioners, such as trainings about (implicit) biases (McNeal 2016; Staats 2016) and intensive coaching for teachers (Gregory et al. 2019). There are varying measures of effectiveness which accompany these various kinds of reform. To be clear, we do not judge many of these reforms to be inherently bad; instead, we note that they are often implemented in ways that prioritize practitioner comfort and eschew a focus on structural, institutionalized racism, and anti-Black racism in particular.

A large swath of reform efforts has focused specifically on the use of suspensions as consequences for disciplinary incidents (for a comprehensive review, see Ritter 2018). For example, school systems in Chicago, Denver, Philadelphia, and the state of California have implemented policy changes that are specific to the practice of suspending students both in school and out of school. Legislators and school boards in states like Arkansas, Maryland, and Texas have restricted the use of suspensions for elementary school students (Cornwell 2015; Ritter 2018). As Ritter (2018) reports, "As of the

2015–16 school year, 23 of the nation's 100 largest school districts had changed policies to require nonpunitive discipline strategies and/or limit suspension use (Steinberg and Lacoe 2017)" (144–145).

Discriminatory discipline is so stark that some school districts and states have implemented policies prohibiting the use of exclusionary discipline for some subjective incidents, such as willful defiance (Washburn 2018). In California, willful defiance is an umbrella term for a range of nonviolent misbehaviors such as tardiness, talking back to authority figures, or dismissive gestures like eye-rolling. Willful defiance, a common justification for suspending students, is a significant contributor to discriminatory use of suspension (Hashim, Strunk, and Dhaliwal 2018). The Los Angeles Unified district and other systems in California have seen decreases in suspensions after banning the use of suspensions for willful defiance (Adams 2015; Washburn 2018) and implementing restorative justice strategies (Hashim et al. 2018), though evidence suggests that discriminatory discipline persists.

REFORM IN ALABAMA

In Alabama, sustained approaches to reform have been slow to gain traction, though reform, like resistance, is happening in pockets around the state. Documents on the Alabama State Department of Education (ALSDE 2014, 2018) website include an overview of PBIS, though it is unclear how widely this program has been implemented, in addition to a document titled "What Every Administrator Needs to Know About Alternatives to Suspension and Expulsion." This report, written by a scholar in Nebraska, points to the problems with the use of exclusionary discipline, especially around disproportionality and "racial and ethnic minorities." Though it is encouraging that disproportionality has been highlighted here, suggested alternatives to suspensions include "mini courses on inappropriate behavior," "increased parental involvement and supervision" in schools, "counselor visits," and "community service," suggestions which locate the problem with students, not with school discipline policies and exclusionary practices themselves. In Alabama, the assumption that school discipline problems are the result of student and parent failings has led to the development of "The Parent Project," which features instructional units with activities and topics for parent support groups designed to aid in "changing behavior and rebuilding family relationships" (ALSDE 2014).

In perhaps one of the highest profile efforts toward reform, a judge in Jefferson County, Alabama, in tandem with a Georgia county judge and with guidance from the Southern Poverty Law Center, prompted a change in the ways that students would be disciplined in schools, including a "stepwise process for responding to misdemeanor offenses" including, warnings, mediation, and then referral to juvenile court (Kupchik 2016, 33). This effort resulted in a 50 percent reduction in court referrals in Jefferson County, a reduction in suspensions from the schools there, and increased graduation rates. Reforms regarding the use of suspensions or other exclusionary practices, however, have been few and far between, despite calls by legal organizations (such as Alabama Appleseed and the Southern Poverty Law Center) for the examination of these practices and work to introduce systems of due process around school discipline consequence hearings.

Further complicating the reform landscape in Alabama is that educational stakeholders and policymakers in the state are often skeptical or mistrustful of education policy that comes from other states, especially those states that are governed by Democrats and/or progressive politicians. Thus, well-intentioned reforms, even if they might ultimately fail to remake education systems, are often not even considered in Alabama. Members of the largest teacher union in the state, the Alabama Education Association, are often loathe to push for any changes in education policies and practices for fear of retribution or retaliation in local contexts. Indeed, many school-based practitioners are often hesitant to admit that they are affiliated with AEA. Additionally, discipline disproportionality across student demographics is not often acknowledged in Alabama; as we have noted in other chapters, there are no disaggregated discipline data provided publicly or to us by the ALSDE. Although routinely collected and compiled by schools and school systems and required to be reported to state-level officials (ALSDE 2010) as well as the Office of Civil Rights (OCR), state databases do not publicly provide data pertaining to discipline incidents or exclusionary discipline by student demographics. This makes it difficult to prompt conversations with policymakers about local contexts, especially those who might be skeptical of data reporting by a federal agency. Finally, school-based practitioners who are privy to their own school-level data are often reluctant to engage in conversations about race or of analyzing race-based discipline disparities (Khalifa and Briscoe 2015). In the following chapter, we zoom back into the system in which Leonard and Marcus worked to take up the race-evasive nature of school discipline reforms there.

RACE-EVASIVE REFORM IN CREEK CITY

School districts are often organized in ways that position building-level administrators as the conduit between policy, established at central office, and classrooms. This positioning is explicit when it comes to discipline, wherein policies often:

compel principals to collect information from teachers and observers, classify the severity of student misconduct, and select consequences aligned to the policy. In doing so, principals often rely on what they perceive to be the "facts of the case" and conceptualize their actions as reinforcing "the basis of order, the bedrock of respect upon which that order stands. Rules are spoken about as inherently neutral, impartially exercised, and impervious to individual feelings or personal responses (Ferguson 2001, 52)." (DeMatthews et al. 2017, 525)

Thus, race-evasiveness—or omitting race from discourse about discipline altogether—is often endorsed as a way to maintain objectivity when enacting discipline policies and doling out consequences, especially in the routine bureaucratic procedures of schools (Khalifa and Briscoe 2015). But, Black students bear the brunt of harsh disciplinary consequences and their deleterious outcomes (U.S. Department of Education 2016), highlighting the ways that purportedly objective, race-neutral policies and practices are anything but.

In Creek City, where Marcus worked as a school administrator and where teachers reflected the general teaching population in that they were primarily white, middle- and upper-class Christian women, there were virtually no conversations about race or ethnicity. Marcus, a Black man, acknowledged that discipline was racialized in his building, noting "there's still a disparity between children of Color and other children." He also indicated that it had not been discussed by administrators and teachers: "Sadly, it has not become a conversation among the faculty." Professional development sessions and faculty meetings with regard to both achievement and discipline data were instead routinely focused on poverty as a driver for disproportionate student outcomes. This is unsurprising given the vast economies that exist around professional development about, for example, Ruby Payne's *Framework for Understanding Poverty*, a hyperfocus on individualism (Ladson-Billings 2006), and bootstraps mentalities. In these discourses, teachers give "primacy to the individual . . . despite the way group membership shapes and defines much of our lives" (Ladson-Billings 2006, 106). Indeed, many of the teachers and administrators at the school system had participated in mandatory professional development sessions focused on "culture of poverty," frequently referencing Payne's "framework" in their discourse about student outcomes. Endorsing these types of frameworks results in teachers' adoption of a "pathology of poor students and hid[ing] behind child poverty as an excuse for why they cannot be successful with some students" (Ladson-Billings 2006, 105). Further, talking about poverty in lieu of racism serves as a more comfortable discourse for white school-based practitioners (Milner 2012, 2013) who may consider themselves as raceless or race-neutral and who are reluctant or resistant to engaging in race-talk. Focusing on poverty while ignoring race is a particularly disappointing discursive pattern given research that highlights the promise of interventions focused on race-consciousness and sense making for interrupting racialized disparities in discipline (Irby 2018). Instead of adopting reforms that would position the school as taking an anti-racist stance, leaders at Marcus's school chose to implement *Capturing Kids' Hearts* (https://flippengroup.com/education/capturing-kids-hearts-1/), a form of PBIS (Stough and Montague 2015), wherein students are rewarded for positive behavior, create social contracts with their teachers and peers, and can "foul" their classmates and teachers for violating agreed-upon norms. Like many school reforms, especially those that are commercialized, this program is race-evasive.

Leonard, another Black school administrator who worked in Creek City schools also had reforms taking place in his building. Leaders at his school had restructured the school day and the way that practitioners considered time during instruction in an effort to cultivate student autonomy. They had also attempted to start restorative justice practices (González 2015), wherein students were able to choose mediation about an incident rather than harsher, more exclusionary consequences, including suspension. This process usually included the student(s), a school counselor, and an administrator. But, restorative justice practices, without sustained integration of interrogating the ways that school policies are racialized and gendered, become focused on student-level interventions rather than systemic patterns in and disproportionate enactment of discipline policy (Anyon et al. 2018). This was the case at Leonard's school, where restorative justice had been implemented in ways that omitted its grounding in racial justice. For example, white students who were caught under the influence of alcohol at a football game were offered the option to participate in a restorative justice circle about their behavior in lieu of facing harsher consequences. A variation of this student-level intervention was also implemented by Leonard's colleague, who proposed an exercise class for students who had "anger management issues." Students were encouraged to drop in during their advisory or homeroom period if they felt they were experiencing anger.

RACED AND RACIST INCIDENTS

We juxtapose the race-evasive nature of these reform interventions at Marcus and Leonard's schools against two high-profile, racist incidents that occurred in the same school system during that time. First, an image of a white student in blackface surfaced on social media, with a racial slur in its caption. School administrators attempted to address the incident by inviting student "representatives" to a meeting/talk circle/facilitated discussion. Administrators chose students to be representatives of their racial groups, including "two white students, a Hispanic student, a Black student, and an Asian student." They sat in a facilitated meeting wherein a white assistant principal at the school asked them whether they ever felt discriminated against because of their racial or ethnic identities; this session was recorded and then broadcast to the school.

The next incident involved a young, white woman student-teacher who saw a Black student in a school hallway with what she thought was a gun; the teacher called the front office and the building was locked down for hours. The student-teacher did not know the student, so she reviewed video footage from the hallways with administrators to identify him. When the student was found, he did not have a gun; instead, he had a hairbrush, echoing plotlines of *The Hate U Give* (Bowen et al. 2018), the movie version of the popular book (Thompson 2017) that had just been released a few months prior.

These incidents serve to highlight deep rooted anti-Black racism in the system, juxtaposed with the race-evasive reform efforts happening there. The race-evasive reform efforts around discipline had little impact on the practice of exclusionary discipline for Black students. Suspensions and expulsions remained consistent over time, and many Black students continued to be suspended repeatedly, with many facing two or more suspensions. The lack of movement in exclusionary discipline trends for Black students in this system, despite the various pockets of reform that had been implemented supports other research that:

> suggests that race-neutral improvement approaches fail to disrupt racial discipline disparities. . . . For example, Positive Behavioral Interventions and Supports (PBIS)—a widely adopted tiered proactive school-wide framework for improving student behavior (Horner et al. 2009)—has been found to reduce the overall use of office referrals, suspensions, and expulsions in elementary school settings, but not discriminatory treatment of students of color (Skiba and Losen 2015). Studies of PBIS' effects in middle schools found that replacing reactive discipline with proactive supports reduced expulsion rates for Latinos and Native Americans, but not for Black students (Skiba and Losen 2015). (Irby 2018, 697)

Thus, any reform that did not consider the ways that anti-Black racism and stereotypes are bound up with school discipline could only have limited impact.

In the next chapter, we turn our attention to a school system in Alabama where Black students were routinely excluded from instruction, via suspensions, as a consequence for minor incidents. We present a portrait of a reform effort designed to address that exclusion that gained momentum and prominence through a multifaceted approach that included both community activism and litigation.

Chapter 9

A Portrait of Reform

Timber County Schools (with Nanyamka A. Shukura, Sangah Lee, and Jasmine S. Betties)

Nanyamka: Eighteen years ago, I was dragged out of the cafeteria by my arm by a School Resource Officer (SRO) from the Atlanta Police Department. My infraction: cutting the cafeteria line and refusing to get out of line when asked to by a school staff member. As I was being escorted to the office, I was told by the officer that I was going to be charged with inciting a riot. While sitting in the office, one of my teachers walked in, saw my face, and asked what was going on. She proceeded to talk to the officer, and the two words she said that day and that ultimately resulted in my being able to go to class were, "Not her." As I continued my time in high school, I came to understand what that teacher did for me that day. She saved my life. She vouched for me. Some of my friends never got that chance. I felt like I received many chances, and I now choose to use my privilege of being able to graduate from high school and go on to college to vouch for the other "Not hers" and "Not hims."

I was smart, though I didn't apply myself at all times, unless I really wanted to participate in something like debate team or cheerleading. I will admit that my behavior while in high school was probably challenging to deal with. I talked back, I often refused to follow orders. I was an average not-following-the-rules teenager. Both my mother and father were actively engaged in my life. I understood right from wrong generally. To loosely quote a keynote speaker I heard in 2016, I appeared to be a fully functioning car until you got behind the wheel and realized my brakes didn't work. The work I do now gives me an opportunity to share my story as an example and witness to how supports, patience, and the will of the adults in my life not to give up on me changed the trajectory of my journey, allowing me to be who I am today: a social justice advocate.

I started working at the Southern Poverty Law Center (SPLC) in August 2010, about three months after graduating from undergrad with a degree in Sociology and a minor in Africana Studies. While in college, I began to learn the "Savage Inequalities" in education (Kozol 1991). I knew that what I observed during my education experience—push out, lack of adequate supports, racist school practices—were happening to droves of students, particularly other Black students. At the time I didn't get the opportunity to explore further than what the class discussed when we reviewed an article linking educational inequality to economic inequality. Then I was granted an internship at a community organization in Chicago that ran a summer program for neighborhood youth. I facilitated a workshop for them about education inequality and, while preparing, my interest in educational inequality continued to grow as I saw the connections between lack of access to quality education and other social ills like inequality in housing and juvenile justice.

Throughout this chapter, you will learn more about the successes and challenges of the varied efforts and strategic work I engaged in while working for SPLC to improve education in the Timber County community. When I started working in the area, I was a young, Black woman, closer in age to a high school senior than I was to a 30-year-old. I was still healing from and unpacking my own education experience. While investigating the allegations made by the plaintiffs in the lawsuit against Timber County Schools, I visited a school to pick up a potential client and some student records.

I walked into the school building wearing a purple shirt. Purple happened to be one of the school colors.

"Young lady, where's the rest of your uniform?"

I turned around, surprised to see the school's assistant principal behind me.

I smiled externally. "I don't go here." Internally I was triggered. Here we go again...

This exchange, emblematic of the ways that administrators often fall into common refrains during the day-to-day runnings of a school building, also highlights the disciplinary policies and practices of Timber County Schools, Alabama, where students, prior to 2013, were routinely issued long-term suspensions (greater than 10 days) for insignificant discipline incidents, such as dress code violations. This exchange also illuminates the ways that this administrator did not know the students in the building, as he had mistaken a community advocate from a legal organization for a student. His readiness to punish Nanyamka for the same infraction he so routinely focused on with students enrolled in the school was an indication of the automaticity with which school administrators can act in punitive ways, in lieu of engaging in humanizing conversation with them.

In this chapter, we focus on the reform efforts of Timber County to highlight the ways that schools, communities, and legal organizations might partner and communicate to disrupt exclusionary practices and their damaging effects for Black students. We contextualize the state of school discipline in the Timber County system and chronicle the negotiation between the system and a legal advocacy organization working in concert with community leaders to reform the removal of students through discipline policy and practice. We examine pre- and post-reform numeric data to explore how the strategic focus on decreasing long-term suspensions, with an eye toward addressing all exclusionary practices, manifested in other troubling patterns with regard to the exclusion of students for disciplinary reasons. We end by interrogating individual-level interventions as well as the limitations of legal remedies to discriminatory practices that are consequences of systemic, institutionalized racism.

We draw from policy documents pertinent to the school system and the reform efforts, publicly available demographic and enrollment data from the Alabama State Department of Education (ALSDE) website, annual School Incident Reports (SIRs) provided to us by the ALSDE for academic years 2010–2016, and the biennial Office of Civil Rights (OCR) discipline reports for the 2009–2016 school years to explore this reform and the ways that a legal advocacy organization, SPLC, worked to build community and stakeholder understanding around the impact of exclusionary discipline, with particular attention to long-term suspensions (more than 10 days), for incidents that were subject to practitioner interpretation.

TIMBER COUNTY SCHOOLS

In the spring of 2010, a group of law fellows working at SPLC visited Timber County. They were following up on a 2009 study funded by the Timber Education Foundation and conducted by the Public Affairs Research Council of Alabama (PARCA) in cooperation with the county school system. At the time, Timber County Schools was the largest system in the state. The PARCA study, focused on student dropout, showed that students with two or more suspensions by sixth grade had a 50 percent dropout rate. The graduation rate for the system was 50 percent, suggesting that suspensions were a key part of the dropout/pushout puzzle and that reducing suspensions could positively impact graduation and dropout/pushout rates. The law fellows discovered that individual principals' overuse of long periods of out-of-school suspension—ranging from weeks to nearly an entire semester—was directly related to academic deficits and credit loss. Students and their families had a right to appeal these suspensions, but the appeals process was cumbersome, rarely effective, and inaccessible to many families because of geographical distance or lack of access to technology. It was not uncommon for suspended students to be arrested if and when they returned to school prematurely, a result of inadequate notification about the terms of their suspensions. Charged with criminal trespassing, they would be introduced to the criminal justice system. All of these factors raised grave concerns about the legally required provision of due process in Timber County.

Spurred by these findings, SPLC attorneys began an inquiry into the disciplinary incidents for which students in Timber County were being suspended, and they enlisted the help of their recently hired community advocate, Nanyamka. She began holding focus groups with students in alternative programs. A respected and well-connected principal at one of the alternative programs helped to arrange these focus groups and community meetings, where students and families made clear that suspensions for minor incidents like dress code violations were frequent, that minor incidents were often escalated to be labeled as willful disobedience, and that they often resulted in long-term suspensions, defined as more than 10 days but not more than a semester. In other words, students in Timber County were routinely excluded from instruction, for more than two full weeks at a time, simply for what they were wearing. The SPLC staff engaged in ongoing efforts to conduct focus groups and work with community leaders and the Timber Area Education Foundation, focusing on relationship building with school leaders and the juvenile court system to collaboratively work on revision to the code of conduct and help implement a School Offense Protocol or a Collaborative Agreement.

Jeremy

During the trips to Timber County, Nanyamka would often visit local community centers and ask if the directors or program leaders knew anyone who experienced exclusionary discipline, or who were simply no longer in school. In February of 2011, the SPLC staff met a Black student at the local Boys and Girls Club as part of ongoing community engagement. Jeremy had endured a long-term suspension for the infraction of skipping. During a class change, he realized he had left his jacket in his last classroom, returned to retrieve it, and was going late to class as a result. There was no due process paperwork; his great-grandmother, who was raising him and wanted to advocate for him, was unable to navigate the system to appeal his suspension. This student's story prompted the team to consider litigation, thus formalizing the Timber Education Campaign. Three staff members comprised the team: a law fellow, a senior staff attorney, and Nanyamka, a community advocate. Jeremy's story, in conjunction with community response to an uptick in media about weapons charges at some local schools that also resulted in students being arrested at school and charged as adults, prompted the Timber Education Campaign team to focus exclusively on revising the school system's code of conduct to eliminate the use of exclusionary discipline for minor offenses and increase the use of alternatives. They also decided to focus on the lack of due process, a legal right in cases of long-term suspension, as a means to put pressure on the school system to make changes to the whole code of conduct and to reduce exclusionary discipline across the board. Nanyamka began to meet with students who had experienced long-term suspensions and were eligible to return to school. In April 2011, she met four more Black students outside of a Boys and Girls Club who had all been long-term suspended from the same high school. She reached out to their parents and guardians seeking permission to further explore what had happened to their children. All consented to further discussion, and ultimately all were on board with pursuing litigation on behalf of their children. Their infractions were similar to Jeremy's: not having their student identification or skipping class. During client interviews with those four, Nanyamka discovered that one of their younger brothers had also been long-term suspended from a middle school for a low-level offense.

In May 2011, the SPLC teams filed a lawsuit against Timber County Schools for those six students. They filed in federal court, in the southern district; their complaint: denial of due process. Seeking injunctive relief, which had the potential to affect nearly 60,000 Timber County students, rather than damages, they submitted both a facial claim, arguing the policy was wrong, and an applied claim, arguing that the policy had been improperly applied. Shortly thereafter, the school district revised their due process policy, so the team dropped their facial claim. In the fall, the team chose to work with community members and leaders to put pressure on the system to engage in a deeper overhaul of the code of conduct. A substantial overhaul was particularly important to wholly address the overuse of both short and long term suspensions.

F.O.R.C.E.

Nanyamka's role on the team was to provide litigation support: paralegal tasks, find and take care of clients and their parents, and work with the community group, which coalesced into FORCE (Fighting for Our Rights to Children's Education) with the motto, "Bringing Value Back to Education." When FORCE held their first meeting in September 2011, 15 people attended. By October, they had more than 300 signatures on a petition seeking changes to the code of conduct. FORCE and Nanyamka held community meetings wherein parent after parent talked about the overuse of suspension in schools and how repeated suspensions pushed their children further and further out of school until they eventually dropped out. The series of community meetings resulted in goals to change the code of conduct to reduce suspensions and to increase avenues for parental engagement and advocacy. FORCE started to speak out at school board meetings, talk to principals, and help identify additional clients for the lawsuit.

In March 2012, FORCE held a community rally, covered by local news outlets, at a local church. With more than 100 attendees, the rally featured many parents who shared their experiences with their children's exclusionary discipline and their struggles to advocate for their children in a context laden with multiple policy levels and inaccessible infrastructure. Following the rally, the collaboration between FORCE and SPLC was solidified. FORCE continued to focus on community efforts, meetings, and consciousness raising. Their efforts generated momentum for know-your-rights trainings, which educated parents on the Timber County Code of Conduct, how to file appeals at the local and federal levels, special education advocacy and rights, education around the discipline data and statistics, and some general tips for advocacy. Know-your-rights trainings were routinely hosted by SPLC advocates in all of the communities in which they worked with parents; the guiding principle being that parents, armed with the right tools, could successfully navigate school discipline systems and advocate for their children. The efforts of FORCE also resulted in the construction of a network for parents, a group on whom they could rely at times when they were unable to get to the schools when their children were in trouble.

The advocacy work of FORCE and the litigation work of the SPLC happened in parallel. Unsurprisingly, following the filing of the lawsuit, SPLC's collaborative efforts with the school system broke down. Hence FORCE took the lead on communications with the school board. Their guiding principles were:

> (1) We strive for Timber County schools to be safe and inclusive environments where children can learn. Our schools must encourage children to reach their full potential. (2) We will take every measure to improve our graduation rate and ensure our students are prepared for success after they leave Timber County schools. It is imperative that suspension is only utilized as a last resort, that disciplinary action is intended to correct the behavioral issues, and that children are not criminalized for minor, nonviolent behaviors. Our children belong in the classroom, not in the streets. (3) FORCE seeks for Timber County schools to implement more preventative services, interventions, and alternatives to suspension. We will advocate for our children to have more resources for conflict resolution programs, more guidance counselors, and more staff members who are well educated on identifying and taking time to understand the individual needs of students. (4) Most importantly, we aim to ensure that parents are fully involved in the decision-making process, and are well informed of their rights,

and that the school informs them when acts of misbehavior initially occur. Parents should NOT be the last to know.

With Nanyamka's guidance, FORCE members continued to meet with school leaders and attend school board meetings. SPLC staff helped FORCE members become facilitators for know-your-rights trainings. They also supported community advocacy efforts to grow the group and push toward their goals. Nanyamka and her colleagues eventually added two clients: a young man who had been long-term suspended during three consecutive school years, for minor incidents, and a young woman who had been long-term suspended for attendance and uniform violations despite documented health concerns that impacted her school attendance. The lawsuit proceeded with seven clients.

A Turning Point

FORCE continued with their advocacy work, consistently attending school board meetings and consistently hearing just "thank you" from a board member at the conclusion of testimony from parents whose children had been the victims of exclusive, long-term, and subjective discipline, as well as from students with direct experience. They garnered media attention and new members as a result of their mobilization and advocacy efforts. Continuing know-your-rights trainings, publishing op-eds and letters to the editor, and submitting testimony to federal commissions, the influence of FORCE in Timber County grew over time. A turning point in their efforts arrived during a school spring 2013 board meeting. At that meeting, Jeanette, a parent, spoke out about her son, Damian, who was pushed out after long-term suspensions. That evening, the board's response was, "we should look at the uniform policy," an acknowledgment that they were feeling the pressure from FORCE and the pending lawsuit. Also that evening, Jeanette who had advocated for Damian at the meeting returned home to learn that her daughter, Danielle, was one of nearly 100 students suspended that day, all from the same school and by the same principal, for uniform violations (Ericson 2013). This mass suspension involved many families, including parents who worked in the system. Response to the mass suspension was mixed, with some community members outraged and others supportive of the school for "holding students accountable." The ongoing presence of FORCE in the media, however, led to more people coming forward about their experiences with harsh, subjective discipline.

The Thursday following the board meeting, FORCE held a press conference featuring Danielle, who had been suspended for wearing a green *and* orange jacket when the dress code called for green *or* orange. Following the press conference, the Timber County Schools superintendent reached out about settlement talks. With the trial set for August 2013 and advocacy efforts continuing on an ongoing basis, settlement conversations began in March with a mediator and clients at the table. The clients shared their experiences and were heard by the leadership team of the school system.

Settlement

By July, there was a signed settlement agreement that included comprehensive reform of the code of conduct, including the removal of "any other offense which the principal may deem reasonable to fall within this category of misconduct" and the elimination of suspension as a possible sanction for three infractions: excessive talking in the classroom, being improperly out of uniform, and possession of nuisance items. The overall goals were to reduce suspensions and increase support for families. The system hired a consultant to guide the reform, steering it toward being more student centered and providing more adequate due process protections. Should students be sent home before their hearings, which should happen only rarely, they would receive credit for days spent out of school prior to their hearing and be permitted to make up assignments upon returning to school. It was made clear that students could bring legal representation or request the presence of a school counselor or parent advocate. To support families, appeals forms were to be revised for clarity and provided at every school, and students were to be treated as innocent until the conclusion of the due process hearing. The settlement required formal training and professional development for teachers and administrators, including working groups to identify research-based alternatives to suspension, to reduce suspensions, and to improve discipline. Also included in the settlement agreement were aspirational goals: reduce the total number of out-of-school suspensions; reduce the number of students who receive two or more out-of-school suspensions in one academic year; reduce the total number of suspensions over 20 days for low- and mid-level offenses; reduce the average number of academic days lost to suspensions; and avoid concentrating suspensions within any group or demographic, including "males, minorities, or students with disabilities" (with the plaintiffs' acknowledgment that they had made no allegation related to discrimination). The settlement agreement also required external monitoring regarding both the settlement terms and the aspirational goals through 2016.

The revised code of conduct was meant to lead to a new culture of practice. The revision included changes beyond the requirements of the settlement agreement, including an explicit statement that held teachers accountable for discipline in their own classrooms. Making this expectation clear in the code of conduct meant that teachers had to attempt to address misconduct in-house and could no longer outsource their students via office referrals and write-ups, thus potentially disrupting some of the mechanisms by which students were punished with exclusionary consequences.

Although these reforms had the potential to improve school experiences for all the students still enrolled in Timber County, the plaintiffs themselves did not directly benefit. One of them graduated in 2013. The rest did not, despite specific guidance in the settlement about the educational services and supports they were to receive. They were simply too far behind academically. Nanyamka is clear that they are freedom fighters; they did not directly benefit from their work and sacrifice or from the work and sacrifice of their families, but the more than 50,000 students enrolled in Timber County Schools have. Timber County's revised code of conduct has since been used as a model for the few other school systems working with SPLC to reduce exclusionary discipline. Given that stakeholders and educators in Alabama often have reservations about adopting education policy from other states, this revised code from Timber County has the potential to beget more local action.

PRECURSORS AND CONSEQUENCES OF THE TIMBER COUNTY SETTLEMENT

As previously stated, we drew from School Incident Reports provided by the ALSDE for 2010–2016 of every disciplinary incident occurring in the system to explore this reform. We narrowed our focus to examine suspensions, as they were the focus of the reform, and categorized which incidents resulting in suspension were subject to practitioner interpretation.

Over the course of the academic years from 2010 to 2016—three academic years before and three academic years after the settlement agreement—students in Timber County Schools, a system with enrollment of approximately 58,000, approximately 50 percent of whom were Black, received 405,848 total days of suspension as consequences for school discipline incidents (see table 9.1). According to testimony offered to the Senate Judiciary Subcommittee on the Constitution, Civil Rights, and Human Rights:

> In [Timber] County, students can be suspended up to 10 days for uniform violations, being unprepared for class, and even talking in the cafeteria. We have heard of students being long-termed suspended, which in [Timber] can be anywhere between 11 days and the end of the semester, for eating a bag of chips in class. . . . In Timber County, you can lose all your credits after you miss 10 days of school in one semester. . . . We see the reality of the school-to-prison pipeline in Timber County. Many Timber children are funneled into the juvenile justice system through our schools. In Timber, many students are arrested for

Table 9.1 Suspensions in Timber County Schools for Subjective Incidents

Year	Total Days	Defiance	Disobedience	Disorderly Conduct	Disruption	Inciting	Profanity	Threats	Other	Total Subjective Days
2010–2011	74,364	0	8,681	4,418	0	0	5,098	8	15,905	34,110
2011–2012	113,120	0	14,167	11,692	0	0	5,968	40	23,708	55,575
2012–2013	107,732	0	15,187	14,544	0	0	5,218	236	22,976	58,161
Pre-reform	295,216	0	38,035	30,654	0	0	16,284	284	62,589	147,846
2013–2014	33,363	0	5,594	3,600	0	0	1,629	24	8,243	19,090
2014–2015	37,124	0	6,823	3,990	0	0	1,714	24	7,452	20,003
2015–2016	39,872	46	8,321	2,993	0	0	2,104	27	7,373	20,864
Post-reform	110,632	46	20,738	10,583	0	0	5,447	75	23,068	59,957
Change	–63%	+	–46%	–66%			–67%	–74%	–63%	–59%

criminal trespassing. This happens when a student comes on the school campus when they are supposed to be on suspension. But, because students don't receive notice, they don't know how long they are suspended or when they are allowed to return to campus.

Some of these assertions are supported by the ALSDE-provided data. Of the 295,216 total days of suspension before the reform, 147,846 (approximately 50 percent) were for subjective infractions (see table 9.1), and at least 18,700 of these days were part of long-term suspensions (Kirby 2013). What is less clear from these numeric data are the number of students arrested for trespassing; Timber County reported no referrals to law enforcement for trespassing in the three years leading up to the settlement agreement. They also reported no referrals to law enforcement for trespassing for the three years after. (We take up broad data discrepancies in chapter 11.)

Following the settlement agreement and revised code of conduct in 2013, the proportion of days of suspension assigned for subjective incidents increased from approximately 50 percent to approximately 54 percent, while the total number of days of suspension assigned for both objective and subjective incidents declined drastically (approximately 63 percent; see table 9.1). As can be seen in table 9.1, apart from an increase for incidents of defiance, the number of suspension days in the system declined dramatically following the 2013 settlement. Regarding the goal of keeping students in classrooms by decreasing suspensions, the reform was largely a success.

However, OCR reports indicate that Black students were disproportionately affected by suspensions, both in- and out-of-school, in the period leading up to the reform and the years immediately after it. Whereas Black students consistently comprised approximately 50 percent of the student enrollment in Timber County, in the two OCR reports immediately prior to the reform approximately 64 percent (2009–2010) and approximately 70 percent (2011–2012) of the students suspended were Black. In the two OCR report cycles following the reform, this disparity remained such that approximately 73 percent (2013–2014) and approximately 70 percent (2015–2016) of the suspended students were Black. This suggests that the call in the settlement to avoid concentrating suspensions among any particular group of students remained unheeded.

UNINTENDED CONSEQUENCES

With the exception of the final aspirational goal focused on avoiding concentrating suspensions among groups of students, the settlement in Timber County, as well as the lawsuit that precipitated it, was race-evasive. That is not to suggest that community efforts were also race-neutral. Nanyamka is clear that, along with some of her team members, she centered race in her discourse in know-your-rights trainings, explanations about the problematic nature of subjective incidents, and explanations of data from the OCR, which is disaggregated by students' demographics, including race. We point out the race-evasive nature of the legal documents related to the case in Timber County to raise questions about the efficacy of legal remedies for problems rooted in white supremacy and anti-Black racism.

Other scholars have also interrogated the extent to which legal interventions can disrupt institutionalized racism (Bell 1980), especially in a sociopolitical context wherein blackness, danger, and criminality are conflated. Reforms that do not necessarily center race and racism as the focus of the conversation—some of which have led to temporary improved outcomes for students and their families—and instead focus on individual-level interventions are often critiqued, even when the targeted individuals are adults, not children. Well-intentioned professional development for teachers about improving the relationships and climate within a school, thereby removing the focus from students and their deficits, still targets the behavior of individuals at the expense of interrogating and addressing the systems that undergird that behavior (Anyon et al. 2018). These efforts also do not include the voices of Black students, parents, and families, those most affected by the application of discipline (Bell 2020). Because individual teachers are agentic, these efforts are likely to narrow race-based discipline gaps, but said gaps are also manifestations of dynamics related to race and power that go well beyond individual practitioners. That is, offering teachers more relationship-building skills or changing their beliefs about their students will not address:

> systemic factors in American educational institutions that work to sustain bias and create challenges for relationship building with youth of color, such as school financing, racial segregation, high stakes testing, teacher quality, tracking, and special education placements (Christine 1993; Mendez, Knoff, and Ferron 2002; Eitle and Eitle 2004; Watts and Erevelles 2004; Arcia 2007). (Anyon et al. 2018, 3)

Without examining systems of race, racism, and power and reimagining possibilities to connect and build relationships with students and families (Davis 2005), reform efforts will be unable to remedy discriminatory discipline (Anyon et al. 2018). They instead may result in unintended consequences, including increases in the use of other forms of exclusionary discipline, like alternative school placements.

Indeed, the numeric data from Timber County suggest unintended consequences from their reform efforts there in that referrals to law enforcement and alternative school placements for subjective infractions (see tables 9.2

A Portrait of Reform   141

Table 9.2 Referrals to Law Enforcement in Timber County Schools for Subjective Incidents

Year	Total Referrals to Law Enforcement	Defiance	Disobedience	Disorderly Conduct	Disruption	Inciting	Profanity	Threats	Other	Total Subjective Referrals to Law Enforcement
2010–2011	0	0	0	0	0	0	0	0	0	0
2011–2012	1	0	0	1	0	0	0	0	0	1
2012–2013	11	0	0	6	0	0	0	0	0	6
Pre-reform	12	0	0	7	0	0	0	0	0	7
2013–2014	4	0	1	2	0	0	0	0	0	3
2014–2015	12	0	0	4	0	0	0	0	0	4
2015–2016	10	0	2	1	0	0	0	0	4	7
Post-reform	26	0	3	7	0	0	0	0	4	14
Change	+117%	0	+	+	0	0	0	0	+	+100%

and 9.3) increased post-reform. The numbers for referrals to law enforcement in the years leading up to the reform effort were small and the district had a history of resisting the placement of more SROs, but the growth in the three years after the reform was dramatic. The number of total referrals more than doubled, and the number of referrals for subjective incidents also doubled (see table 9.2). That pattern continued and became even more dramatic. In 2016–2017, there were 271 referrals to law enforcement in the system, 105 (approximately 39 percent) of which were for disorderly conduct. In 2017–2018 and 2018–2019, those number grew still more: 352 total, 154 (approximately 44 percent) for disorderly conduct and 486 total, 252 (approximately 52 percent) for disorderly conduct, respectively.

And, the total number of days of alternative school placement increased from 46,759 in the three years before the reform to 53,674 in the three years after. Similarly, the number of days of alternative school placement for subjective incidents also increased, from 18,203 to 22,244, an increase of 22 percent. This increase is attributed to increased alternative school placements for disobedience, disorderly conduct, and threats, while the number of days for other incidents decreased (see table 9.3). Language in the settlement agreement suggests the decline in "other" was accounted for by a change in policy that meant students could not be subjected to exclusionary discipline practices for dress code/uniform violations, excessive talking, the possession of "nuisance" items, or simply at the principal's discretion.

As we have noted elsewhere, the ALSDE does not make disaggregated data regarding disciplinary incidnes and consequences publicly available, nor were they willing to share them with us. Their lack of availability contributes to the static nature of removal and discriminatory discipline practices since it is difficult to ask stakeholders to consider reform when data are lacking. Although some data are reported to the OCR, those data fail to link incidents and consequences, again obscuring patterns about how school discipline operates in racialized ways. Likewise, the legal discourse that drove the settlement in Timber County was largely race-evasive. Although that decision may have been pragmatic at the time of the lawsuit, the data since the reform suggest that failure to address the root causes of discriminatory discipline (institutionalized anti-Black racism) meant that exclusionary practices shifted form. Rather than relying on suspensions, school administrators used law enforcement referrals and alternative school placements to remove students, a disproportionate number of whom were Black. These shifts once again reveal the malleability of racism and the ways it affects Black students in particular. That is, reform, as part of the grammar of school discipline, still takes place within a system predicated on white supremacy and anti-Black racism, leaving inequity intact while also perpetuating it.

A Portrait of Reform

Table 9.3 Days in Alternative School in Timber County Schools for Subjective Incidents

Year	Total Days	Defiance	Disobedience	Disorderly Conduct	Disruption	Inciting	Profanity	Threats	Other	Total Subjective Days
2010–2011	17,767	0	588	3,408	0	0	556	0	1,520	6,072
2011–2012	15,005	0	1,103	3,176	0	0	275	0	2,201	6,755
2012–2013	13,942	0	372	2,615	0	0	260	0	2,129	5,367
Pre-reform	46,759	0	2,063	9,199	0	0	1,091	0	5,850	18,203
2013–2014	23,780	0	702	5,331	0	0	236	96	1,678	8,043
2014–2015	16,040	0	1,417	4,208	0	0	172	111	1,878	7,786
2015–2016	13,854	0	901	3,650	0	0	449	310	1,105	6,415
Post-reform	53,674	0	3,020	13,189	0	0	857	517	4,661	22,244
Change	+15%	0	+46%	+43%	0	0	−21%	+	−20%	+22%

Timber County Schools and its students experienced a reform rooted in "the need to provide services . . . to address the real conditions and the real needs of actual people caught up in the system" (Meiners 2011, 550). This reform, unfortunately, was not able to rectify the broader anti-Black racism that was operating, much like the race-evasive reforms in the system where Leonard and Marcus worked had little impact on the exclusionary practices there. Thus, in the final part of the book, we encourage practitioners and policymakers to take up and engage with the idea of repair as we rethink the role of discipline and punishment in public schools in Alabama.

OPPORTUNITIES FOR REFLECTION AND ACTION REGARDING REFORM

As Love (2019) so aptly writes, "reform ain't justice" (10). Multifaceted strategies are needed, including those aimed at all forms of school policies and practices that dehumanize, brutalize, and exclude, requiring attention to structural and institutionalized white supremacy and racism in educational institutions. Here we encourage practitioners to consider, for example, how mass exclusion of students from schools functions to exacerbate community and social problems, much as mass incarceration does. How might educators decriminalize certain offenses so that students are not further disconnected from peers, teachers, and schools? Might they imagine alternatives to punishment that are focused on relationships, rather than relying on retribution? How might practitioners come to know their own rights and potentials for activism for the communities in which their schools are located, and how might they support students and parents' efforts to do the same? What lessons might they take from the failures of race-evasive reforms to galvanize their work as school and community activists? Finally, how might practitioners form and draw on partnerships with community organizers and legal advocates who act in service to justice and equity to reimagine discipline in schools and repair the damage it has done to communities?

Part IV

REPAIR

Chapter 10

The 4th R

In previous parts of the book, we asked that practitioners engage with questions around their philosophies of schooling and discipline. We asked that they dig into the details of their discipline data to prompt conversations about the racialized nature of school discipline and that they reflect, individually and collectively, on their preconceived notions and prevailing narratives about students of Color, and particularly Black students. These asks were meant to push practitioners to reimagine the interpersonal work of schooling and invest deeply in relationships with the students in their care, acknowledging the ways that white supremacy and anti-Black racism inform the processes of school discipline. In this final part of the book, we offer a prescriptive (Tyack and Tobin 1994) to the grammar of school discipline directed at the way things should be in schools: we ask that readers build upon that reflection and relationship-focused work toward repair. That is, we suggest that the fourth "R" that is thus far absent from the grammar of school discipline, but which has the most potential to disrupt, is *repair*.

The concept of repair is often rooted in righting the wrongs inflicted by the legacy of enslavement and the theft of Black property, labor, and livelihood through our contemporary societal structures (for treatment of reparations in the 21st century, see Araujo 2017). According to the National Coalition of Blacks for Reparations in America (N'COBRA 2016):

> Reparations is a process of repairing, healing and restoring a people injured because of their group identity and in violation of their fundamental human rights by governments, corporations, institutions and families. . . . Reparations can be in as many forms as necessary to equitably (fairly) address the many forms of injury caused by chattel slavery and its continuing vestiges. The material forms of reparations include cash payments, land, economic development,

and repatriation resources particularly to those who are descendants of enslaved Africans. Other forms of reparations for Black people of African descent include funds for scholarships and community development; creation of multi-media depictions of the history of Black people of African descent and textbooks for educational institutions that tell the story from the African descendants' perspective; development of historical monuments and museums; the return of artifacts and art to appropriate people or institutions; exoneration of political prisoners; and, the elimination of laws and practices that maintain dual systems in the major areas of life including the punishment system, health, education and the financial/economic system. The forms of reparations received should improve the lives of African descendants in the United States for future generations to come; foster economic, social and political parity; and allow for full rights of self-determination. (para. 1)

In the United States, reparations rectify the anti-Black racism embedded in our society, including the injustices that occur in public education. With regard to reparations in education, the National African American Reparations Commission (NAARC 2015) documents the historical wrongs that come with the denial of education to Black people during the period of enslavement and continuing today:

Africans in America have acquired knowledge, produced great inventors, built institutions and developed extraordinary leaders despite calculated efforts to deny Black people an education and/or the propagation of misinformation designed to destroy identity, self-esteem and instill obedience to an oppressive system. During enslavement Africans could be punished or even killed for learning to read. Post-emancipation the vast majority of Black young people have been confined to separate and severely under-resourced schools during legal and de facto segregation. These conditions prevail today in what is sometimes called "poor performing schools." (para. 24)

Added to ongoing segregation of Black students into underfunded, under-resourced schools is the denial of education that comes with removal of students in the name of discipline. Removing students from their classrooms and schools, as we have argued throughout this book, summarily denies students opportunities for education. Acknowledging and atoning for that removal is the first step of repair.

As previously stated, reparations to communities often take account of financial costs, something seen as controversial to many (Harris 2002), perhaps especially in the Deep South. The inclusion of financial costs in efforts to make reparations for the grammar of school discipline may make sense because the economic impact is substantial. How much should be paid?

Scholars and policymakers make aggregate estimates of the economic costs of exclusionary discipline. Their estimates are often rooted in the assumption that exclusion from school leads to dropping out, which in turn leads to fewer job opportunities, decreased earning power, and less potential for economic mobility. While we do not mean to suggest that repair should be calculated in terms of capitalist labor politics, these estimates offer a starting place to assigning a monetary value to the denial of opportunities that result from exclusionary school discipline policy and practice. A report issued by the Center for Civil Rights Remedies estimates that "suspensions cost the nation more than $35 billion in lost tax revenue and increased social expenditures" (Rumberger and Losen 2016, para. 1). This estimate is conservative, as it only accounts for the cost of suspensions for tenth graders for one year.

When seeking to answer the question regarding how much should be paid, we might also look to estimates of the actual costs of removal, via exclusionary discipline. Schools, school systems, and states invest in removal, though they could elect to reinvest those funds to make reparations. The total investment in exclusionary discipline has been calculated for states like Texas, Florida, and California. In Texas, researchers have estimated that the annual economic effect of exclusionary discipline is approximately $680 million when considering exclusionary discipline as a precursor and antecedent to student dropout. Inasmuch as exclusionary discipline also affects grade retention, they estimated $31.6 million in additional schooling costs (Marchbanks et al. 2013). Researchers also calculated the "security and monitoring" costs—the costs of school security and policing across 11 districts in Texas—along with the costs in each district for out-of-school suspensions, alternative school referrals, and educational services provided to students who had been expelled. On average, these 11 districts spent $156.08 per student in 2010–2011 on discipline and security (Texas Appleseed 2011).

Researchers have not yet calculated the costs of exclusionary school discipline in Alabama. We note, however, that the Alabama State Department of Education (ALSDE) reported that, for the 2018 fiscal year, the state average per pupil expenditure was $9,698 ($53.88 per student, per school day, assuming a 180-day school year), an increase from the 2016 fiscal year expenditures of $9,213 per student ($51.18 per student, per school day). We suggest these figures may also offer a place to start when considering the monetary values of a school day, acknowledging, of course, the costs of lost educational opportunity are compounded and are certainly more than the state investment per student per day. We also suggest a comprehensive accounting of expenditures for exclusionary discipline, surveillance technology, and school-based police. We also emphasize the local, community-incurred costs for the financial benefit for a select few Alabamians by way of the criminalization of citizens (Dyer 2000), subsequent incarceration, and prison labor in both public and private (SPLC 2017), for-profit prisons (Gotsch and Basti 2018).

While economic reparations have garnered attention and are attractive—rightly so—we suggest that school practitioners and researchers also take up a broader ethos of repair in their local contexts, with individual students and families and in their classrooms, schools, and communities. What might repair look like in the nested structures of schooling? How might teachers repair relationships with individual students, engaging student resistance in ways that are productive rather than leaning into removal? How might administrators repair relationships with those same students, and their families, especially if they are ultimately responsible for decision-making about disciplinary consequences? How might school systems repair the trauma inflicted on students and families through the use of corporal punishment? How might school systems repair relationships impacted by the harm done to students and families by exclusionary and discriminatory discipline practices? In an effort to guide school communities' paths towards repair, we chart the broad principles—restitution, compensation, rehabilitation, satisfaction, and guarantees of non-repetition (Generally Assembly of the U.N., 2005)—as they relate to the removal, resistance, and reform that comprise the grammar of school discipline in Alabama (see table 10.1). We emphasize that, while many of these suggestions are fiscal in nature, repair can and must encompass a broad range of community-driven actions[1]. This ethos of repair will need to be local and contextualized; there is no one-size-fits-all solution for the problems in the grammar of school discipline. Rather, stakeholders must identify the damage done by the removal of students in the name of discipline by soliciting community knowledge. Although we offer suggestions about what repair might look like, we reiterate that community knowledge must be the source for answers about how to acknowledge and redress the harms of school discipline.

Reparations are worthwhile so that the benefits of repair are experienced by Black students and families who are adversely affected by the grammar of school discipline. We believe it is also worthwhile to consider how to repair the humanity of school-based practitioners, a humanity which is compromised in the enactment of the white supremacist removal of Black students from education. Indeed, when we enact oppression, we do not just damage the humanities of the oppressed; we also damage our own humanity. In particular, white school-based practitioners must critically examine educative work to "consider whether it brings us closer to humanization or makes us more dehumanized" (Matias and Allen 2016, 49), recognizing that the anti-Black project of school discipline is damaging to all. As Love (2019) indicates, abolishing the conditions that make it possible to inflict harm on Black and Brown folx is a push for everyone's humanity.

Table 10.1 Aligning the Grammar of School Discipline with the Principles of Reparations

	Restitution	Compensation	Rehabilitation	Satisfaction	Guarantees of Non-Repetition
Removal	Decarcerate students who have been removed to adult and juvenile justice facilities. Replace removed and excluded students back in their classrooms and schools. Allocate fiscal resources to prepare policymakers and school-based practitioners to contend with the centrality of removal in our current policies and practices of school discipline as well as its white supremacist and anti-Black racist roots. Sustain this preparation and professional development to push toward a reimagining of schooling contexts that center relationships, rather than removal and denial of education.	Calculate the fiscal costs of exclusion in a community/school system and allocate financial resources to families and communities adversely affected by removal.	Provide and fund medical and psychological care, legal and social services for students and families adversely affected by removal.	Acknowledge the racialized removal taking place in Alabama public schools. Make available comprehensive public data that report school discipline incidents, the consequences ascribed to those incidents, and the demographic data about students who received these consequences. State department officials must make those data publicly available to all Alabamians.	Abolish the disciplinary policies and practices that prompt removal and exclusion, including the presence of law enforcement officers in public schools that criminalize students and introduce them to broader carceral systems. Divest from school-police partnerships, alternative school models, and juvenile justice facilities.

(Continued)

Table 10.1 Aligning the Grammar of School Discipline with the Principles of Reparations (Continued)

	Restitution	Compensation	Rehabilitation	Satisfaction	Guarantees of Non-Repetition
Resistance	Place students in schools that are welcoming to resistance to injustice and that are working to be more just spaces vis-à-vis curricula and pedagogies. Allocate fiscal resources to preparing policymakers and school-based practitioners to contend with interpretations of student behaviors as "defiant," "disobedient," "disorderly," and their roots in white supremacy and anti-Black racism. Sustain this preparation and professional development to push toward reframing of student behaviors that center asset-based, rather than deficit-based, thinking.	Calculate the fiscal and other cognitive and emotional costs associated with labeling students as resistant, especially in cases where those labels have introduced students to juvenile and adult criminal and legal systems. Compensate students and families for those costs.	Provide and fund medical and psychological care, legal and social services and supports for students and families who are resisting unjust schooling contexts.	Acknowledge that students' resistance is often justified, rooted in their rejection of oppressive, dehumanizing practices and irrelevant curricula and instruction.	Restructure school policies and practices, in tandem with communities, to identify perceived resistance as productive and communicative, rather than as deserving of punishment and removal.
Reform	Identify where reform efforts have simply shifted patterns rather than disrupting them. Redirect in-place funding and professional development for reform models focused on individual students and practitioners (e.g., PBS/PBIS, "implicit bias" training) to instead examine systemic policies that remove and penalize resistance.	Calculate the fiscal costs, in addition to other community costs, of failed reform efforts. Redirect funds and efforts to developing school-community partnerships.	Provide and fund medical and psychological care, legal and social services for students and families who have been harmed by reform. Provide and fund ongoing practitioner reflection and professional development toward humility with students and families, who should set the terms of reparation and healing.	Acknowledge that reforms predicated on behaviors of individual students (e.g., PBS/PBIS, "implicit bias" training) will never remedy a racist problem or the problem of racism. Race-evasive reforms that fail to address systemic, underlying causes will reinstate white supremacy.	Allocate resources to build and sustain school-family partnerships in lieu of expenditures on popular, corporatized reform models. Establish community oversight of schools.

For our part as scholars and practitioners in our state of Alabama, we view the writing of this book as a first effort toward repair. Numeric data from ALSDE and the Office of Civil Rights, taken together with our narrative data from school administrators and students in alternative schools, construct a clear portrait of the grammar of school discipline: the mechanisms by which Black students are removed from schools, resistance in the face of that removal, and efforts toward reform that may have benefits for some, but dire consequences for others. We also have presented humanizing portraits of the students who are removed and the practitioners who are charged with their removal in order to prompt reflection and action about the ways in which school discipline is a manifestation of anti-Black racism in public schools in Alabama.

Our efforts toward repair are not, however, without their own tensions. Indeed, we too are affected by the grammar of school discipline. In the next chapter, we further explore these tensions, including the inherent racial tension we had to navigate to undertake this work. In doing so, we trouble the methodological, theoretical, and axiological aspects of our work as white scholars studying white supremacist, anti-Black school structures. We attend to the ways in which our privileged positions mean that our investigations are inherently exploitative, particularly of those students and school-based practitioners with whom we built (and continue to build) caring relationships, and the ways we stand to benefit from that exploitation. We also take up the problematics inherent in our use of portraiture.

NOTES

1. For further resources, school-based practitioners might access the "Reparations Now Toolkit" at https://m4bl.org/policy-platforms/reparations/.

Chapter 11

Self-Portraiture, Problematic Positions, and Politics

In this chapter, we make explicit the procedural and methodological challenges we had in conducting research about school discipline in Alabama. We also work to engage in calls for "uncomfortable reflexivity" (Pillow 2003) to position ourselves in our research project, taking up the critiques we might face by virtue of our racial identities and our power as white researchers, as we construct research and portraits that are inevitably filtered through our white gazes. We then consider what reparative work in schools looks like in an era of more visible white supremacy and racism in the public domain.

DATA DENIALS AND DISCREPANCIES

In 2016, we began to think more carefully about discipline, and the ways that anti-Black racism shapes discriminatory discipline, after sharing stories of our own K-12 teaching experiences with one another and after meeting youth who had been removed from middle and high schools to alternative education. We started to click around in the available data about Alabama to explore what the numeric data about school discipline could tell us about our state. Over the course of the years since, we encountered a series of data denials and discrepancies. First, we had numerous difficulties in obtaining data. We began by exploring the public-facing School Incident Report (SIR) data on the Alabama State Department of Education (ALSDE) website. These data afforded us the ability to explore the number and type of incidents at both the system and the school levels in a given academic year. The only consequence that we could explore with these incident-level data was referral to law enforcement. Thus, to further explore the ways in which certain incidents were consequenced, as well as to try and ascertain the students involved, we sent a series of requests to the ALSDE via numerous contacts for SIR data that linked incidents and all state-defined consequences and that were disaggregated by students' racial and other demographic characteristics. We were repeatedly assured that they would be sent; eventually, the ALSDE did provide us, via one of our coauthors, with SIR data, which were what we used in the reporting of this book. Those data were not disaggregated by student demographics, but they did include the days of suspension, collapsed to include both out-of-school and in-school, days of alternative school placement, number of expulsions, and instances of corporal punishment by incident type in addition to information about referral to law enforcement. Interestingly, as of the time of the writing of this chapter, some of the SIR data from years prior to 2014 had been removed from the ALSDE website, and we have witnessed multiple versions and iterations of public-facing data over the last several years.

Moreover, there were discrepancies between the data files we had been sent, via a coauthor, and the data that were available on the public-facing website. The data files we were sent reported varied numbers for incidents and consequences; some were lower than the public-facing data reports, and some were higher. When we began to cross-reference the data we had been provided with data that some individual systems posted on their public-facing websites, ostensibly for the same academic time-periods, we also noticed discrepancies that were again without pattern: some numbers were higher; others were lower.

Our next step was to begin cross-referencing state-level data with those data available from the Office of Civil Rights (OCR), where data were disaggregated, but in much different forms. We could tell, for example, what types of exclusionary discipline were used for which groups of students, but were unable to link incidents with consequences. We also noticed discrepancies. For example, we noticed that many schools for which there were no reported referrals to law enforcement in the state-provided data had reported school-based arrests to the OCR. Some schools that had not reported any days of alternative school placement to the OCR had alternative schools full of students and SIRs indicating many days of alternative school placement. Officials at the OCR attributed this to different periods of reporting or poor data entry and advised us to direct our questions to the ALSDE, which we did, and received no response. We also attempted to contact various related entities including sheriff's departments and school resource officer representatives; our calls were not returned. Attempting to reconcile these datasets was, as we indicated during a conference presentation one year, "a mess," a sentiment echoed by many in our audience who had attempted to examine their own state-level data in conjunction with that which had been provided to the OCR.

As we explored the numeric data further, we made the decision to rely heavily on the state-provided data, despite the fact that they were incomplete, and to supplement our findings with data from the OCR as they are only released every other year and had not been released for any school years since 2015–2016. OCR data contained student demographic information and consequences, but not the incidents for which the consequences were assigned. Importantly, though, the federal data indicated that 136 of 137 reporting school systems in Alabama in 2015–2016 disproportionately used at least one and usually multiple forms of exclusionary discipline (in-school suspension, out-of-school suspension, expulsions, alternative school referrals, law enforcement referrals, school-based arrests, or corporal punishment) with Black students.

For the bulk of this project, we focused our analyses on the intersection between exclusionary discipline and subjective incidents, analyses we could not have done with OCR data alone. To restate, state-level data had only incidents and aggregate consequences, making the number of students and their demographic information involved impossible to ascertain; the federal-level data had student demographic data and specific consequences, but we were unable to examine the incidents for which students were issued those consequences. Thus, the ALSDE, by maintaining an internally different reporting system than what is required for the OCR, further obfuscates patterns in discipline data that we know to be racialized and gendered. Indeed, it would be more efficient to align processes for data for reporting at the state and federal levels, but this would render disparities readily visible to public stakeholders and laypeople. Instead, the data, as they are reported, do not easily yield to traditional forms of numeric or statistical analysis.

Given this, we anticipate that we will encounter criticisms of the central argument in this book—that Black students are systematically removed from Alabama classrooms—on the basis that the numeric data we were able to access and have provided to support those claims are disparate, incompatible, and unsuited to the kinds of statistical analyses required to demonstrate correlations and likelihoods. However, the Public Affairs Research Council of Alabama (PARCA) was able to conduct analyses based on disaggregated discipline data provided directly to them by the ALSDE. Their report (2020) indicates that, indeed, Black students are disciplined more frequently and more harshly than their white peers. We also argue that the lack of disaggregated data provided to us or made available to the public is an intentional whitewashing of the ways in which school discipline and its grammar are discriminatory. Rather than being dissuaded by the state of the data, we chose to analyze the absences therein, drawing on much research literature to fill in the gaps and enacting a commitment to "challenge racism-neutral and racism-evasive approaches to studying racial disparities by centering current research that makes visible the normalized facets of racism in K–12 schools" (Kohli, Pizarro, and Nevárez 2017, 182). We responded to this absence of data by way of portraiture, amplifying and magnifying practitioners and students' accounts of discriminatory discipline, as well as descriptions of the contexts in which harsh, exclusionary discipline occurs.

PORTRAITURE AS A RESPONSE

When we started this project, it was clear, early on, that few scholars had taken up discipline in Alabama as a focus of inquiry. We wondered why; school discipline and the school-to-prison pipeline were common topics at regional and national conferences and in publications. We quickly began to understand how discipline reporting at the state level obfuscates discriminatory discipline and how the method of reporting was not structured to yield to statistical analyses. It is challenging to persuade stakeholders and policymakers in the absence of numeric data. Moreover, if numeric data were available, history tells us that they are not enough to dismantle systems built on white supremacy. Absent a widespread push toward the abolition of exclusionary discipline, and we do not anticipate one in Alabama, we hope we have provided opportunities for practitioners to consider the small moves toward racial justice that they might make: intervening in removal, engaging resistance, pushing for reform, and committing to reparations. We also hope we have offered a path that others can take up to make sense of available data, replacing absences in data with the voices of educators and students to feature those whose perspectives are often dismissed. That is, we hope to have provided a model for the roles of theory and stories in making sense of data that may be highly redacted and intentionally sanitized by supplementing and even supplanting them with the portraits of those people whose lives are shaped by what happens in schools.

Portraiture (Lawrence-Lightfoot 1983; Lawrence-Lightfoot and Davis 1997) as a method is rooted in aesthetic tendencies, works to integrate ethnographic and naturalistic inquiry with representations of participants that are empathic. Representing research via portraiture can function "as a source of empowerment for schools, communities, and researchers. When constructing portraits, the researcher highlights those habits and contributors to the ethos of the site" (Chapman 2005, 32). In this book, we have worked to explore the context of Alabama to add to the conversation about school discipline in U.S. public schools, choosing to focus on stories that illuminate its grammar, stories of removal, resistance to oppressive practices, and reform. We have also endeavored to provide opportunities for practitioners to consider where they might do the same and how they might extend that work toward reparations in their school communities.

Even so, we wish to acknowledge that the portraits we have presented here, in our attempt at (moving toward) repair, are also incomplete:

> Partiality is not in and of itself a negative aspect of the research. Rather, this partiality provides the portraitist the space to acknowledge her or his presence—physically, psychologically, spiritually, and emotionally—in the research, thereby dismantling the notion that the researcher is the only knower and expert on the lives and experiences of the participants. (Dixson, Chapman, and Hill 2005, 17)

In the following sections, we position ourselves, further acknowledging our presence in the project, and unpack the problems and dilemmas we faced.

COMPLICITY AND RESISTANCE

Here, we take up the call, via self-portraiture, to examine the ways that we are complicit in anti-Black racism and the problem and grammar of school discipline. Lawrence-Lightfoot (2005) asserts that "one of the most powerful characteristics of portraiture is its ability to embrace contradictions, its ability to document the beautiful/ugly experiences that are so much a part of the texture of human development and social relationships" (9).

In chapter 5, we wrote of the ways that we found moments of joy with students as they navigated often hostile schooling contexts; in other words: the beautiful. Here, we focus on the ugly to lay bare the ways that we are also part of that hostile landscape. We do this work in order to provide further examples of how educators must make themselves vulnerable, documenting both the beautiful and ugly, in critiquing the ways that school-based policies and practices are steeped in whiteness and taken for granted, and how they are enacted in anti-Black ways.

Just as the alternative school students with whom we worked were forced to navigate the betweenness of adulthood and childhood, we too navigated tensions in the space we shared with them. We consistently felt glad to be with them and compelled to make their time with us as positive as possible, while we also felt that our presence in their school made us complicit in their mistreatment. We both belonged and didn't; we were interlopers with real relationships with students but without real power to shape their overall school experiences. We were racial and community outsiders, and we represented an institution that marginalizes members from the Black community in our region. Further, when we witnessed practitioners enact harsh disciplinary consequences in this context, we feared advocating for students in explicit ways, a fear rooted in the risk that we might have the privileges that we were afforded in our work there revoked for doing so. That is, in that hypersurveilled, punitive environment where we existed as outsiders, we feared that any critique of the school model and those within it might jeopardize our position at the school and the freedoms that we had in our classes. Most of all, we feared that vocalizing a critique would negatively impact the students in our classes in that they would no longer be privy to the moments of connection, joy, and warmth that our classroom context, at times, provided. Were we to speak up, students would incur the most risk and the most potential consequence.

Namely, we understand our work and presence in the alternative school as simultaneously complicit and resistant. Our engagement at once legitimized the school and its role in the removal of students from their traditional schools and afforded us occasional opportunities to resist the oppressive climate of the school. We were able to engage in discussion-based pedagogies, whereas students were often forbidden to speak. We took students outdoors, whereas their movements in the building were highly controlled and surveilled. We prioritized students' interests above the rigid instructional expectations of the school administrators. Our dual role as insiders and outsiders, teachers who were employed by a local university, meant we could embed resistance in our complicity. We engaged with the same Black students who had been labeled bad, defiant, and disrespectful by other school-based personnel, but we never felt those things in our sustained interactions with them, whether in our roles as their teachers or as researchers in other teachers' classrooms. Instead, we saw students engage in play, collective action to address environmental concerns in their neighborhoods, and relationship-building with one another and us (interactions that included personal questions, personal disclosure, profanity, and even extracurricular rides to get pregnancy tests and books at the library). But, by merely being there, we were implicitly condoning their removal from the schools for which they were zoned and all of the social and extracurricular opportunities that are bound up with traditional school attendance, instantiating the process and effects of removal.

A next tension was that we worked with Black students in the context of an agriscience class where we routinely worked outside, in a garden. We acknowledge the critiques of the school garden movement, including the ways these programs put students of Color to work "in the fields" (Flanagan 2010) potentially at the expense of more rigorous curricula, and that much of the discourse around food systems is race-evasive (Guthman 2008). We worked to integrate topics about racial and environmental justice in our classes in an effort to mitigate some of these critiques, despite there being no real standards to which we could anchor these curricular decisions.

Just as the school leaders we highlighted had to navigate the tensions of enacting oppressive policy in their school buildings at the expense of the well-being of the students there, we navigated tensions in managing our dual roles as researchers and practitioners. We invested in the lives of students and school leaders even as we represented the college and institution responsible for preparing many practitioners in school communities in Alabama, the same practitioners who had removed the students with whom we worked. We attempted to manage these often coinciding roles by journaling, debriefing with peers who also identified as scholar-practitioners, and taking (some of) our interpretations back to students and practitioners, (re)evaluating them in light of the feedback and insight they offered.

We also have been complicit in the problem of school discipline beyond just our working in the context of alternative schools in Alabama. For example, Carey made use of taken-for-granted discipline policies and practices during her time teaching in a public high school in Alabama, relying on school administrators to handle, and often remove, what she perceived to be difficult disciplinary challenges in her class. Similarly, Hannah, while teaching in a public high school in North Carolina, sometimes relied on school policies regarding tardies, detentions, and suspensions, which inevitably contributed to the removal of Black and Brown students from her classroom and the broader school community.

We experienced many of these tensions as unresolvable, the inherent challenges of engaging in antiracist work as white scholars within existing structures and contextual constraints. We sit with them now, acknowledging them for ourselves and our reader, to reflect on how we are also part of the grammar of school discipline.

WHO BENEFITS?

Much like the students featured in chapter 9, those who were freedom fighters in the reform efforts in Timber County, the alternative school students we have written about are also unwitting freedom fighters who will not benefit directly from this work. The whiteness mixed into the mortar and infused in the air of their school buildings is also part of the fabric of the institution of higher education in which we work, an institution that affords us many privileges: much higher than state median incomes, guaranteed employment, the option to work in the comfort of the arm chairs of the ivory tower, and access to schools across the state, schools we can leave just as easily as we can enter. Just as whiteness has given rise to the exclusion of students, particularly Black students, from their traditional schools, whiteness, in conjunction with the neoliberal accountability and profit-focused structures of higher education, has given rise to the pressure that we exploit these students in the name of scholarship, lest we "perish" instead of "publish." This requirement, of course, positions the work we do *with* students as something less than scholarship and the work we, as white scholars, do *about* them as valuable, the *real* work of faculty.

The stories we have worked to document and relay here do not belong to us. They belong to students and practitioners who remain unidentified in this text. The ethical conventions of our profession require that we mask (i.e., "protect") their identities through the use of pseudonyms; few will know who they really are. The same conventions also require that we similarly protect the schools and systems that mistreat them. We also acknowledge that our use of portraiture is additionally problematic since the stories of students we have written are our versions of their stories, and we inhabit white bodies, always already complicit in the oppression of people of Color, benefiting from both whiteness and the ways that we inhabit it. In our research methods classes, we often engage graduate students in discussions about "who gets to tell whose stories, and for whom?" As researchers, while we try to bring to the fore the racist grammar that perpetuates anti-Black school discipline, our engagement with these data and the texts we have drawn on to support our analyses happens through a white gaze (Yancy 2016). We have been reluctant to tell some of the stories here, as we know they are filtered through our own white gaze, and our decision to do so will garner valid criticism. What license do we, as white women, have to invoke portraits of Black educators and students whose lives are "already caught up in narratives prescripted by the state" (Raiford 2019, para. 4)? Research exploits—glorifies pain for the education of others—and documents trauma in ways that overshadow justice work in schools. In our portraiture, we risk further positioning Black students as marginalized and victimized rather than joyous and resilient. We are sure that we have recentered whiteness in ways that remain invisible to us in this project, despite our best attempts to draw on analytical frames designed to help us see. We have felt white fragility (DiAngelo 2018), including defensiveness, anger, and even tears when given critiques about our work as teachers, researchers, and white women working toward antiracist praxis, and expect to do so again in the future. We acknowledge that our work toward unpacking the ways we inhabit whiteness is ongoing, never-ending, and always difficult, and we take these words by Christine Clark (1999) to heart: "As an antiracist racist I believe that I should always feel conflicted, full of contradictions, never as though I have 'arrived'" (92).

THIS SOCIOPOLITICAL MOMENT

Our presentation of the grammar of school discipline in Alabama comes at a contested sociopolitical moment. As we look to the future of school discipline policies and practices in Alabama, we anticipate that Black students will continue to experience discriminatory discipline in the forms of brutality, exclusion from instruction, and introduction to the juvenile justice system (the school-to-prison pipeline, the school/prison nexus) unless substantive attention is paid to the mechanisms by which students are disciplined, the ways in which related data are reported, the unintended consequences that come with well-intentioned reform, and the possibilities afforded by repair.

We have engaged, and will continue to engage, in abolitionist imaginings and scholar-activism focused on the idea of repair. We do this, in part, to repair the damage done to our humanity in the times when we have been complicit in the oppression of people of Color, times when we have condoned or taken no notice of their removal, ignored or misread their resistance, and permitted white supremacy and anti-Black racism to persist, even in the midst of reform. Our humanity is undermined, isolated, and traumatized by witnessing and failing to intervene in racist policies and practices; we cannot at once experience being fully human in the midst of the dehumanization of others.

Though we see continued race-evasive discourse in the plans for moving public education forward (backward?) in Alabama, this discourse paradoxically continues to occur in a moment beyond the era of race-evasiveness. As Matias and Newlove (2017) argue, we have now entered:

> a moment of emboldened en/whitening epistemology that is characterized by the perverse re-appropriation of civil rights and socially just terminologies and concepts—once used to support the rights of People of Color—to instead strengthen white nationalism. Although we recognize that whiteness ideology was ever present during any period, we argue that during this epistemological moment, whiteness is returning to an emboldened state, which, if left uncontested, can reproduce many discriminatory acts. (921)

We thus acknowledge that there are forces at work in systems in Alabama that are historically rooted and (re)surgent: there are pockets where it is no longer undesirable to be labeled a racist. These pockets have always existed, but they are once again highly visible in the public, overtly and proudly state-sanctioned much as they were in the time of George Wallace and Bull Connor, though the rhetoric has morphed. There was a time not so long ago when few public employees would have responded to racial stereotypes with "these are facts" even if that's what they believed; a fear of being labeled a racist may have prevented them from doing so. But there is ever-increasing space in the public domain for people to proudly espouse overtly anti-Black ideas, be deemed legitimate thinkers, and to garner broad public support for election to the highest offices in the land. What does it mean for our opportunities for reflection and action when, ideologically, no reflection and action are deemed necessary because things are working just as they should within a white supremacist order? Conversely, it is not enough to condemn overtly white supremacist and anti-Black sentiment and ideology. Continued examination of the ways that whiteness and the stereotypes and dominant narratives that serve it distort the ability to acknowledge and honor the humanity of all is also widely needed.

We hope that this text serves as a model for what it can look like to engage with data, even dehumanized or sanitized data, in humanizing ways. We ask practitioners and scholars to take up portraiture, or other humanizing methods, when considering and analyzing numeric data generated in classrooms and schools. It is easy to fall into the habit of thinking about numeric data points and patterns as abstractions, removed from real-life experiences. Turning to humanizing methods can support our efforts to remember that numbers are really just reductionist representations of *actual* people whose lives are altered, often negatively, by the practices and policies implied in the patterns.

The assumption we made at the onset of this project was that Alabama, at best, would be reflective of national trends in discipline; given the sociopolitical and historical context here, we expected things to be worse, and perhaps they are. Better, worse, these gradients are no matter. What we know, based on the overwhelming volume of research about the school-to-prison pipeline, school/prison nexus, and our carceral state in addition to the voices of those affected firsthand by school discipline, some of whom we have included in this book, is that school discipline affects us all: students, practitioners, families. This is not to suggest that these effects are uniformly or equally shared. As we have demonstrated in this book, school discipline policies and practices burden Black students and families in Alabama in outrageous ways, much as the criminal justice system does. What might it mean, though, for those who are seemingly oblivious to those burdens to begin to recognize, reconcile, repair, and abolish them? What might it mean for white people in particular to feel responsible for the well-being of all (Applebaum 2010)?

Here in Alabama, police profile our Black friends and neighbors, arresting and publicly humiliating them. ICE officials raid and terrorize communities nearby to our university. Locals on grand juries indict their neighbors for drug charges that would be legal and/or decriminalized in nearby states, while also voting to further restrict addiction, health care, and mental health services, and to support the expansion of prisons. Alabama is often scapegoated as the worst of places, the most oppressive, the easiest to dismiss as a lost cause. It's also the site where many abolitionists and organizers have chosen to do their work, offering us hope. Alabama, often a great shame to our nation, is also a site of great resilience and resistance, and it could be a site of great restoration and reparation. What happens in Alabama happens everywhere.

We close this book, writing from Alabama, in the midst of a global pandemic and a renewed uprising against state-sanctioned violence. We have all been asked to engage in physical distancing, and in some cases, isolation for the well-being of all. Having written most of this book literally together, the two of us are now mostly separated, as mandated by the response to the Covid-19 pandemic and the precautions we are taking within our communities. We have sheltered in place, watched schools and universities close, and witnessed many students, faculty, and staff forced to return to school buildings despite the risks of doing so. We acknowledge that many are existing in a state of exclusion, some removed from many of the most important people in their lives—friends, family, colleagues, teachers, and students—and others excluded from decision-making that affects their lives in physical and material ways.

In this moment, we also see increasing rates of Black and Brown students disciplined in virtual environments for many of the same incidents that they are in the face-to-face classroom: removed from Zoom and Google meetings for "defiant" behavior; suspended for dress-code violations while in their own homes; penalized for being late to their computers. We are also witnessing a new era of surveillance. Teachers glimpse a small snapshot of students' home lives and take license to report their families to social services. Administrators monitor students' private chats for any wrongdoing and refer them to School Resource Officers for those messages. In this moment of heightened surveillance of Black students' behaviors, and the loss of sacred living spaces to this surveillance, we urge practitioners to examine our philosophies of discipline, punishment, and correction, contextualizing them with the need for humanizing practices with students and families. In this moment, we are all poised to develop more empathy for the students routinely removed from schools and classrooms, away from their teachers and classmates. This moment offers insight into the motives for resistance and reform and into the need for relationship-building and repair. In the midst of these new approaches to teaching and learning across classrooms and online spaces, we have an opportunity to reimagine the grammars that dictate our institutions, to remake the routines that comprise our life together.

References

Adams, Jane Meredith. 2015. "California Student Suspension Rate Drops as 'Willful Defiance' Punishments Decline." *EdSource*, November 23, 2015. https://edsourc e.org/2015/california-student-suspension-rate-drops-as-willful-defiance-punishme nts-decline/90989.

Addington, Lynn A. 2019. "Black Girls Doing Time for White Boys' Crime? Considering Columbine's Security Legacy Through an Intersectional Lens." *Journal of Contemporary Criminal Justice* 35 (3): 296–314. https://doi.org/10 .1177/1043986219840205.

Advancement Project, Education Law Center – PA, FairTest, The Forum for Education and Democracy, Juvenile Law Center, NAACP Legal Defense and Educational Fund, Inc. 2011. "Federal Policy, ESEA Reauthorization, and the School-to-Prison Pipeline." Last modified March, 2011. https:// https://www.elc -pa.org/wp-content/uploads/2013/11/FederalPolicy_ESEA_and_SchoolToPrison Pipeline.03.09.11.pdf.

Alabama Appleseed Center for Law and Justice. 2019. "Hall Monitors with Handcuffs: How Alabama's Unregulated, Unmonitored School Resource Officer Program Threatens the State's Most Vulnerable Children." Accessed November 28, 2020. https://alabamaappleseed.org/wp-content/uploads/2019/08/Alabama-Apples eed-Hall-Monitors-with-Handcuffs.pdf.

Alabama Juvenile Justice Task Force. 2017. "Final Report." Accessed November 28, 2020. http://lsa.state.al.us/PDF/Other/JJTF/JJTF-Final-Report.pdf.

Alabama State Department of Education [ALSDE]. 2008-2016. "Enrollment Data." Accessed January 27, 2020. http://web.alsde.edu/PublicDataReports/Default.aspx.

Alabama State Department of Education [ALSDE]. 2010. "SIR Guide and Overview of Major Reporting Elements." Accessed November 28, 2020. https://www.alsde .edu/sec/pss/Discipline/SIR%20Overview%20and%20Summary.pdf.

Alabama State Department of Education [ALSDE]. 2011. "Innovative Pathways to Graduation Guide: A Bridge for Success." Accessed November 28, 2020. https:/

/www.alsde.edu/sec/pss/Alternative%20Education/IPGG%20Document%20%20Final%202006-28-11%2010.18.pdf.

Alabama State Department of Education [ALSDE]. 2014. "The Implementation Guide for the Alabama Parent Project Program." Accessed November 28, 2020. https://www.alsde.edu/sec/pss/Discipline/PARENT%20PROJECT%20IMPLEMENTATION%20GUIDE.pdf.

Alabama State Department of Education [ALSDE]. 2017. "Education Report Card." Accessed November 28, 2020. https://reportcard.alsde.edu/Alsde/SelectSchool.

Alabama State Department of Education [ALSDE]. 2018. "What Every Administrator Needs to Know about Alternatives to Suspension and Expulsion." Accessed November 28, 2020. https://www.alsde.edu/sec/pss/PBS/Alternatives_to_Suspensions.pdf.

Allen, Quaylan, and Kimberly A. White-Smith. 2014. "'Just as Bad as Prisons': The Challenge of Dismantling the School-to-Prison Pipeline through Teacher and Community Education." *Equity & Excellence in Education* 47 (4): 445–460. https://doi.org/10.1080/10665684.2014.958961.

American Academy of Pediatrics. 2013. "Out-of-School Suspension and Expulsion." *Pediatrics* 131 (3): e1000–e1007. https://doi.org/10.1542/peds.2012-3932.

American Psychological Association Zero Tolerance Task Force. 2008. "Are Zero Tolerance Policies Effective in Schools?: An Evidentiary Review and Recommendations." *American Psychologist* 63 (9): 852–862. https://doi.org/10.1037/0003-066x.63.9.852.

Anderson, Amy J., and Hannah Carson Baggett. 2020. "'I Just Put My Head Down, But They Still Get on to Me': Navigating Silence in an Alternative School in Alabama." *Journal of Critical Thought and Praxis* 9 (1). https://doi.org/10.31274/jctp.9563.

Anderson, Carol. 2018. *One Person, No Vote: How Voter Suppression Is Destroying Our Democracy.* New York: Bloomsbury Publishing.

Anderson, Kaitlin P., and Gary W. Ritter. 2020. "Do School Discipline Policies Treat Students Fairly? Evidence from Arkansas." *Educational Policy* 34 (5): 707–734. https://doi.org/10.1177/0895904818802085.

Anderson, Kaitlin P., Gary W. Ritter, and Gema Zamarro. 2019. "Understanding a Vicious Cycle: The Relationship between Student Discipline and Student Academic Outcomes." *Educational Researcher* 48 (5): 251–262. https://doi.org/10.3102/0013189x19848720.

Anfara Jr, Vincent A., Katherine R. Evans, and Jessica N. Lester. 2013. "Restorative Justice in Education: What We Know So Far." *Middle School Journal* 44 (5): 57–63. https://doi.org/10.1080/00940771.2013.11461873.

Annamma, Subini Ancy. 2017. *The Pedagogy of Pathologization: Dis/Abled Girls of Color in the School-Prison Nexus.* New York: Routledge.

Annamma, Subini Ancy, Yolanda Anyon, Nicole M. Joseph, Jordan Farrar, Eldridge Greer, Barbara Downing, and John Simmons. 2019. "Black Girls and School Discipline: The Complexities of Being Overrepresented and Understudied." *Urban Education* 54 (2): 211–242. https://doi.org/10.1177/0042085916646610.

References

Annamma, Subini, Tamara Handy, Amanda L. Miller, and Elizabeth Jackson. 2020. "Animating Discipline Disparities Through Debilitating Practices: Girls of Color and Inequitable Classroom Interactions." *Teachers College Record* 122 (5).

Annamma, Subini Ancy, Darrell D. Jackson, and Deb Morrison. 2017. "Conceptualizing Color-Evasiveness: Using Dis/Ability Critical Race Theory to Expand a Color-Blind Racial Ideology in Education and Society." *Race Ethnicity and Education* 20 (2): 147–162. https://doi.org/10.1080/13613324.2016.1248837.

Anyon, Jean. 1980. "Social Class and the Hidden Curriculum of Work." *Journal of Education*, 162 (1): 67–92. https://doi.org/10.1080/13613324.2016.1248837.

Anyon, Yolanda, Chalane Lechuga, Debora Ortega, Barbara Downing, Eldridge Greer, and John Simmons. 2018. "An Exploration of the Relationships between Student Racial Background and the School Sub-Contexts of Office Discipline Referrals: A Critical Race Theory Analysis." *Race Ethnicity and Education* 21 (3): 390–406. https://doi.org/10.1080/13613324.2017.1328594.

Anyon, Yolanda, Duan Zhang, and Cynthia Hazel. 2016. "Race, Exclusionary Discipline, and Connectedness to Adults in Secondary Schools." *American Journal of Community Psychology* 57 (3/4): 342–352. https://doi.org/10.1002/ajcp.12061.

Applebaum, Barbara. 2010. *Being White, Being Good: White Complicity, White Moral Responsibility, and Social Justice Pedagogy*. Plymouth, UK: Lexington Books.

Araujo, Ana Lucia. 2017. *Reparations for Slavery and the Slave Trade: A Transnational and Comparative History*. New York: Bloomsbury.

Arcia, Emily. 2006. "Achievement and Enrollment Status of Suspended Students: Outcomes in a Large, Multicultural School District." *Education and Urban Society* 38 (3): 359–369. https://doi.org/10.1177/0013124506286947.

Avildsen, John G. (Director). 1989. *Lean on Me* [Motion Picture]. United States: Warner Home Video.

Baggett, Hannah Carson. 2016. "Student Enrollment in World Languages: L'Égalité des Chances?" *Foreign Language Annals* 49 (1): 162–179. https://doi.org/10.1111/flan.12173.

Baggett, Hannah Carson. 2021. "Nobody Likes Me, Everybody Hates Me (Worms)." *Qualitative Inquiry*: 1–5. https://doi.org/10.1177/1077800419884959.

Baggett, Hannah Carson, and Carey E. Andrzejewski. 2017. "'Man, Somebody Tell that Kid to Shut Up': Youth Participatory Action Research at a Rural Alternative School in the Deep South." *Critical Questions in Education* 8 (4): 401–417.

Baggett, Hannah Carson, and Carey E. Andrzejewski. 2020a. "Bravery and YPAR in a Rural Alternative School." In *Educating for Social Justice: Field Notes from Rural Communities* edited by Rebekah A. Cordova and William M. Reynolds, 72–85. Boston: Sense.

Baggett, Hannah Carson, and Carey E. Andrzejewski. 2020b. "An Exploration of White Fear and School Discipline in Alabama." *Whiteness and Education* 5 (1): 74–90. https://doi.org/10.1080/23793406.2019.1697964.

Balfanz, Robert, Vaughan byrnes, and Joanna Fox. 2014. "Sent Home and Put Off-Track: The Antecedents, Disproportionality, and Consequences of Being

Suspended in 9th Grade." *Journal of Applied Research on Children: Informing Policy for Children at Risk* 5 (2): article 13.

Barnard, Charles H., and John Jones. 1987. "Farm Real Estate Values in the United States by Counties, 1850-1982." Washington, DC: United States Department of Agriculture, Economic Research Service. Accessed November 28, 2020. https://www.card.iastate.edu/land-value/history/Barnard-and-Jones-1987-Farm-real-estate-values-in-the-United-States-by-counties-1850-1982.pdf.

Bartlett, Lesley, Marla Frederick, Thaddeus Gulbrandsen, and Enrique Murillo. 2002. "The Marketization of Education: Public Schools for Private Ends." *Anthropology & Education Quarterly* 33 (1): 5–29. https://doi.org/10.1525/aeq.2002.33.1.5.

Bass, Jack. 1993. *Taming the Storm: The Life and Times of Judge Frank M. Johnson, Jr. and the South's Fight Over Civil Rights.* New York: Doubleday.

Beger, Randall R. 2002. "Expansion of Police Power in Public Schools and the Vanishing Rights of Students." *Social Justice* 29 (1/2): 119–130. Accessed November 28, 2020. http://www.jstor.org/stable/29768123.

Bell, Charles. 2020. "'Maybe if They Let Us Tell the Story I Wouldn't Have Gotten Suspended': Understanding Black Students' and Parents' Perceptions of School Discipline." *Children and Youth Services Review* 110. https://doi.org/10.1016/j.childyouth.2020.104757.

Bell, Derrick A. 1980. "Brown v. Board of Education and the Interest-Convergence Dilemma." *Harvard Law Review* 93 (3): 518–533. https://doi.org/10.2307/1340546.

Bell, Derrick A. 1992. *Faces at the Bottom of the Well.* New York: Basic Books.

Bellinger, L. Boyd, Nicole Darcangelo, Stacey S. Horn, Erica R. Meiners, and Sarah Schriber. 2016. "Ecologies of School Discipline for Queer Youth: What Listening to Queer Youth Teaches Us About Transforming School Discipline." In *Inequality in School Discipline*, edited by Russell J. Skiba, Kavitha Mediratta, and M. Karega Rausch, 135–152. New York: Palgrave Macmillan.

Bennett, William John, John J. DiIulio, and John P. Walters. 1996. *Body Count: Moral Poverty and How to Win America's War Against Crime and Drugs.* New York: Simon and Schuster.

Bertrand, Marianne, and Sendhil Mullainathan. 2004. "Are Emily and Greg More Employable than Lakisha and Jamal? A Field Experiment on Labor Market Discrimination." *American Economic Review* 94 (4): 991–1013. https://doi.org/10.1257/0002828042002561.

Blake, Jamilia J., Bettie Ray Butler, Chance W. Lewis, and Alicia Darensbourg. 2011. "Unmasking the Inequitable Discipline Experiences of Urban Black Girls: Implications for Urban Educational Stakeholders." *Urban Review* 43 (2): 90–106. https://doi.org/10.1007/s11256-009-0148-8.

Blake, Jamilia J., and Rebecca Epstein. 2019. "Listening to Black Women and Girls: Lived Experiences of Adultification Bias." Georgetown Law: Center On Poverty and Inequality: Initiative on Gender Justice & Opportunity. Accessed December 1, 2020. https://genderjusticeandopportunity.georgetown.edu/wp-content/uploads/2020/06/Listening-to-Black-Women-and-Girls.pdf.

Blake, Tom. (Transcriptionist). 2003, March. "Madison County, Alabama: Largest Slaveholders from 1860 Slave Census Schedules and Surname Matches for African

Americans on 1870 Census." Accessed November 28, 2020 http://freepages.roo tsweb.com/~ajac/genealogy/almadison.htm.

Bonilla-Silva, Eduardo. 2003. *Racism Without Racists: Colorblind Racism and the Persistence of Racial Inequality in America*. New York: Rowman and Littlefield.

Bonilla-Silva, Eduardo. 2012. "The Invisible Weight of Whiteness: The Racial Grammar of Everyday Life in America." *Ethnic and Racial Studies* 35 (2): 173–194. https://doi.org/10.1080/01419870.2011.613997.

Bourdieu, Pierre, and Jean Claude Passeron. 1977. *Reproduction in Society, Education, and Culture* (2nd ed.). Thousand Oaks, CA: Sage.

Bowen, Marty, Wyck Godfrey, Robert Teitel (Producer), and George Tillman, Jr. (Producer and Director). 2018. *The Hate U Give* [Motion Picture]. United States: Fox 2000 Pictures.

Brayboy, Bryan McKinley Jones. 2005. "Transformational Resistance and Social Justice: American Indians in Ivy League Universities." *Anthropology & Education Quarterly* 36 (3): 193–211.

Brenan, Megan. 2018. "Most U.S. Teachers Oppose Carrying Guns in Schools." *Gallup News*, March 16, 2018. https://news.gallup.com/poll/229808/teachers-oppose-carrying-guns-schools.aspx.

Brockenbrough, Ed. 2015. "'The Discipline Stop': Black Male Teachers and the Politics of Urban School Discipline." *Education and Urban Society* 47 (5): 499–522. https://doi.org/10.1177/0013124514530154.

Brown, Anthony L. 2012. "On Human Kinds and Role Models: A Critical Discussion about the African American Male Teacher." *Educational Studies* 48 (3): 296–315. https://doi.org/10.1080/00131946.2012.660666.

Brown, Ben. 2006. "Understanding and Assessing School Police Officers: A Conceptual and Methodological Comment." *Journal of Criminal Justice* 34 (6): 591–604. https://doi.org/10.1016/j.jcrimjus.2006.09.013.

Browne, Simone. 2015. *Dark Matters: On the Surveillance of Blackness*. Durham, NC: Duke University Press.

Browne-Dianis, Judith. 2011. "Stepping Back from Zero Tolerance." *Educational Leadership* 69 (1): 24–28.

Bryk, Anthony S., Penny Bender Sebring, David Kerbow, Sharon Rollow, and John Q. Easton. 1998. *Charting Chicago School Reform: Democratic Localism as a Lever for Social Change*. Boulder, CO: Westview Press.

Bullock, Heather E., and Harmony A. Reppond. 2018. "Of 'Takers' and 'Makers': A Social Psychological Analysis of Class and Classism." In *Oxford Handbook of Social Psychology and Social Justice*, edited by Phillip L. Hammack, 223–244. New York: Oxford University Press.

Butler, Judith. (1993). "Endangered/Endangering: Schematic Racism and White Paranoia." In *Reading Rodney King/Reading Urban Uprising*, edited by Robert Gooding-Williams, 15–22. New York: Routledge.

Butler, Bettie Ray, and Nicholas P. Triplett. 2019. "The Influence of Administrative Leadership on Racial Disparities in School Discipline." In *Convictions of Conscience: How Voices from the Margins Inform Public Actions and Educational*

Leadership, edited by Brenda J. McMahon and Lisa R. Merriweather, 55–74. Charlotte, NC: Information Age Publishing.

Caraballo, Limarys. 2019. "Being 'Loud': Identities-in-Practice in a Figured World of Achievement." *American Educational Research Journal* 56 (4): 1281–1317. https://doi.org/10.3102/0002831218816059.

Carpenter, Bradley W., Beth E. Bukoski, Matthew Berry, and Amanda M. Mitchell. 2017. "Examining the Social Justice Identity of Assistant Principals in Persistently Low-Achieving Schools." *Urban Education* 52 (3): 287–315. https://doi.org/10.1177/0042085915574529.

Carter, Prudence L., Russell Skiba, Marriella I. Arredondo, and Mica Pollock. 2017. "You Can't Fix What You Don't Look At: Acknowledging Race in Addressing Racial Discipline Disparities." *Urban Education* 52 (2): 207–235. https://doi.org/10.1177/0042085916660350.

Carver, Priscilla Rouse, Laurie Lewis, and Peter Tice. 2010. "Alternative Schools and Programs for Public School Students at Risk of Educational Failure: 2007–08 (NCES 2010-026)." Washington, DC: U.S. Government Printing Office. Accessed November 28, 2020 https://nces.ed.gov/pubs2010/2010026.pdf.

Casella, Ronnie. 2003a. "Punishing Dangerousness through Preventive Detention: Illustrating the Institutional Link between School and Prison." In *New Directions for Youth Development: Deconstructing the School-to-Prison Pipeline*, edited by Johanna Wald and Daniel J. Losen, 55–70. San Francisco: Jossey-Bass.

Casella, Ronnie. 2003b. "Security, Schooling, and the Consumer's Choice to Segregate." *The Urban Review* 35 (2): 129–148. https://doi.org/DOI:10.1023/A:1023761612855.

Chapman, Thandeka K. 2005. "Expressions of 'Voice' in Portraiture." *Qualitative Inquiry* 11 (1): 27–51. https://doi.org/10.1177/1077800404270840.

Chapman, Thandeka K. 2007. "Interrogating Classroom Relationships and Events: Using Portraiture and Critical Race Theory in Education Research." *Educational Researcher* 36 (3): 156–162. https://doi.org/10.3102/0013189x07301437.

Charles, Kerwin Kofi, Jonathan Guryan, and Jessica Pan. 2018. "The Effects of Sexism on American Women: The Role of Norms vs. Discrimination (No. w24904)." National Bureau of Economic Research. Accessed November 29, 2020 https://www.nber.org/papers/w24904.

Charles, Safiya. 2019. "Demoralized and Disconnected: Black Girls Are Being Pushed Out of Schools: Here's How." *Montgomery Advertiser,* December 27, 2019. https://www.montgomeryadvertiser.com/story/news/2019/12/27/black-girls-pushed-out-schools-ayanna-pressley-act-juvenile-justice-reform/2662361001/.

Child Trends. 2014. "Child Trends Databank: Attitudes toward Spanking: Indicators on Children and Youth." Accessed November 28, 2020. https://www.childtrends.org/wp-content/uploads/2015/03/indicator_1427477229.49.pdf.

Childs, Karen Elfner, Don Kincaid, Heather Peshak George, and Nicholas A. Gage. 2016. "The Relationship between School-Wide Implementation of Positive Behavior Intervention and Supports and Student Discipline Outcomes." *Journal of Positive Behavior Interventions* 18 (2): 89–99. https://doi.org/ v DOI: 10.1177/109

Chmielewski, Jennifer F., Kimberly M. Belmonte, Michelle Fine, M., and Brett G. Stoudt. 2016. "Intersectional Inquiries with LGBTQ and Gender Nonconforming Youth of Color: Participatory Research on Discipline Disparities at the Race/Sexuality/Gender Nexus." In *Inequality in School Discipline: Research and Practice to Reduce Disparities*, edited by Russell J. Skiba, Kavitha Mediratta, and M. Karega Rausch, 171–188New York: Palgrave Macmillan.

Christie, Christine A., C. Michael Nelson, and Kristine Jolivette. 2004. "School Characteristics Related to the Use of Suspension." *Education and Treatment of Children* 27 (4): 509–526.

Clark, Christine. 1999. "The Secret: White Lies Are Never Little." In *Becoming and Unbecoming White: Owning and Disowning a Racial Identity*, edited by Christine Clark and James O'Donnell, 92–110. Santa Barbara, CA: Praeger.

Coates, Ta-Nehisi. 2014. "The Case for Reparations." *The Atlantic* 313 (5): 54–71. Accessed November 18, 2020. https://www.theatlantic.com/magazine/archive/2014/06/the-case-for-reparations/361631/.

Coates, Ta-Nehisi. 2015. *Between the World and Me*. New York: Spiegel and Grau.

Cobb-Clark, Deborah A., Sonja C. de New (née Kassenboehmer), Trinh Le, Duncan McVicar, and Rong Zhang. 2015. "Is There an Educational Penalty for Being Suspended from School?" *Education Economics* 23 (4): 376–395. https://doi.org/10.2139/ssrn.2364166.

Cohen, Cathy J. 2004. "Deviance as Resistance: A New Research Agenda for the Study of Black Politics." *Du Bois Review: Social Science Research on Race* 1 (1): 27–45. https://doi.org/10.1017/s1742058x04040044.

Coles, Justin A., and Tunette Powell. 2020. "A BlackCrit Analysis on Black Urban Youth and Suspension Disproportionality as Anti-Black Symbolic Violence." *Race Ethnicity and Education* 23 (1): 113–133. https://doi.org/10.1080/13613324.2019.1631778.

Cooper, Camille Wilson. 2003. "The Detrimental Impact of Teacher Bias: Lessons Learned from the Standpoint of African American Mothers." *Teacher Education Quarterly* 30 (2): 101–116.

Cornelius, Janet. 1983. "'We Slipped and Learned to Read:' Slave Accounts of the Literacy Process, 1830-1865." *Phylon* 44 (3): 171–186. https://doi.org/10.2307/274930.

Cornwell, Paige. 2015. "Seattle School Board Halts Suspensions for Elementary Students." *The Seattle Times*, September 23, 2015. http://www.seattletimes.com/seattle-news/education/seattle-school-board-halts-suspensions-for-elementary-students/.

Crain, Trisha Powell. 2017. "Alabama Second in Nation in School District Secessions, Report Says." *Al.com*, June 21, 2017. https://www.al.com/news/2017/06/alabama_second_in_nation_in_sc.html.

Crain, Trisha Powell. 2017. "Suspensions Feed the Achievement Gap in Alabama Schools." *Al.com*, August 14, 2017. https://www.al.com/news/2017/08/the_discipline_gap_why_suspens.html.

Crenshaw, Kimberlé Williams, Priscilla Ocen, and Jyoti Nanda. 2015. "Black Girls Matter: Pushed Out, Overpoliced, and Underprotected." Center for Intersectionality and Social Policy Studies and African American Policy Forum. Accessed November 28, 2020. http://static1.squarespace.com/static/53f20d90e4b0b80451158d8c/t/54d2d22ae4b00c506cffe978/1423102506084/BlackGirlsMatter_Report.pdf.

Crone, Deanne A., Leanne S. Hawken, and Robert H. Horner. 2015. *Building Positive Behavior Support Systems in Schools: Functional Behavioral Assessment* (2nd ed.). New York: Guilford Publications.

Cuban, Larry. 1993. *How Teachers Taught: Constancy and Change in American Classrooms, 1890-1990.* New York: Teachers College Press.

Curran, F. Chris. 2016. "Estimating the Effect of State Zero Tolerance Laws on Exclusionary Discipline, Racial Discipline Gaps, and Student Behavior." *Educational Evaluation and Policy Analysis* 38 (4): 647–668. https://doi.org/10.3102/0162373716652728.

Curran, F. Chris, and James Kitchin. 2018. "Estimating the Relationship between Corporal Punishment Use and School Suspensions: Longitudinal Evidence from the Civil Rights Data Collection." *Peabody Journal of Education* 93 (2): 139–160. https://doi.org/10.1080/0161956x.2018.1435036.

Dancy, T. Elon. 2014. "The Adultification of Black Boys: What Educational Settings Can Learn from Trayvon Martin." In *Trayvon Martin, Race, and American Justice*, edited by Kenneth J. Fasching-Varner, Rema E. Reynolds, Katrice A. Albert, and Lori L. Martin, 49–55. Rotterdam, The Netherlands: Brill Sense.

Darling-Hammond, Linda. (2004). "The Color Line in American Education: Race, Resources, and Student Achievement." *Du Bois Review: Social Science Research on Race* 1 (2): 213–246. https://doi.org/10.1017/s1742058x0404202x.

Darling-Hammond, Linda. 2007. "Race, Inequality and Educational Accountability: The Irony of 'No Child Left Behind.'" *Race Ethnicity and Education* 10 (3): 245–260. https://doi.org/10.1080/13613320701503207.

Darling-Hammond, Linda. 2010. *The Flat World and Education: How America's Commitment to Equity Will Determine Our Future.* New York: Teachers College Press.

Davis, Angela Y. 1981. "Rape, Racism and the Capitalist Setting." *The Black Scholar* 12 (6): 39–45. https://doi.org/10.1080/00064246.1981.11414219.

Davis, Angela Y. 2005. *Abolition Democracy: Prisons, Democracy, and Empire.* New York: Seven Stories.

DeMatthews, David E. 2018. *Community Engaged Leadership for Social Justice: A Critical Approach in Urban Schools.* New York: Routledge.

DeMatthews, David E., Roderick L. Carey, Arturo Olivarez, and Kevin Moussavi Saeedi. 2017. "Guilty as Charged? Principals' Perspectives on Disciplinary Practices and the Racial Discipline Gap." *Educational Administration Quarterly* 53 (4): 519–555. https://doi.org/10.1177/0013161x17714844.

DiAngelo, Robin. 2011. "White Fragility." *International Journal of Critical Pedagogy* 3 (3): 54–70.

Diamond, John B., and Amanda E. Lewis. 2019. "Race and Discipline at a Racially Mixed High School: Status, Capital, and the Practice of Organizational Routines." *Urban Education* 54 (6): 831–859. https://doi.org/10.1177/0042085918814581.

Dillard, Cynthia B. 1995. "Leading with Her Life: An African American Feminist (Re)Interpretation of Leadership for an Urban High School Principal." *Educational Administration Quarterly* 31 (4): 539–563. https://doi.org/10.1177/0013161X9503100403.

Dillard, Cynthia B. 2016. "We Are Still Here: Declarations of Love and Sovereignty in Black Life Under Siege." *Educational Studies* 52 (3): 201–215. https://doi.org/10.1080/00131946.2016.1169737.

Dilulio, John. 1995. "The Coming of the Super-Predators." *Washington Examiner*, November 27, 1995. https://www.washingtonexaminer.com/weekly-standard/the-coming-of-the-super-predators.

Dimitriadis, Greg. 2011. "Studying Resistance: Some Cautionary Notes." *International Journal of Qualitative Studies in Education* 24 (5): 649–654. https://doi.org/10.1080/09518398.2011.600260.

Dixon-Román, Ezekiel J. 2014. "Deviance as Pedagogy: From Nondominant Cultural Capital to Deviantly Marked Cultural Repertoires." *Teachers College Record* 116 (8): 1–30.

Dixson, Adrienne D., Thandeka K. Chapman, and Djanna A. Hill. 2005. "Research as an Aesthetic Process: Extending the Portraiture Methodology." *Qualitative Inquiry* 11 (1): 16–26. https://doi.org/10.1177/1077800404270836.

Dumas, Michael J. 2016. "Against the Dark: Antiblackness in Education Policy and Discourse." *Theory into Practice* 55 (1): 11–19. https://doi.org/10.1080/00405841.2016.1116852.

Dumas, Michael J., and Joseph Derrick Nelson. 2016. "(Re)Imagining Black Boyhood: Toward a Critical Framework for Educational Research." *Harvard Educational Review* 86 (1): 27–47. https://doi.org/10.17763/0017-8055.86.1.27.

Dunn, Alyssa Hadley, Beth Sondel, and Hannah Carson Baggett. 2019. "'I Don't Want to Come Off as Pushing an Agenda': How Contexts Shaped Teachers' Pedagogy in the Days after the 2016 U.S. Presidential Election." *American Educational Research Journal* 56 (2): 444–476. https://doi.org/10.3102/0002831218794892.

Dunning-Lozano, Jessica L. 2018. "School Discipline, Race, and the Discursive Construction of the 'Deficient' Student." *Sociological Spectrum* 38 (5): 326–345. https://doi.org/10.1080/02732173.2018.1532364.

Dupper, David R., and Amy E. Montgomery Dingus. 2008. "Corporal Punishment in U.S. Public Schools: A Continuing Challenge for School Social Workers." *Children and Schools* 30 (4): 243–250. https://doi.org/10.1093/cs/30.4.243.

Dyer, Joel. 2000. *The Perpetual Prison Machine: How America Profits from Crime*. Boulder, CO: Westview Press.

Eitle, Tamela McNulty, and David James Eitle. 2004. "Inequality, Segregation, and the Overrepresentation of African Americans in School Suspensions." *Sociological Perspectives* 47 (3): 269–287. https://doi.org/10.1525/sop.2004.47.3.269.

Elliott, Sinikka, and Megan Reid. 2019. "Low-Income Black Mothers Parenting Adolescents in the Mass Incarceration Era: The Long Reach of Criminalization." *American Sociological Review* 84 (2): 197–219. https://doi.org/10.1177/0003122419833386.

Emihovich, Catherine A. 1983. "The Color of Misbehaving: Two Case Studies of Deviant Boys." *Journal of Black Studies* 13 (3): 259–274. https://doi.org/10.1177/002193478301300301.

Epstein, Rebecca, Jamilia J. Blake, and Thalia González, T. 2017. "Girlhood Interrupted: The Erasure of Black Girls' Childhood." Center on Poverty and Inequality, Georgetown Law. Accessed November 28, 2020. https://www.blendedandblack.com/wp-content/uploads/2017/08/girlhood-interrupted.pdf.

Ericson, Sally Pearsall. 2013. "LeFlore Magnet High School Suspends 100 Students for Dress Code Violations; Do You Agree? (Poll)." *Al.com*, March 26, 2012. https://www.al.com/live/2013/03/leflore_magnet_high_school_sus.html.

Espelage, Dorothy L., and Susan M. Swearer (Eds.). 2004. *Bullying in American Schools: A Social-Ecological Perspective on Prevention and Intervention*. Mahwah, NJ: Lawrence Erlbaum.

Evans-Winters, Venus, E. 2005. *Teaching Black Girls: Resiliency in Urban Classrooms*. New York: Peter Lang.

Evans-Winters, Venus E., and Magaela C. Bethune, M. C. (Eds.). 2014. *(Re)Teaching Trayvon: Education for Racial Justice and Human Freedom*. Rotterdam, The Netherlands: Sense Publishing.

Fabelo, Tony, Michael D. Thompson, Martha Plotkin, Dottie Carmichael, Miner P. Marchbanks III, M. P., and Eric A. Booth. 2011. "Breaking Schools' Rules: A Statewide Study of How School Discipline Relates to Students' Success and Juvenile Justice Involvement." The Council of State Governments: Justice Center and Public Policy Research Institute. Accessed November 30, 2020. https://safesupportivelearning.ed.gov/resources/breaking-school-rules-statewide-study-how-school-discipline-relates-students-success-and#:~:text=Breaking%20School%20Rules%3A%20A%20Statewide%20Study%20of%20How,students%E2%80%99%20academic%20performance%20and%20juvenile%20justice%20system%20involvement.

Farmer, Sarah. 2010. "Criminality of Black Youth in Inner-City Schools: 'Moral panic', Moral Imagination, and Moral Formation." *Race Ethnicity and Education* 13 (3): 367–381. https://doi.org/10.1080/13613324.2010.500845.

Fasching-Varner, Kenneth J., Roland W. Mitchell, Lori L. Martin, and Karen P. Bennett-Haron. 2014. "Beyond School-to-Prison Pipeline and Toward an Educational and Penal Realism." *Equity & Excellence in Education* 47 (4): 410–429. https://doi.org/10.1080/10665684.2014.959285.

Fasching-Varner, Kenneth J., Rema E. Reynolds, Katrice A. Albert, and Lori L. Martin. (Eds.). 2014. *Trayvon Martin, Race, and American Justice: Writing Wrong*. Boston: Sense Publishers.

Fedders, Barbara. 2017. "Schooling at Risk." *Iowa Law Review* 103 (3): 871–923. Accessed November 30, 2020. https://ilr.law.uiowa.edu/assets/Uploads/ILR-103-3-Fedders.pdf.

Fenning, Pamela, and Jennifer Rose. 2007. "Overrepresentation of African American Students in Exclusionary Discipline: The Role of School Policy." *Urban Education* 42 (6): 536–559. https://doi.org/10.1177/0042085907305039.

Ferguson, Ann Arnett. 2001. *Bad Boys: Public Schools in the Making of Black Masculinity*. Ann Arbor, MI: University of Michigan Press.

References

Fine, Michelle. 1991. *Framing Dropouts: Notes on the Politics of an Urban Public High School*. Albany, NY: State University of New York Press.

Finn, Jeremy D., Reva M. Fish, and Leslie A. Scott. 2008. "Educational Sequelae of High School Misbehavior." *The Journal of Educational Research* 101 (5): 259–274. https://doi.org/10.3200/joer.101.5.259-274.

Fisher, Benjamin W., and Emily A. Hennessy. 2016. "School Resource Officers and Exclusionary Discipline in U.S. High Schools: A Systematic Review and Meta-Analysis." *Adolescent Research Review* 1 (3): 217–233. https://doi.org/10.1007/s40894-015-0006-8.

Flanagan, Caitlin. 2010. "Cultivating Failure: How School Gardens Are Cheating Our Most Vulnerable Students." *The Atlantic*, January/February, 2010. https://www.theatlantic.com/magazine/archive/2010/01/cultivating-failure/307819/.

Flennaugh, Terry K., Kristy S. Cooper Stein, and Dorinda J. Carter Andrews. 2018. "Necessary but Insufficient: How Educators Enact Hope for Formerly Disconnected Youth." *Urban Education* 53 (1): 113–138. https://doi.org/10.1177/0042085917714515.

Flynt, Wayne. 2004. *Alabama in the Twentieth Century*. Tuscaloosa, AL: University of Alabama Press.

Foley, Douglas E. 1990. *Learning Capitalist Culture: Deep in the Heart of Tejas*. Philadelphia: University of Pennsylvania Press.

Foley, Douglas E. 1991. "Rethinking School Ethnographies of Colonial Settings: A Performance Perspective of Reproduction and Resistance." *Comparative Education Review* 35 (3): 532–551. https://doi.org/10.1086/447051.

Font, Sarah A., and Elizabeth T. Gershoff. 2017. "Contextual Factors Associated with the Use of Corporal Punishment in U.S. Public Schools." *Children and Youth Services Review* 79: 408–417. https://doi.org/10.1016/j.childyouth.2017.06.034.

Fornili, Katherine Smith. 2018. "Racialized Mass Incarceration and the War on Drugs: A Critical Race Theory Appraisal." *Journal of Addictions Nursing* 29 (1): 65–72. https://doi.org/10.1097/jan.0000000000000215.

Forsyth, Craig J., Raymond W. Biggar, York A. Forsyth, and Holly Howat. 2015. "The Punishment Gap: Racial/Ethnic Comparisons in School Infractions by Objective and Subjective Definitions." *Deviant Behavior* 36 (4): 276–287. https://doi.org/10.1080/01639625.2014.935623.

Frankenberg, Ruth. 1993. *White Women, Race Matters: The Social Construction of Whiteness*. Minneapolis, MN: University of Minnesota Press.

Frankenberg, Erica, Genevieve Siegel Hawley, Jongyeon Ee, and Gary Orfield. 2017. "Southern Schools: More than a Half-Century after the Civil Rights Revolution." The Civil Rights Project. Accessed November 30, 2020. https://www.civilrightsproject.ucla.edu/research/k-12-education/integration-and-diversity/southern-schools-brown-83-report.

Fuentes, Annette. (2003). "Discipline and Punish: Zero Tolerance Policies Have Created a 'Lockdown Environment' in Schools." *The Nation* 277: 17–20. Accessed November 19, 2020. https://www.thenation.com/article/archive/discipline-and-punish/.

Furman, Cara E. 2020. "Interruptions: Cultivating Truth-Telling as Resistance with Pre-Service Teachers." *Studies in Philosophy and Education* 39 (1): 1–17. https://doi.org/10.1007/s11217-019-09681-0.

Garrison, Timothy. 2007. "From Parent to Protector: The History of Corporal Punishment in American Public Schools." *Journal of Contemporary Legal Issues* 16 (fall): 115–119.

General Assembly resolution 60/147, *Basic Principles and Guidelines on the Right to a Remedy and Reparation for Victims of Gross Violations of International Human Rights Law and Serious Violations of International Humanitarian Law*, A/RES/60/147 (16 December 2005), available from undocs.org/en/A/RES/60/147.

George, Janel A. 2015. "Stereotype and School Pushout: Race, Gender and Discipline Disparities." *Arkansas Law Review* 68 (1): 101–129.

Gershoff, Elizabeth T. 2010. "More Harm than Good: A Summary of Scientific Research on the Intended and Unintended Effects of Corporal Punishment on Children." *Law and Contemporary Problems* 73: 31–56.

Gershoff, Elizabeth T., and Sarah A. Font. 2016. "Corporal Punishment in U.S. Public Schools: Prevalence, Disparities in Use, and Status in State and Federal Policy." *Social Policy Report* 30 (1): 1–26.

Gershoff, Elizabeth T., and Andrew Grogan-Kaylor. 2016. "Spanking and Child Outcomes: Old Controversies and New Meta-Analyses." *Journal of Family Psychology* 30 (4): 453–469. https://doi.org/10.1037/fam0000191

Gershoff, Elizabeth T., Kelly M. Purtell, and Igor Holas. 2015. *Corporal Punishment in U.S. Public Schools: Legal Precedents, Current Practices, and Future Policy*. New York: Springer.

Gibbs Grey, ThedaMarie D., and Lisa M. Harrison. 2020. "Call Me Worthy: Utilizing Storytelling to Reclaim Narratives about Black Middle School Girls Experiencing Inequitable School Discipline." *Equity & Excellence in Education*. https://doi.org/10.1080/10665684.2020.1764880.

Gillborn, David. 2018. "Heads I Win, Tails You Lose: Anti-Black Racism as Fluid, Relentless, Individual and Systemic. *Peabody Journal of Education* 93 (1): 66–77. https://doi.org/10.1080/0161956x.2017.1403178.

Gilliam, Walter S., Angela N. Maupin, Chin R. Reyes, Maria Accavitti, and Frederick Shic. 2016. "Do Early Educators' Implicit Biases Regarding Sex and Race Relate to Behavior Expectations and Recommendations of Preschool Expulsions and Suspensions?" Yale Child Study Center, September 28, 2016. Accessed November 30, 2020. https://medicine.yale.edu/childstudy/zigler/publications/Preschool%20Implicit%20Bias%20Policy%20Brief_final_9_26_276766_5379_v1.pdf.

Gilmore, Ruth Wilson. 2007. *Golden Gulag: Prisons, Surplus, Crisis, and Opposition in Globalizing California*. Los Angeles: University of California Press.

Giroux, Henry. 1983. "Theories of Reproduction and Resistance in the New Sociology of Education: A Critical Analysis. *Harvard Educational Review* 53 (3): 257–293. https://doi.org/10.17763/haer.53.3.a67x4u33g7682734.

Girvan, Erik J., Cody Gion, Kent McIntosh, and Keith Smolkowski. 2017. "The Relative Contribution of Subjective Office Referrals to Racial Disproportionality in School Discipline." *School Psychology Quarterly* 32 (3): 392–404. https://doi.org/10.1037/spq0000178.

Gleich-Bope, Deborah. 2014. "Truancy Laws: How Are They Affecting Our Legal Systems, Our Schools, and the Students Involved?" *The Clearing House: A Journal of Educational Strategies, Issues and Ideas* 87 (3): 110–114. https://doi.org/10.1080/00098655.2014.891885.

Glenn, Myra C. 1984. *Campaigns Against Corporal Punishment: Prisoners, Sailors, Women, and Children in Antebellum America*. Albany, NY: SUNY Press.

Goff, Phillip Atiba, Matthew Christian Jackson, Brooke Allison Lewis Di Leone, Carmen Marie Culotta, and Natalie Ann DiTomasso. 2014. "The Essence of Innocence: Consequences of Dehumanizing Black Children. *Journal of Personality and Social Psychology* 106 (4): 526–545. https://doi.org/10.1037/a0035663.

González, Thalia. 2015. "Socializing Schools: Addressing Racial Disparities in Discipline through Restorative Justice." In *Closing the School Discipline Gap: Equitable Remedies for Excessive Exclusion*, edited by Daniel J. Losen, 151–165. New York: Teachers College Press.

Goss v. Lopez. 1975. 419 U.S. 565.

Gotanda, Neil. 1991. "A Critique of Our Constitution Is Color-Blind." *Stanford Law Review* 44: 1–68. https://doi.org/10.2307/1228940.

Gotanda, Neil. 2004. "Reflections on Korematsu, Brown and White Innocence." *Temple Political and Civil Rights Law Review* 13: 663–674.

Gotsch, Kara, and Vinay Basti. 2018. "Capitalizing on Mass Incarceration: U.S. Growth in Private Prisons." The Sentencing Project. Accessed November 30, 2020. https://www.sentencingproject.org/publications/capitalizing-on-mass-incarceration-u-s-growth-in-private-prisons/.

Grahame, Peter R., and David W. Jardine. 1990. "Deviance, Resistance, and Play: A Study in the Communicative Organization of Trouble in Class." *Curriculum Inquiry* 20 (3): 283–304. https://doi.org/10.2307/1180227.

Green, Ambra L., Deanna K. Maynard, and Sondra M. Stegenga. 2017. "Common Misconceptions of Suspension: Ideas and Alternatives for School Leaders." *Psychology in the Schools* 55 (4): 419–428. https://doi.org/10.1002/pits.22111.

Gregory, James F. 1995. "The Crime of Punishment: Racial and Gender Disparities in the Use of Corporal Punishment in U.S. Public Schools. *Journal of Negro Education* 64 (4): 454–462. https://doi.org/10.2307/2967267.

Gregory, Anne, James Bell, and Mica Pollock. 2014. "How Educators Can Eradicate Disparities in School Discipline: A Briefing Paper on School-Based Interventions." The Equity Project at Indiana University, Center for Evaluation and Education Policy. Accessed November 30, 2020. https://safesupportivelearning.ed.gov/sites/default/files/Discipline_Dispartities_How_to_Eradicate_Disparities_in_School_Discipline.pdf.

Gregory, Anne, and Edward Fergus. 2017. "Social and Emotional Learning and Equity in School Discipline." *The Future of Children* 27 (1): 117–136. https://doi.org/10.1353/foc.2017.0006.

Gregory, Anne, Erik A. Ruzek, Jamie DeCoster, Amori Yee Mikami, and Joseph P. Allen. 2019. "Focused Classroom Coaching and Widespread Racial Equity in School Discipline." *AERA Open* 5 (4): 1–15. https://doi.org/10.1177/2332858419897274.

Gregory, Anne, Russell J. Skiba, and Pedro A. Noguera. 2010. "The Achievement Gap and the Discipline Gap: Two Sides of the Same Coin?" *Educational Researcher* 39 (1): 59–68. https://doi.org/10.3102/0013189x09357621.

Gregory, Anne, and Aisha R. Thompson. 2010. "African American High School Students and Variability in Behavior Across Classrooms." *Journal of Community Psychology* 38 (3): 386–402. https://doi.org/10.1002/jcop.20370.

Gregory, Anne, and Rhona S. Weinstein. 2008. "The Discipline Gap and African Americans: Defiance or Cooperation in the High School Classroom." *Journal of School Psychology* 46 (4): 455–475. https://doi.org/10.1016/j.jsp.2007.09.001.

Grotjahn, Jess, and Chelsea Brentzel. 2018. "Gov. Ivey Announced Plan to Allow Trained School Administrators to Be Armed, Questions About Plan Remain." *WHNT News 19*, June 1, 2018. https://whnt.com/2018/06/01/alabama-will-allow-trained-school-administrators-to-be-armed-on-campus/.

Guthman, Julie. 2008. "'If They Only Knew': Color Blindness and Universalism in California Alternative Food Institutions." *The Professional Geographer* 60 (3): 387–397. https://doi.org/10.1080/00330120802013679.

Gutiérrez, Kris D. 2006. "White Innocence: A Framework and Methodology for Rethinking Educational Discourse and Inquiry." *International Journal of Learning* 12 (10): 223–229. https://doi.org/10.18848/1447-9494/cgp/v12i10/48224.

Gutiérrez, Kris D., and Nathanlia E. Jaramillo. 2006. "Looking for Educational Equity: The Consequences of Relying on Brown." *Yearbook of the National Society for the Study of Education* 105 (2): 173–189. https://doi.org/10.1111/j.1744-7984.2006.00081.x.

Haney López, Ian F. 2000. "The Social Construction of Race." In *Critical Race Theory: The Cutting Edge*, edited by Richard Delgado and Jean Stefancic, 238–248. Philadelphia: Temple University Press.

Hannah-Jones, Nikole. 2014. "Segregation Now…" *The Atlantic*, May, 2014. https://www.theatlantic.com/magazine/archive/2014/05/segregation-now/359813/.

Hannah-Jones, Nikole. 2016. "Choosing a School for My Daughter in a Segregated City." *The New York Times*, June 9, 2016. https://www.nytimes.com/2016/06/12/magazine/choosing-a-school-for-my-daughter-in-a-segregated-city.html.

Hannah-Jones, Nikole. 2017. "The Resegregation of Jefferson County" *The New York Times, The Education Issue*, September 6, 2017. https://www.nytimes.com/2017/09/06/magazine/the-resegregation-of-jefferson-county.html.

Harris, Cheryl I. 1993. "Whiteness as Property." *Harvard Law Review* 106 (8): 1707–1791. https://doi.org/10.2307/1341787.

Harris, Lee A. 2002. "Reparations as a Dirty Word: The Norm Against Slavery Reparations." *University of Memphis Law Review* 33: 409–448. https://doi.org/10.2139/ssrn.433020.

Harrison, Lisa. 2017. "Redefining Intersectionality Theory through the Lens of African American Young Adolescent Girls' Racialized Experiences." *Youth and Society* 49 (8): 1023–1039. https://doi.org/10.1177/0044118x15569216.

Hartman, Saidiya. 2007. *Lose Your Mother: A Journey along the Atlantic Slave Route*. New York: Farrar, Straus and Giroux.
Harvey, Gordon. 2018. "Public Education in Alabama after Desegregation." Accessed November 30, 2020. http://www.encyclopediaofalabama.org/article/h-3421.
Hashim, Ayesha K., Katharine O. Strunk, and Tasminda K. Dhaliwal. 2018. "Justice for All? Suspension Bans and Restorative Justice Programs in the Los Angeles Unified School District." *Peabody Journal of Education* 93 (2): 174–189. https://doi.org/10.1080/0161956x.2018.1435040.
Haynes, Chayla, Saran Stewart, and Evette Allen. 2016. "Three Paths, One Struggle: Black Women and Girls Battling Invisibility in U.S. Classrooms." *The Journal of Negro Education* 85 (3): 380–391. https://doi.org/10.7709/jnegroeducation.85.3.0380.
Heitzeg, Nancy A. 2009. "Education or Incarceration: Zero Tolerance Policies and the School to Prison Pipeline." *Forum on Public Policy Online* 2009 (2). Accessed November 30, 2020. https://files.eric.ed.gov/fulltext/EJ870076.pdf.
Hines-Datiri, Dorothy, and Dorinda J. Carter Andrews. 2020. "The Effects of Zero Tolerance Policies on Black Girls: Using Critical Race Feminism and Figured Worlds to Examine School Discipline." *Urban Education* 55 (10): 1419–1440. https://doi.org/10.1177/0042085917690204.
Hinton, Elizabeth. 2015. "Creating Crime: The Rise and Impact of National Juvenile Delinquency Programs in Black Urban Neighborhoods." *Journal of Urban History* 41 (5): 808–824.
Hirschfield, Paul J. 2008. "Preparing for Prison? The Criminalization of School Discipline in the U.S.A." *Theoretical Criminology* 12 (1): 79–101. https://doi.org/10.1177/1362480607085795.
Hoffman, Stephen. 2014. "Zero Benefit: Estimating the Effect of Zero Tolerance Discipline Policies on Racial Disparities in School Discipline." *Educational Policy* 28 (1): 69–95. https://doi.org/10.1177/0895904812453999.
Holden, George W., Kaci L. Wright, and Deborah D. Sendek. 2018. "History of and Progress in the Movement to End Corporal Punishment in the United States." In *Corporal Punishment of Children*, edited by Bernadette Saunders, Pernilla Leviner, and Bronwyn Naylor, 293–320. Leiden, Netherlands: Brill Nijhoff.
hooks, bell. 2014. *Teaching to Transgress: Education as the Practice of Freedom*. New York: Routledge.
Huang, Francis L. 2020. "Prior Problem Behaviors Do Not Account for the Racial Suspension Gap. *Educational Researcher* 49 (7): 493–502. https://doi.org/10.3102/0013189X20932474.
Human Rights Watch and the ACLU. 2008. "A Violent Education: Corporal Punishment in U.S. Public Schools." Accessed November 30, 2020. https://www.aclu.org/violent-education-corporal-punishment-children-us-public-schools.
Hyman, Irwin A. 1995. "Corporal Punishment, Psychological Maltreatment, Violence, and Punitiveness in America: Research, Advocacy, and Public Policy." *Applied and Preventive Psychology* 4 (2): 113–130. https://doi.org/10.1016/s0962-1849(05)80084-8.

Hyman, Irwin A., and Donna C. Perone. 1998. "The Other Side of School Violence: Educator Policies and Practices that May Contribute to Student Misbehavior. *Journal of School Psychology* 36 (1): 7–27. https://doi.org/10.1016/s0022-4405(97)87007-0.

Irby, Decoteau J. 2013. "Net-Deepening of School Discipline." *The Urban Review* 45 (2): 197–219. https://doi.org/10.1007/s11256-012-0217-2.

Irby, Decoteau J. 2014. "Revealing Racial Purity Ideology: Fear of Black–White Intimacy as a Framework for Understanding School Discipline in Post-Brown Schools." *Educational Administration Quarterly* 50 (5): 783–795. https://doi.org/10.1177/0013161x14549958.

Irby, Decoteau J. 2018. "Mo' Data, Mo' Problems: Making Sense of Racial Discipline Disparities in a Large Diversifying Suburban High School." *Educational Administration Quarterly* 54 (5): 693–722. https://doi.org/10.1177/0013161x18769051.

Irvine, Jacqueline Jordan. 1990. *Black Students and School Failure: Policies, Practices, and Prescriptions*. New York: Greenwood Press.

Irwin, Katherine, Janet Davidson, and Amanda Hall-Sanchez. 2013. "The Race to Punish in American Schools: Class and Race Predictors of Punitive School-Crime Control." *Critical Criminology* 21 (1): 47–71. https://doi.org/10.1007/s10612-012-9171-2.

Jacobs, Margaret D. 2009. *White Mother to a Dark Race: Settler Colonialism, Maternalism, and the Removal of Indigenous Children in the American West and Australia, 1880-1940*. Lincoln, NE: University of Nebraska Press.

James, Carl E. 2012. "Students 'At Risk': Stereotypes and the Schooling of Black Boys." *Urban Education* 47 (2): 464–494. https://doi.org/10.1177/0042085911429084.

James, Nathan, and Gail McCallion. 2013. "School Resource Officers: Law Enforcement Officers in Schools (Report No. 7-5700)." Congressional Research Service. Accessed November 30, 2020. https://fas.org/sgp/crs/misc/R43126.pdf.

Javdani, Shabnam. 2019. "Policing Education: An Empirical Review of the Challenges and Impact of the Work of School Police Officers." *American Journal of Community Psychology* 63 (3/4): 253–269. https://doi.org/10.1002/ajcp.12306.

Jennings, Michael E. 2014. "Trayvon Martin and the Myth of Superpredator: A Note on African American Males as Problems in American Society." In *Trayvon Martin, Race, and American Justice*, edited by Kenneth J. Fasching-Varner, Rema E. Reynolds, Katrice A. Albert, and Lori L. Martin, 191–196. Rotterdam: Sense.

Johnson, Sarah Lindstrom, Jessika Bottiani, Tracy E. Waasdorp, and Catherine P. Bradshaw. 2018. "Surveillance or Safekeeping? How School Security Officer and Camera Presence Influence Students' Perceptions of Safety, Equity, and Support." *Journal of Adolescent Health* 63 (6): 732–738. https://doi.org/10.1016/j.jadohealth.2018.06.008.

Kafka, Judith. 2011. *The History of "Zero Tolerance" in American Public Schooling*. New York: Palgrave.

Kanstroom, Daniel. 2007. *Deportation Nation: Outsiders in American History*. Cambridge, MA: Harvard University Press.

Katznelson, Ira. 2005. *When Affirmative Action Was White: An Untold History of Racial Inequality in Twentieth-Century America*. New York: W. W. Norton and Company.

Keierleber, Mark. 2019. "Some Florida School Districts Are Forming Their Own Police Forces, Despite Safety Questions." *The Trace*, October 16, 2019. https ://www.thetrace.org/2019/10/florida-school-police-departments-parkland-shoo ting/.

Kendi, Ibram X. 2017. *Stamped from the Beginning: The Definitive History of Racist Ideas in America*. New York: Bold Type Books.

Kennedy, Brianna L., Melanie M. Acosta, and Olivia Soutullo. 2019. "Counternarratives of Students' Experiences Returning to Comprehensive Schools from an Involuntary Disciplinary Alternative School." *Race Ethnicity and Education* 22 (1): 130–149. https://doi.org/10.1080/13613324.2017.1376634.

Kennedy, Brianna L., Amy S. Murphy, and Adam Jordan. 2017. "Title I Middle School Administrators' Beliefs and Choices About Using Corporal Punishment and Exclusionary Discipline." *American Journal of Education* 123 (2): 243–280. https://doi.org/10.1086/689929.

Kennedy-Lewis, Brianna L. 2014. "Using Critical Policy Analysis to Examine Competing Discourses in Zero Tolerance Legislation: Do We Really Want to Leave No Child Behind?" *Journal of Education Policy* 29 (2): 165–194. https://do i.org/10.1080/02680939.2013.800911.

Kennedy-Lewis, Brianna L., Douglas Whitaker, and Olivia Soutullo. 2016. "'Maybe that Helps Folks Feel Better About What They're Doing': Examining Contradictions Between Educator Presumptions, Student Experiences, and Outcomes at an Alternative School." *Journal of Education for Students Placed At Risk* 21 (4): 230–245. https://doi.org/10.1080/10824669.2016.1220308.

Khalifa, Muhammad. 2015. "Can Blacks Be Racists? Black-On-Black Principal Abuse in an Urban School Setting." *International Journal of Qualitative Studies in Education* 28 (2): 259–282. https://doi.org/10.1080/09518398.2014.916002.

Khalifa, Muhammad. 2018. *Culturally Responsive School Leadership*. Cambridge, MA: Harvard Education Press.

Khalifa, Muhammad A., and Felicia Briscoe. 2015. "A Counternarrative Autoethnography Exploring School Districts' Role in Reproducing Racism: Willful Blindness to Racial Inequities." *Teachers College Record* 117 (8): 1–34.

Khalifa, Muhammad A., Mark Anthony Gooden, and James Earl Davis. 2016. "Culturally Responsive School Leadership: A Synthesis of the Literature." *Review of Educational Research* 86 (4): 1272–1311. https://doi.org/10.3102 /0034654316630383.

Kim, Jeong-Hee. 2010. "Understanding Student Resistance as a Communicative Act." *Ethnography and Education* 5 (3): 261–276. https://doi.org/10.1080/174578 23.2010.511349.

Kim, Jeong-Hee, and Kay Ann Taylor. 2008. "An Alternative for Whom: Rethinking Alternative Education to Break the Cycle of Educational Inequality." *Journal of Educational Research* 101 (4): 207–219. https://doi.org/10.3200/joer.101.4.207-2 19.

King, Jr., John B. 2016. "Letter to States Calling for an End to Corporal Punishment in Schools." U.S. Department of Education. Accessed November 30, 2020. https://www2.ed.gov/policy/gen/guid/school-discipline/files/corporal-punishment-dcl-11-22-2016.pdf.

Kirby, Brendan. 2013. "Mobile School System Agrees to Sweeping Changes in Suspension Policies to Settle Lawsuit." *Al.com*, June 28, 2013. https://www.al.com/live/2013/06/mobile_school_system_agrees_to.html.

Klein, Alyson. 2018. "Arming School Staff Is 'Incredibly Dangerous,' Advocates Tell School Safety Commission." *Education Week*, August 28, 2018. http://blogs.edweek.org/edweek/campaign-k-12/2018/08/school_safety_alabama_guns_teachers_arm_commission_listening_session.html.

Kohli, Rita, Marcos Pizarro, and Arturo Nevárez. 2017. "The 'New Racism' of K–12 Schools: Centering Critical Research on Racism." *Review of Research in Education* 41 (1): 182–202. https://doi.org/10.3102/0091732x16686949.

Kosciw, Joseph G., Emily A. Greytak, Adrian D. Zongrone, Caitline M. Clark, and Nhan L. Truong. 2018. "The 2017 National School Climate Survey: The Experiences of Lesbian, Gay, Bisexual, Transgender, and Queer Youth in Our Nation's Schools." Gay, Lesbian and Straight Education Network (GLSEN). Accessed November 30, 2020. https://www.glsen.org/sites/default/files/2019-10/GLSEN-2017-National-School-Climate-Survey-NSCS-Full-Report.pdf.

Kozol, Jonathan. 1991. *Savage Inequalities: Children in America's Schools*. New York: Crown Publishing.

Kupchik, Aaron. 2010. *Homeroom Security: School Discipline in an Age of Fear*. New York: New York University Press.

Kupchik, Aaron. 2016. *The Real School Safety Problem: The Long-Term Consequences of Harsh School Punishment*. Oakland, CA: University of California Press.

Kupchik, Aaron, and Thomas J. Mowen. (2016). "Hurting Families." In *The Real School Safety Problem: The Long-Term Consequences of Harsh School Punishment*, written by Aaron Kupchik, 56–72. Oakland, CA: University of California Press.

Kupchik, Aaron, and Geoff K. Ward. 2011. "Reproducing Social Inequality Through School Security: Effects of Race and Class on School Security Measures." *Proceedings from The 106th Annual Meeting of the American Sociological Association*. Las Vegas, NV.

Kupchik, Aaron, and Geoff Ward. 2014. "Race, Poverty, and Exclusionary School Security: An Empirical Analysis of U.S. Elementary, Middle, and High Schools." *Youth Violence and Juvenile Justice* 12 (4): 332–354. https://doi.org/10.1177/1541204013503890.

Kwon, Soo Ah. 2006. "Youth of Color Organizing for Juvenile Justice." In *Beyond Resistance: Youth Activism and Community Change*, edited by Shawn Ginwright, Pedro Noguero, and Julio Cammarota, 215–228. New York: Routledge.

Kwon, Soo Ah. 2013. *Uncivil Youth: Race, Activism, and Affirmative Governmentality*. Durham: Duke University Press.

Lacoe, Johanna, and Michael P. Steinberg. 2018. "Rolling Back Zero Tolerance: The Effect of Discipline Policy Reform on Suspension Usage and Student Outcomes."

Peabody Journal of Education 93 (2): 207–227. https://doi.org/10.1080/0161956x .2018.1435047.

Ladson-Billings, Gloria. 2004. "Landing on the Wrong Note: The Price We Paid for Brown." *Educational Researcher* 33 (7): 3–13. https://doi.org/10.3102/001318 9X033007003.

Ladson-Billings, Gloria. 2006. "From the Achievement Gap to the Education Debt: Understanding Achievement in U.S. Schools." *Educational Researcher* 35 (7): 3–12. https://doi.org/10.3102/0013189x035007003.

Ladson-Billings, Gloria. 2011. "Boyz to Men? Teaching to Restore Black Boys' Childhood." *Race Ethnicity and Education* 14 (1): 7–15. https://doi.org/10.1080/1 3613324.2011.531977.

Lambda Legal. 2012. "Protected and Served?" Accessed November 30, 2020. https://www.lambdalegal.org/protected-and-served.

Langberg, Jason, Barbara Fedders, and Drew Kukorowski. 2011. "Law Enforcement Officers in Wake County Schools: The Human, Educational, and Financial Costs." Advocates for Children's Services. Accessed November 30, 2020. http://www.greatschoolsinwake.org/wp-content/uploads/2012/08/Law-Enforcement-Officers-in-Wake-County-Schools-The-Human-Educational-and-Financial-Costs.pdf.

Larson, Jeff, Nikole Hannah-Jones, and Mike Tigas. 2014. "School Segregation After Brown." *Propublica*, May 1, 2014. http://projects.propublica.org/segregation-now/?utm_source=etandutm_medium=emailandutm_campaign=dailynewsletter.

Lawrence-Lightfoot, Sara. 1983. *The Good High School*. New York: Basic Books.

Lawrence-Lightfoot, Sara. 2005. "Reflections on Portraiture: A Dialogue Between Art and Science." *Qualitative Inquiry* 11 (1): 3–15. https://doi.org/10.1177 /1077800404270955.

Lawrence-Lightfoot, Sara, and Jessica Hoffman Davis. 1997. *The Art and Science of Portraiture*. San Francisco: Jossey-Bass.

Lehr, Camilla A., Chee Soon Tan, and Jim Ysseldyke. 2009. "Alternative Schools: A Synthesis of State-Level Policy and Research." *Remedial and Special Education* 30 (1): 19–32. https://doi.org/10.1177/0741932508315645.

Lensmire, Timothy J. 2010. "Ambivalent White Racial Identities: Fear and an Elusive Innocence." *Race Ethnicity and Education* 13 (2): 159–172. https://doi.org/10.1080 /13613321003751577.

Leonardo, Zeus. 2013. *Race Frameworks: A Multidimensional Theory of Racism and Education*. New York: Teachers College Press.

Lesko, Nancy. 2012. *Act Your Age!: A Cultural Construction of Adolescence*. London: Routledge.

Leslie, Virginia Kent Anderson 1986. A Myth of the Southern Lady: Antebellum Proslavery Rhetoric and the Proper Place of Woman. In *Southern Women*, 37–52. London: Routledge.

Lewis-McCoy, R. L'Heureux. 2014. *Inequality in the Promised Land: Race, Resources, and Suburban Schooling*. Redwood City, CA: Stanford University Press.

Lim., Woojin. 2020. "George Yancy: To Be Black in the U.S. Is to Have a Knee Against Your Neck Each Day." *Truthout*, July 18, 2020. https://truthout.org/arti

cles/george-yancy-to-be-black-in-the-us-is-to-have-a-knee-against-your-neck-each-day/?fbclid=IwAR1O5jvuCxxmsbVcpgX_y0NZi7AEpnT0LIuSr2_MD3Fa1r_uiY3mXuHHT5A.

Loder, Tondra L. 2005. "African American Women Principals' Reflections on Social Change, Community Othermothering, and Chicago Public School Reform." *Urban Education* 40 (3): 298–320. https://doi.org/10.1177/0042085905274535.

Losen, Daniel, and Edley, Christopher. 2001. "The Role of Law in Policing Abusive Disciplinary Practices: Why School Discipline Is a Civil Rights Issue." In *Zero Tolerance: Resisting the Drive for Punishment in Our Schools*, edited by William Ayers, Bernadine Dohrn, and Rick Ayers, 256–264. New York: The New Press.

Losen, Daniel J. (Ed.). 2014. *Closing the School Discipline Gap: Equitable Remedies for Excessive Exclusion*. New York: Teachers College Press.

Losen, Daniel J., and Jonathan Gillespie. 2012. "Opportunities Suspended: The Disparate Impact of Disciplinary Exclusion from School." Civil Rights Project. Accessed November 30, 2020. https://civilrightsproject.ucla.edu/resources/projects/center-for-civil-rights-remedies/school-to-prison-folder/federal-reports/upcoming-ccrr-research.

Losen, Daniel J., and Russell J. Skiba. 2010. "Suspending Education: Urban Middle Schools in Crisis." Southern Poverty Law Center. Accessed November 30, 2020. https://www.splcenter.org/sites/default/files/d6_legacy_files/downloads/publication/Suspended_Education.pdf.

Love, Betina L. 2019. *We Want to Do More Than Survive: Abolitionist Teaching and the Pursuit of Educational Freedom*. Boston: Beacon Press.

Mallett, Christopher A. 2016. "The School-to-Prison Pipeline: A Critical Review of the Punitive Paradigm Shift." *Child and Adolescent Social Work Journal* 33 (1): 15–24. https://doi.org/10.1007/s10560-015-0397-1.

Marchbanks III, Miner P., Jamilia J. Blake, Eric A. Booth, Dottie Carmichael, Allison L. Seibert, and Tony Fabelo. 2013. "The Economic Effects of Exclusionary Discipline on Grade Retention and High School Dropout." In *Closing the School Discipline Gap: Equitable Remedies for Excessive Exclusion*, edited by Daniel J. Losen, 59–74. New York: Teachers College Press.

Marsh, L. Trenton S., and Noguera, Pedro A. 2018. Beyond Stigma and Stereotypes: An Ethnographic Study on the Effects of School-Imposed Labeling on Black Males in an Urban Charter School. *The Urban Review* 50 (3): 447–477. https://doi.org/10.1007/s11256-017-0441-x.

Matias, Cheryl E. 2016. *Feeling White: Whiteness, Emotionality, and Education*. Boston: Sense Publishers.

Matias, Cheryl E. (Ed.). 2019. *Surviving Becky(ies): Pedagogies for Deconstructing Whiteness and Gender*. Lanham, MD: Lexington Books.

Matias, Cheryl E., and Ricky Lee Allen. 2016. Loving Whiteness to Death: Sadomasochism, Emotionality, and the Possibility of Humanizing Love." In *Feeling White: Whiteness, Emotionality, and Education*, written by Cheryl E. Matias, 45–67. Rotterdam, The Netherlands: Sense Publishers.

Matias, Cheryl E., and Robin DiAngelo. 2013. Beyond the Face of Race: Emo-Cognitive Explorations of White Neurosis and Racial Cray-Cray." *The Journal of Educational Foundations* 27 (3/4): 3–20.

Matias, Cheryl E., and Peter M. Newlove. 2017. Better the Devil You See, Than the One You Don't: Bearing Witness to Emboldened En-Whitening Epistemology in the Trump Era." *International Journal of Qualitative Studies in Education* 30 (10): 920–928. https://doi.org/10.1080/09518398.2017.1312590.

Mattsson, K. (2009). Not Me, Yet Part of Me – Destabilizing the Silence of Visual Whiteness." In *Body Claims*, edited by Janne Bromseth, Lisa Folkmarson Käll, and Katarina Mattsson, 134–153. Uppsala: Centre for Gender Research, Uppsala University.

Mazzei, Patricia. 2019. "Florida Moves Toward Arming Teachers, Despite Opposition from Parkland Students." *The New York Times*, April 21, 2019. https://www.nytimes.com/2019/04/23/us/florida-teacher-armed.html.

McCarthy, Martha M. 2005. "Corporal Punishment in Public Schools: Is the United States Out of Step?" *Educational Horizons* 83 (4): 235–240.

McElrath, Karen, Lori Guevara, Zahra Shekarkhar, and Joe M. Brown. 2020. "Out-of-School Suspensions: Counter-Narratives from the Student Perspective." *Journal of Qualitative Criminal Justice and Criminology* 8 (3): 1–32. https://doi.org/10.21428/88de04a1.ee4217b2.

McMahon, Brenda. 2007. "Educational Administrators' Conceptions of Whiteness, Anti-Racism, and Social Justice." *Journal of Educational Administration* 45 (6): 684–696. https://doi.org/10.1108/09578230710829874.

McNeal, Laura R. 2016. "Managing Our Blind Spot: The Role of Bias in the School-to-Prison Pipeline." *Arizona State Law Journal* 48: 285–311.

Meadows-Fernandez, Rochaun. 2020. "Why Won't Society Let Black Girls Be Children?" *The New York Times*, April 17, 2020. https://www.nytimes.com/2020/04/17/parenting/adultification-black-girls.html.

Meiners, Erica R. 2007. *Right to Be Hostile: Schools, Prisons, and the Making of Public Enemies*. New York: Routledge.

Meiners, Erica R. 2011. "Ending the School-to-Prison Pipeline/Building Abolition Futures." *The Urban Review* 43 (4): 547–565. https://doi.org/10.1007/s11256-011-0187-9.

Meiners, Erica R. 2016. *For the Children?: Protecting Innocence in a Carceral State*. Minneapolis: University of Minnesota Press.

Mills, Charles W. 1997. *The Racial Contract*. New York: Cornell University Press.

Milner, IV, H. Richard. 2012. "Beyond a Test Score: Explaining Opportunity Gaps in Educational Practice." *Journal of Black Studies* 43 (6): 693–718. https://doi.org/10.1177/0021934712442539.

Milner, IV, H. Richard. 2013. "Analyzing Poverty, Learning, and Teaching Through a Critical Race Theory Lens." *Review of Research in Education* 37 (1): 1–53. https://doi.org/10.3102/0091732x12459720.

Mitchell, Mary M., and Catherine P. Bradshaw. 2013. "Examining Classroom Influences on Student Perceptions of School Climate: The Role of Classroom

Management and Exclusionary Discipline Strategies." *Journal of School Psychology* 51 (5): 599–610. https://doi.org/10.1016/j.jsp.2013.05.005.

Monahan, Kathryn C., Susan VanDerhei, Jordan Bechtold, and Elizabeth Cauffman. 2014. "From the School Yard to the Squad Car: School Discipline, Truancy, and Arrest." *Journal of Youth and Adolescence* 43 (7): 1110–1122. https://doi.org/10.1007/s10964-014-0103-1.

Morgan, Emily, Nina Salomon, Martha Plotkin, and Rebecca Cohen. 2014. "The School Discipline Consensus Report: Strategies from the Field to Keep Students Engaged in School and Out of the Juvenile Justice System." The Council of State Governments Justice Center, New York, NY. Accessed December 1, 2020. https://safesupportivelearning.ed.gov/sites/default/files/The_School_Discipline_Consensus_Report.pdf.

Moriearty, Perry L., and William Carson. 2012. "Cognitive Warfare and Young Black Males in America." *Journal of Gender, Race, and Justice* 15 (2): 281–313.

Morris, Monique W. 2016. *Pushout: The Criminalization of Black Girls in Schools*. New York: The New Press.

Morris, Edward W., and Brea L. Perry. 2016. "The Punishment Gap: School Suspension and Racial Disparities in Achievement." *Social Problems* 63 (1): 68–86. https://doi.org/10.1093/socpro/spv026.

Morrison, Gale M., and Barbara D'Incau. 1997. "The Web of Zero-Tolerance: Characteristics of Students Who Are Recommended for Expulsion from School." *Education and Treatment of Children* 20 (3): 316–335.

Morrison, Toni. 1992. *Playing in the Dark: Whiteness and the Literary Imagination*. Cambridge, MA: Harvard University Press.

Muhammad, Khalil Gibran. 2010. *The Condemnation of Blackness: Race, Crime, and the Making of Modern Urban America*. Cambridge, MA: Harvard University Press.

Na, Chongmin, and Denise C. Gottfredson. 2013. "Police Officers in Schools: Effects on School Crime and the Processing of Offending Behaviors." *Justice Quarterly* 30 (4): 619–650. https://doi.org/10.1080/07418825.2011.615754.

National African American Reparations Commission [NAARC]. 2015. "NAARC Rolls Out Preliminary 10 Points Reparations Plan." Accessed December 1, 2020. https://ibw21.org/initiative-posts/naarc-posts/naarc-rolls-out-preliminary-10-point-reparations-plan/.

National Association of School Resource Officers [NASRO]. (n.d.). "Frequently Asked Questions." Accessed December 1, 2020. https://www.nasro.org/faq/.

National Center for Education Statistics [NCES]. 2002. "Public Alternative Schools and Programs for Students at Risk of Education Failure: 2000–01." U.S. Department of Education. Accessed December 1, 2020. https://nces.ed.gov/pubs2002/2002004.pdf.

National Coalition of Blacks for Reparations in America [N'COBRA]. 2016. "What is Reparations." Accessed December 1, 2020. https://www.ncobraonline.org/reparations/.

National Cotton Council of America [NCC]. 2018. "Top County's Production." Accessed April 5, 2019. http://www.cotton.org/econ/cropinfo/cropdata/county-db.cfm.

National Juvenile Defender Center [NJDC]. 2018. "Practice and Policy Resources: Alabama." Accessed November 19, 2020. http://njdc.info/practice-policy-resources/state-profiles/alabama/.

National Women's Law Center [NWLC]. 2016. "An Open Letter to End Corporal Punishment in Schools." Accessed November 19, 2020. https://nwlc.org/resources/open-letter-calling-for-end-to-corporal-punishment-in-schools/?utm_content=andutm_medium=emailandutm_name=andutm_source=govdeliveryandutm_term=.

Newcomb, Whitney Sherman, and Arielle Niemeyer. 2015. "African American Women Principals: Heeding the Call to Serve as Conduits for Transforming Urban School Communities." *International Journal of Qualitative Studies in Education* 28 (7): 786–799. https://doi.org/10.1080/09518398.2015.1036948.

Niche. 2020. "2021 Best School Districts in Alabama." Accessed December 1, 2020. https://www.niche.com/k12/search/best-school-districts/s/alabama/.

Nicholson-Crotty, Sean, Zachary Birchmeier, and David Valentine. 2009. "Exploring the Impact of School Discipline on Racial Disproportion in The Juvenile Justice System." *Social Science Quarterly* 90 (4): 1003–1018. https://doi.org/10.1111/j.1540-6237.2009.00674.x.

Nielsen, Linda. 1979. "Let's Suspend Suspensions: Consequences and Alternatives." *The Personnel and Guidance Journal* 57 (9): 442–445. https://doi.org/10.1002/j.2164-4918.1979.tb05432.x.

Noguera, Pedro A. 1995. "Preventing and Producing Violence: A Critical Analysis of Responses to School Violence." *Harvard Educational Review* 65 (2): 189–213. https://doi.org/10.17763/haer.65.2.e4615g5374044q28.

Noguera, Pedro A. 2008. "Benefits of Learning." In *Everyday Antiracism: Getting Real about Race in School*, edited by Mica Pollock, 132–138. New York: The New Press.

Noguera, Pedro A. 2009. *The Trouble with Black Boys...and Other Reflections on Race, Equity, and the Future of Public Education*. San Francisco: Jossey-Bass.

Noguera, Pedro A., Eve Tuck, and K. Wayne Yang. 2013. "Organizing Resistance into Social Movements." In *Youth resistance research and theories of change*, edited by Eve Tuck and K. Wayne Young, 71–81. New York: Routledge.

Nolan, Kathleen. 2011. *Police in the Hallways: Discipline in an Urban High School*. Minneapolis: University of Minnesota Press.

Noltemeyer, Amity, and Caven S. McLoughlin. 2010. "Patterns of Exclusionary Discipline by School Typology, Ethnicity, and Their Interaction." *Penn GSE Perspectives on Urban Education* 7 (1): 27–40.

Noltemeyer, Amity L., Rose Marie Ward, and Caven Mcloughlin. 2015. "Relationship between School Suspension and Student Outcomes: A Meta-Analysis." *School Psychology Review* 44 (2): 224–240. https://doi.org/10.17105/spr-14-0008.1.

Oakes, Jeannie. 2005. *Keeping Track: How Schools Structure Inequality* (2nd ed.). New Haven, CT: Yale University Press.

Office of Civil Rights Biennial Civil Rights Data Collection project. Accessed December 1, 2020. http://ocrdata.ed.gov.

Okonofua, Jason A., and Jennifer L. Eberhardt. 2015. "Two Strikes: Race and the Disciplining of Young Students." *Psychological Science* 26 (5): 617–624. https://doi.org/10.1177/0956797615570365.

Okonofua, Jason A., Gregory M. Walton, and Jennifer L. Eberhardt. 2016. "A Vicious Cycle: A Social-Psychological Account of Extreme Racial Disparities in School Discipline." *Perspectives on Psychological Science* 11 (3): 381–398. https://doi.org/10.1177/1745691616635592.

Orfield, Gary, and Erica Frankenberg. 2013. *Educational Delusions?: Why Choice Can Deepen Inequality and How to Make Schools Fair*. Oakland, CA: University of California Press.

Orfield, Gary, and Chungmei Lee. 2005. "Why Segregation Matters: Poverty and Educational Inequality." The Civil Rights Project. Accessed December 1, 2020. https://www.civilrightsproject.ucla.edu/research/k-12-education/integration-and-diversity/why-segregation-matters-poverty-and-educational-inequality.

Orfield, Gary, and Chungmei Lee. 2007. "Historic Reversals, Accelerating Resegregation, and the Need for New Integration Strategies." The Civil Rights Project. Accessed December 1, 2020. https://civilrightsproject.ucla.edu/research/k-12-education/integration-and-diversity/historic-reversals-accelerating-resegregation-and-the-need-for-new-integration-strategies-1/orfield-historic-reversals-accelerating.pdf.

Orozco, Richard, and Jesus Jaime Diaz. 2016. "'Suited to Their Needs': White Innocence as a Vestige of Segregation." *Multicultural Perspectives* 18 (3): 127–133. https://doi.org/10.1080/15210960.2016.1185610.

Owen, Stephen S., and Kenneth Wagner. 2006. "Explaining School Corporal Punishment: Evangelical Protestantism and Social Capital in a Path Model." *Social Justice Research* 19 (4): 471–499. https://doi.org/10.1007/s11211-006-0024-6.

Owens, Jayanti, and Sara S. McLanahan. 2020. "Unpacking the Drivers of Racial Disparities in School Suspension and Expulsion." *Social Forces* 98 (4): 1548–1577. https://doi.org/10.1093/sf/soz095.

Palmer, Brian. 2013. "Why Do We Suspend Misbehaving Students?: Don't They Want to Go Home." *Slate*, March 15, 2013. https://slate.com/human-interest/2013/03/why-do-we-suspend-children-from-school.html.

Palmer, Neal A., and Emily A. Greytak. 2017. "LGBTQ Student Victimization and Its Relationship to School Discipline and Justice System Involvement." *Criminal Justice Review* 42 (2): 163–187. https://doi.org/10.1177/0734016817704698.

Paperson, La. 2011. "A Disrupting Darkness: Youth Resistance as Racial Wisdom." *International Journal of Qualitative Studies in Education* 24 (7): 805–815. https://doi.org/10.1080/09518398.2011.632786.

Patton, Stacey. 2017. "Corporal Punishment in Black Communities: Not an Intrinsic Cultural Tradition but Racial Trauma." *Children, Youth, and Family News*, APA, April 2017. Accessed December 1, 2020. https://www.apa.org/pi/families/resources/newsletter/2017/04/racial-trauma.

Peguero, Anthony A., and Zahra Shekarkhar. 2011. "Latino/a Student Misbehavior and School Punishment." *Hispanic Journal of Behavioral Sciences* 33 (1): 54–70. https://doi.org/10.1177/0739986310388021.

Perry, Brea L., and Edward W. Morris. 2014. "Suspending Progress: Collateral Consequences of Exclusionary Punishment in Public Schools." *American Sociological Review* 79 (6): 1067–1087. https://doi.org/10.1177/0003122414556308.

Perry, Theresa, Claude Steele, and Asa Hilliard, III. 2003. *Young, Gifted, and Black: Promoting High Achievement among African-American Students.* Boston: Beacon Press.

Peters, April L. 2012. "Leading through the Challenge of Change: African-American Women Principals on Small School Reform." *International Journal of Qualitative Studies in Education* 25 (1): 23–38. https://doi.org/10.1080/09518398.2011.647722.

Pillow, Wanda. 2003. "Confession, Catharsis, or Cure? Rethinking the Uses of Reflexivity as Methodological Power in Qualitative Research." *International Journal of Qualitative Studies in Education* 16 (2): 175–196. https://doi.org/10.1080/0951839032000060635.

Porowski, Allan, Rosemarie O'Connor, and Jia Lisa Luo. 2014. "How Do States Define Alternative Education?" U.S. Department of Education, Institute of Education Sciences, National Center for Education Evaluation and Regional Assistance, September 2014. Accessed December 1, 2020. https://files.eric.ed.gov/fulltext/ED546775.pdf.

Powell, Tunette, and Justin A. Coles. 2020. "'We Still Here': Black Mothers' Personal Narratives of Sense Making and Resisting Antiblackness and the Suspensions of Their Black Children." *Race Ethnicity and Education.* https://doi.org/10.1080/13613324.2020.1718076.

Public Affairs Research Council of Alabama (PARCA). 2020. "School Discipline and Race in Alabama." Accessed December 1, 2020. http://parcalabama.org/school-discipline-and-race-in-alabama/.

Public Counsel 2015. "Fix School Discipline: How We Can Fix School Discipline: Toolkit For Educators." Los Angeles, CA: Public Counsel. Accessed December 1, 2020. http://www.fixschooldiscipline.org/educator-toolkit/.

Quillian, Lincoln, Devah Pager, Ole Hexel, and Arnfill H. Midtbøen. 2017. "Meta-Analysis of Field Experiments Shows No Change in Racial Discrimination in Hiring Over Time." *Proceedings of the National Academy of Sciences* 114 (41): 10870–10875. https://doi.org/10.1073/pnas.1706255114.

Raby, Rebecca. 2005. "What Is Resistance?" *Journal of Youth Studies* 8 (2): 151–171. https://doi.org/10.1080/13676260500149246.

Raffaele Mendez, Linda M. 2003. "Predictors of Suspension and Negative School Outcomes: A Longitudinal Investigation." *New Directions for Youth Development* 99: 17–33. https://doi.org/10.1002/yd.52.

Raider-Roth, Miriam, Vicki Stieha, and Billy Hensley. 2012. "Rupture and Repair: Episodes of Resistance and Resilience in Teachers' Learning." *Teaching and Teacher Education* 28 (4): 493–502. https://doi.org/10.1016/j.tate.2011.11.002.

Raiford, Leigh. 2019. "Nia in Two Acts." *The New Inquiry*, July 26, 2019. Accessed November 19, 2020. https://thenewinquiry.com/nia-in-two-acts/.

Rausch, M. Karega, and Russell J. Skiba. (2005). "The Academic Cost of Discipline: The Contribution of School Discipline to Achievement." Paper presented at the

Annual meeting of the American Educational Research Association, Montreal, Quebec, Canada.

Reed, Latish Cherie. 2012. "The Intersection of Race and Gender in School Leadership for Three Black Female Principals." *International Journal of Qualitative Studies in Education* 25 (1): 39–58. https://doi.org/10.1080/09518398.2011.647723.

Richie, Beth E. 2012. *Arrested Justice: Black Women, Violence, and America's Prison Nation*. New York: NYU Press.

de los Ríos, Cati V., Jorge López, and Ernest Morrell. 2015. "Toward a Critical Pedagogy of Race: Ethnic Studies and Literacies of Power in High School Classrooms." *Race and Social Problems* 7 (1): 84–96. https://doi.org/10.1007/s12552-014-9142-1.

Ritter, Gary W. 2018. "Reviewing the Progress of School Discipline Reform." *Peabody Journal of Education* 93 (2): 133–138. https://doi.org/10.1080/0161956x.2018.1435034.

Robbins, Christopher G. 2008. *Expelling Hope: The Assault on Youth and the Militarization of Schooling*. Albany, NY: SUNY Press.

Roberts, Dorothy E. 1997. "Unshackling Black Motherhood." *Michigan Law Review* 95 (4): 938–964. https://doi.org/10.2307/1290050.

Rocque, Michael. 2010. "Office Discipline and Student Behavior: Does Race Matter?" *American Journal of Education* 116 (4): 557–581. https://doi.org/10.1086/653629.

Rodriguez, Sophia. 2017. "'My Eyes Were Opened to the Lack of Diversity in Our Best Schools': Re-Conceptualizing Competitive School Choice Policy as a Racial Formation." *The Urban Review* 49 (4): 529–550. https://doi.org/10.1007/s11256-017-0415-z.

Rothstein, Richard. 2017. *The Color of Law: A Forgotten History of How Our Government Segregated America*. New York: Liveright Publishing.

Ruglis, Jessica. 2011. "Mapping the Biopolitics of School Dropout and Youth Resistance." *International Journal of Qualitative Studies in Education* 24 (5): 627–637. https://doi.org/10.1080/09518398.2011.600268.

Rumberger, Russell W., and Daniel J. Losen. 2016. "The High Cost of Harsh Discipline and Its Disparate Impact." Civil Rights Project. Accessed December 1, 2020. https://www.civilrightsproject.ucla.edu/resources/projects/center-for-civil-rights-remedies/school-to-prison-folder/federal-reports/the-high-cost-of-harsh-discipline-and-its-disparate-impact/UCLA_HighCost_6-2_948.pdf.

Ruzzi, Betsy Brown, and Jacqueline Kraemer. 2006. "Academic Programs in Alternative Education: An Overview." National Center on Education and the Economy (NJ1). Accessed December 1, 2020. http://ncee.org/wp-content/uploads/2010/04/AcademicProg.pdf.

Ryan, Francis J. 1994. "From Rod to Reason: Historical Perspectives on Corporal Punishment in the Public School, 1642-1994." *Educational Horizons* 72 (2): 70–77.

Saltman, Kenneth J., and David A. Gabbard (Eds.). 2003. *Education as Enforcement: The Militarization and Corporatization of Schools*. New York: Routledge.

Sanburn, Josh. 2014. "All the Ways Darren Wilson Described Being Afraid of Michael Brown." *Time*, November 25, 2014. Accessed November 19, 2020. https://time.com/3605346/darren-wilson-michael-brown-demon/.

SchoolDigger. 2018. "Alabama School District Rankings." Accessed November 19, 2020. https://www.schooldigger.com/go/AL/districtrank.aspx.

Selman, Kaitlyn J. 2017. "Imprisoning 'Those' Kids: Neoliberal Logics and the Disciplinary Alternative School." *Youth Justice* 17 (3): 213–231. https://doi.org/10.1177/1473225417712607.

Selman, Kaitlyn J. 2018. "Punishment as Pedagogy: An Exploration of the Disciplinary Alternative School" (Unpublished doctoral dissertation). Old Dominion University, Norfolk, VA. Accessed December 1, 2020. https://doi.org/10.25777/h1d5-c183.

Sensoy, Özlem, and Robin DiAngelo. 2017. *Is Everyone Really Equal?: An Introduction to Key Concepts in Social Justice Education*. New York: Teachers College Press.

Shedd, Carla. 2015. *Unequal City: Race, Schools, and Perceptions of Injustice*. New York: Russell Sage.

Sherfinski, David. 2018. "Percentage of Public Schools with Resource Officers on the Rise: Report." *The Washington Times*, March 29, 2018. Accessed November 19, 2020. https://www.washingtontimes.com/news/2018/mar/29/percentage-public-schools-resource-officers-rise-r/.

Shyman, Eric. 2018. "Smoke and Mirrors: A Thematically Based Polemic of Whiteness and the Myth of Desegregation in U.S. School Reform." *Whiteness and Education* 3 (2): 122–140. https://doi.org/10.1080/23793406.2018.1545247.

Siddle Walker, Vanessa. 2000. "Valued Segregated Schools for African American Children in the South, 1935-1969: A Review of Common Themes and Characteristics." *Review of Educational Research* 70 (3): 253–285. https://doi.org/10.3102/00346543070003253.

Siddle Walker, Vanessa. 2001. "African American Teaching in the South: 1940–1960." *American Educational Research Journal* 38: 751–779. https://doi.org/10.3102/00028312038004751.

Siddle Walker, Vanessa. 2019. "What Black Educators Built." *Educational Leadership* 76 (7): 12–18.

Simmons, Lizbet. 2016. *The Prison School: Educational Inequality and School Discipline in the Age of Mass Incarceration*. Berkeley, CA: University of California Press.

Skiba, Russell J. 2000. "Zero Tolerance, Zero Evidence: An Analysis of School Disciplinary Practice: Policy Research Report." *Indiana Education Policy Center*, report RR-SRS2. https://eric.ed.gov/?id=ED469537.

Skiba, Russell J., Mariella I. Arredondo, and Natasha T. Williams. 2014. "More Than a Metaphor: The Contribution of Exclusionary Discipline to a School-to-Prison Pipeline." *Equity & Excellence in Education* 47 (4): 546–564. https://doi.org/10.1080/10665684.2014.958965.

Skiba, Russell. J., Choong-Geun Chung, Mega Trachok, Timberly L. Baker, Adam Sheya, and Robin L. Hughes. 2014. Parsing Disciplinary Disproportionality: Contributions of Infraction, Student, and School Characteristics to Out-of-School

Suspension and Expulsion." *American Educational Research Journal* 51 (4): 640–670. https://doi.org/10.3102/0002831214541670.

Skiba, Russell J., Suzanne E. Eckes, and Kevin Brown. 2009. "African American Disproportionality in School Discipline: The Divide Between Best Evidence and Legal Remedy. *New York Law School Legal Review* 54: 1071–1088.

Skiba, Russell J., Robert S. Michael, Abra Carroll Nardo, and Reece L. Peterson. 2002. "The Color of Discipline: Sources of Racial and Gender Disproportionality in School Punishment." *The Urban Review* 34 (4): 317–342. https://doi.org/10.1023/A:1021320817372.

Skiba, Russell J., and Reece L. Peterson. 2000. "School Discipline at a Crossroads: From Zero Tolerance to Early Response." *Exceptional Children* 66 (3): 335–346. https://doi.org/10.1177/001440290006600305.

Skiba, Russell, and M. Karega Rausch. 2004. "The Relationship Between Achievement, Discipline, and Race: An Analysis of Factors Predicting ISTEP Scores." Center for Evaluation and Education Policy. Accessed December 1, 2020. https://files.eric.ed.gov/fulltext/ED488899.pdf.

Skiba, Russell J., and M. Karega Rausch. 2013. "Zero Tolerance, Suspension, and Expulsion: Questions of Equity and Effectiveness." In *Handbook of Classroom Management*, edited by Carolyn M. Evertson and Carol S. Weinstein, 1073–1100. New York: Routledge.

Skiba, Russell, Ada Simmons, Lori Staudinger, Marcus Rausch, Gayle Dow, and Renae Feggins. 2003. "Consistent Removal: Contributions of School Discipline to the School-Prison Pipeline." In School to Prison Pipeline Conference: Harvard Civil Rights Project, Boston, MA.

Skiba, Russell J., and Natasha T. Williams. 2014. "Are Black Kids Worse? Myths and Facts about Racial Differences in Behavior." *The Equity Project at Indiana University*, 1–8. Accessed November 19, 2020. https://indrc.indiana.edu/tools-resources/pdf-disciplineseries/african_american_differential_behavior_031214.pdf.

Smiley, CalvinJohn, and David Fakunle. 2016. "From 'Brute' to 'Thug': The Demonization and Criminalization of Unarmed Black Male Victims in America." *Journal of Human Behavior in the Social Environment* 26 (3/4): 350–366. https://doi.org/10.1080/10911359.2015.1129256.

Snapp, Shannon D., Jennifer M. Hoenig, Amanda Fields, and Stephen T. Russell. 2015. "Messy, Butch, and Queer: LGBTQ Youth and the School-to-Prison Pipeline." *Journal of Adolescent Research* 30 (1): 57–82. https://doi.org/10.1177/0743558414557625.

Sojoyner, Damian M. 2013. "Black Radicals Make for Bad Citizens: Undoing the Myth of the School to Prison Pipeline." *Berkeley Review of Education* 4 (2): 241–263. https://doi.org/10.5070/b84110021.

Solorzano, Daniel G., and Dolores Delgado Bernal. 2001. "Examining Transformational Resistance Through a Critical Race and LatCrit Theory Framework: Chicana and Chicano Students in an Urban Context." *Urban Education* 36 (3): 308–342. https://doi.org/10.1177/0042085901363002.

Sosa, Teresa, and Mark Latta. 2019. "'What Are We Trying to Accomplish?': Student Resistance as Racial Wisdom." *Equity & Excellence in Education* 52 (1): 108–128. https://doi.org/10.1080/10665684.2019.1635053.

References

Southern Poverty Law Center [SPLC]. 2017. "Private Prisons: The Wrong Choice for Alabama." Accessed December 1, 2020. https://www.splcenter.org/20171030/private-prisons-wrong-choice-alabama.

Southern Poverty Law Center [SPLC] and The Civil Rights Project [CRP]. 2019. "The Striking Outlier: The Persistent, Painful and Problematic Practice of Corporal Punishment in Schools." Accessed December 1, 2020. https://www.splcenter.org/sites/default/files/com_corporal_punishment_final_web_0.pdf.

Staats, Cheryl. 2016. "Understanding Implicit Bias: What Educators Should Know." *American Educator* 39 (4): 29–43.

Stevenson, Howard C. 2014. *Promoting Racial Literacy in Schools: Differences that Make a Difference*. New York: Teachers College Press.

Stinchcomb, Jeanne B., Gordon Bazemore, and Nancy Riestenberg. 2006. "Beyond Zero Tolerance: Restoring Justice in Secondary Schools." *Youth Violence and Juvenile Justice* 4 (2): 123–147. https://doi.org/10.1177/1541204006286287.

Stough, Laura M., and Marcia L. Montague. 2015. "How Teachers Learn to Be Classroom Managers." In *Handbook of Classroom Management* (2nd ed.), edited by Edmund T. Emmer and Edward J. Sabornie, 446–458. New York: Routledge.

Stovall, David. 2016. "Schools Suck, but They're Supposed To: Schooling, Incarceration and the Future of Education." *Journal of Curriculum and Pedagogy* 13 (1): 20–22. https://doi.org/10.1080/15505170.2016.1138252.

Straus, Murray A. 1994. *Beating the Devil Out of Them*. Piscataway, NJ: Transaction Publishers.

Suh, Suhyun, and Jingyo Suh. 2007. "Risk Factors and Levels of Risk for High School Dropouts." *Professional School Counseling* 10 (3): 297–306. https://doi.org/10.1177/2156759x0701000312.

Strunk, Kamden K., Leslie Anne Locke, and Georgianna L. Martin. 2017. *Oppression and Resistance in Southern Higher and Adult Education*. New York: Palgrave Macmillan.

Taylor, Keeanga-Yamahtta. 2019. *Race for Profit: How Banks and the Real Estate Industry Undermined Black Homeownership*. Chapel Hill, NC: The UNC Press.

Taylor, Catherine A., Lauren Hamvas, and Ruth Paris. 2011. "Perceived Instrumentality and Normativeness of Corporal Punishment Use Among Black Mothers." *Family Relations* 60 (1): 60–72. https://doi.org/10.1111/j.1741-3729.2010.00633.x.

Texas Appleseed. 2011. "Breaking Rules, Breaking Budgets: Cost of Exclusionary Discipline in 11 Texas School Districts." Accessed December 1, 2020. http://www.njjn.org/uploads/digital-library/Breaking-Rules-Breaking-Budgets--Cost-of-Exclusionary-Discipline-in-11-Texas-School-Districts_TxAppleseed.pdf.

Thandeka. 2001. *Learning to Be White: Money, Race, and God in America*. New York: Continuum.

Theoharis, George. 2007. "Social Justice Educational Leaders and Resistance: Toward a Theory of Social Justice Leadership." *Educational Administration Quarterly* 43 (2): 221–258.

Theriot, Matthew T. 2009. "School Resource Officers and the Criminalization of Student Behavior." *Journal of Criminal Justice* 37 (3): 280–287. https://doi.org/10.1016/j.crimjus.2009.04.008.

Theriot, Matthew T., and David R. Dupper. 2010. "Student Discipline Problems and the Transition from Elementary to Middle School." *Education and Urban Society* 42 (2): 205–222. https://doi.org/10.1177/0013124509349583.

Thompson, Angie. 2017. T*he Hate U Give*. New York: Balzer and Bray.

Tillman, Linda C. 2004. "African American Principals and the Legacy of Brown." *Review of Research in Education* 28 (1): 101–146. https://doi.org/10.3102/0091732x028001101.

Toure, Judith, and Dana Thompson Dorsey. 2018. "Stereotypes, Images, and Inclination to Discriminatory Action: The White Racial Frame in the Practice of School Leadership." *Teachers College Record* 120 (2): 37–49.

Townsend, Tiffany G., Torsten B. Neilands, Anita Jones Thomas, and Tiffany R. Jackson. 2010. "I'm No Jezebel; I Am Young, Gifted, and Black: Identity, Sexuality, and Black Girls." *Psychology of Women Quarterly* 34 (3): 273–285. https://doi.org/10.1111/j.1471-6402.2010.01574.x.

Trepagnier, Barbara. 2006. *Silent Racism: How Well-Meaning White People Perpetuate the Racial Divide*. Boulder, CO: Paradigm Publishers.

Triplett, Nicholas P., Ayana Allen, and Chance W. Lewis. 2014. "Zero Tolerance, School Shootings, and the Post-Brown Quest for Equity in Discipline Policy: An Examination of How Urban Minorities Are Punished for White Suburban Violence." *Journal of Negro Education* 83 (3): 352–370. https://doi.org/10.7709/jnegroeducation.83.3.0352.

Truong, Nhan L., Adrian D. Zongrone, and Joseph G. Kosciw. 2020. "Erasure and Resilience: The Experiences of LGBTQ Students of Color. Black LGBTQ Youth in U.S. Schools." New York: Gay, Lesbian and Straight Education Network (GLSEN). Accessed December 1, 2020. https://www.glsen.org/sites/default/files/2020-06/Erasure-and-Resilience-Black-2020.pdf.

Tuck, Eve. 2011. "Humiliating Ironies and Dangerous Dignities: A Dialectic of School Pushout." *International Journal of Qualitative Studies in Education* 24 (7): 817–827. https://doi.org/10.1080/09518398.2011.632785.

Tuck, Eve, and K. Wayne Yang. 2011. "Youth Resistance Revisited: New Theories of Youth Negotiations of Educational Injustices." *International Journal of Qualitative Studies in Education* 24 (5): 521–530. https://doi.org/10.1080/09518398.2011.600274.

Tuck, Eve, and K. Wayne Yang (Eds.). 2013. *Youth Resistance Research and Theories of Change*. New York: Routledge.

Tyack, David B. 1974. *The One Best System: A History of American Urban Education*. Cambridge, MA: Harvard University Press.

Tyack, David. (1976). "Ways of Seeing: An Essay on the History of Compulsory Schooling." *Harvard Educational Review* 46 (3): 355–389. https://doi.org/10.17763/haer.46.3.v73405527200106v.

Tyack, David, and Michael Berkowitz. 1977. "The Man Nobody Liked: Toward a Social History of the Truant Officer, 1840-1940." *American Quarterly* 29 (1): 31–54. https://doi.org/10.2307/2712260.

Tyack, David, and William Tobin. 1994. "The 'Grammar' of Schooling: Why Has It Been So Hard to Change?" *American Educational Research Journal* 31 (3): 453–479. https://doi.org/10.3102/00028312031003453.

Tye, Barbara Benham. 1998. "The Deep Structure of Schooling: What It Is and How It Works." *The Clearing House* 71 (6): 332–334. https://doi.org/10.1080/000986 59809599585.

Tyson, Karolyn. 2011. *Integration Interrupted: Tracking, Black Students, and Acting White After Brown.* New York: Oxford University Press.

United Nations, Committee on the Rights of the Child (CRC). 2007. "CRC General Comment No. 8 (2006): The Right of the Child to Protection from Corporal Punishment and Other Cruel or Degrading Forms of Punishment (U.N. CRC/C/GC/8)." Accessed December 1, 2020. http://www.refworld.org/docid/460bc7772.html.

U.S. Department of Education. 2016. "2013-2014 Civil Rights Data Collection: A First Look." Accessed December 1, 2020. http://www2.ed.gov/about/offices/list/ocr/docs/2013-14-first-look.pdf.

U.S. Department of Education. 2018. "2015-2016 Civil Rights Data Collection: School Climate and Safety." Accessed December 1, 2020. https://www2.ed.gov/about/offices/list/ocr/docs/school-climate-and-safety.pdf.

U.S. Department of Justice. 2020. "Department of Justice Awards $2.2 Million for Innovative Community Policing Projects." The U.S. Attorney's Office, Northern District of Alabama. Accessed December 1, 2020. https://www.justice.gov/usao-ndal/pr/department-justice-awards-22-million-innovative-community-policing-projects.

U.S. Government Accountability Office [USGAO]. 2018. "K-12 Education: Discipline Disparities for Black Students, Boys, and Students with Disabilities." Accessed December 1, 2020. https://www.gao.gov/assets/700/690828.pdf.

Van Acker, Richard. 2007. "Antisocial, Aggressive, and Violent Behavior in Children and Adolescents within Alternative Education Settings: Prevention and Intervention." *Preventing School Failure* 51 (2): 5–12. https://doi.org/10.3200/psfl.51.2.5-12.

Vanderhaar, Judi, Marco Munoz, and Joseph Petrosko. 2014. "Reconsidering the Alternatives: The Relationship between Suspension, Disciplinary Alternative School Placement, Subsequent Juvenile Detention, and the Salience of Race." *Journal of Applied Research on Children* 5 (2): article 14.

Villenas, Sofia, and Donna Deyhle. 1999. "Critical Race Theory and Ethnographies Challenging the Stereotypes: Latino Families, Schooling, Resilience and Resistance." *Curriculum Inquiry* 29 (4): 413–445. https://doi.org/10.1111/0362-6784.00140.

Vitale, Alex S. 2017. *The End of Policing.* Brooklyn: Verso Books.

Wald, Johanna, and Daniel J. Losen. 2003. "Defining and Redirecting a School-to-Prison Pipeline." *New Directions for Youth Development* 99: 9–15.

Walker, Danielle, Cheryl E. Matias, and Robin Brandehoff. 2017. ""Who You Callin' Smartmouth?" Misunderstood Traumatization of Black and Brown Girls." *Bank Street, Occasional Paper Series* no. 38: article 6. Accessed December 1, 2020. https://educate.bankstreet.edu/cgi/viewcontent.cgi?article=1127&context=occasional-paper-series.

Wallace, Jr. John M., Sara Goodkind, Cynthia M. Wallace, and Jerald G. Bachman. 2008. "Racial, Ethnic, and Gender Differences in School Discipline Among U. S. High School Students: 1991-2005." *Negro Educational Review* 59 (1/2): 47–62.

Ward, Geoff, Nick Petersen, Aaron Kupchik, and James Pratt. 2019. "Historic Lynching and Corporal Punishment in Contemporary Southern Schools." *Social Problems*. https://doi.org/10.1093/socpro/spz044.

Ward, Stephanie Francis, and Etienne Delessert. 2014. "Less Than Zero: Schools Are Rethinking Zero Tolerance Policies and Questioning Whether the Discipline Is Really Effective." *ABA Journal* 100: 55–61.

Washburn, David. 2018. "Countdown to Expand Ban on 'Willful Defiance' Suspensions in California Schools." *EdSource*, February 15, 2018. https://edsource.org/2018/youth-advocates-pushing-to-expand-californias-ban-on-willful-defiance-suspensions/593754.

Wasserman, Lewis M. 2011. "Corporal Punishment in K-12 Public School Settings: Reconsideration of Its Constitutional Dimensions Thirty Years After Ingraham v. Wright." *Touro Law Review* 26, 1029–1101.

Weeks, Stephen. B. 1915. *History of Public School Education in Alabama*. Washington, DC: U.S. Government Printing Office. Accessed December 1, 2020. https://files.eric.ed.gov/fulltext/ED541810.pdf.

Weissman, Marsha. 2015. *Prelude to Prison: Student Perspectives on School Suspension*. Syracuse, NY: Syracuse University Press.

Welch, Kelly. 2007. "Black Criminal Stereotypes and Racial Profiling." *Journal of Contemporary Criminal Justice* 23 (3): 276–288. https://doi.org/10.1177/1043986207306870.

Welch, Kelly, and Allison Ann Payne. 2010. "Racial Threat and Punitive School Discipline." *Social Problems* 57 (1): 25–48. https://doi.org/10.1525/sp.2010.57.1.25.

Welch, Kelly, and Allison Ann Payne. 2012. "Exclusionary School Punishment: The Effect of Racial Threat on Expulsion and Suspension." *Youth Violence and Juvenile Justice* 10 (2): 155–171. https://doi.org/10.1177/1541204011423766.

Welch, Kelly, and Allison Ann Payne. 2018. "Zero Tolerance School Policies." In *The Palgrave International Handbook of School Discipline, Surveillance, and Social Control*, edited by Joe Deakin, Emmeline Taylor, and Aaron Kupchik, 215–234. Basingstoke, U.K.: Palgrave Macmillan.

Welsh, Richard O., and Shafiqua Little. 2018. "The School Discipline Dilemma: A Comprehensive Review of Disparities and Alternative Approaches." *Review of Educational Research* 88 (5): 752–794. https://doi.org/10.3102/0034654318791582.

Wentzel, Kathryn R. 2002. "Are Effective Teachers Like Good Parents? Teaching Styles and Student Adjustment in Early Adolescence. *Child Development* 73 (1): 287–301. https://doi.org/10.1111/1467-8624.00406.

Whitaker, Amir, and Daniel J. Losen. 2019. "The Striking Outlier: The Persistent, Painful and Problematic Practice of Corporal Punishment in Schools." The Civil Rights Project. Accessed December 1, 2020. https://escholarship.org/uc/item/9d19p8wt.

Whites-Koditchek, Sarah. 2019. "Neighbor States Stop Paddling Disabled Students, Alabama Schools Still Swinging Away." *Al.com*, December 17, 2019. https://www.al.com/reckon/2019/12/neighbor-states-stop-paddling-disabled-students-alabama-schools-still-swinging-away.html.

Whitford, Denise K., Antonis Katsiyannis, and Jennifer Counts. 2016. "Discriminatory Discipline: Trends and Issues." *NASSP Bulletin* 100 (2): 117–135. https://doi.org/10.1177/0192636516677340.

Will, Madeline. 2019. "Survey: Teachers Are Conflicted about the Role of Suspensions." *Education Week*, July 30, 2019. http://blogs.edweek.org/teachers/teaching_now/2019/07/survey_teachers_conflicted_role_suspensions.html?cmp=eml-enl-tu-news1andM=58898435andU=2921994andUUID=23900cd37094e4aa67af1226716382dd.

Willis, Paul. 1977. *Learning to Labour*. Nafferton: Saxon House Press.

Winans, Amy E. 2005. "Local Pedagogies and Race: Interrogating White Safety in the Rural College Classroom." *College English* 67 (3): 253–273. https://doi.org/10.2307/30044636.

Winn, Maisha T. 2010. "'Betwixt and Between': Literacy, Liminality, and the Celling of Black Girls." *Race Ethnicity and Education* 13 (4): 425–447. https://doi.org/10.1080/13613321003751601.

Winn, Maisha T. 2011. *Girl Time: Literacy, Justice, and the School-to-Prison Pipeline. (Teaching for Social Justice)*. New York: Teachers College Press.

Wolf, Kerrin C., and Aaron Kupchik. 2017. "School Suspensions and Adverse Experiences in Adulthood." *Justice Quarterly* 34 (3): 407–430. https://doi.org/10.1080/07418825.2016.1168475.

Wun, Connie. 2018. "Angered: Black and Non-Black Girls of Color at the Intersections of Violence and School Discipline in the United States." *Race Ethnicity and Education* 21 (4): 423–437. https://doi.org/10.1080/13613324.2016.1248829.

Yancy, George. 2016. *Black Bodies, White Gazes: The Continuing Significance of Race in America* (2nd ed.). Lanham, MD: Rowman and Littlefield.

Young, Jemimah L., Jamaal R. Young, and Bettie Ray Butler. 2018. "A Student Saved Is NOT a Dollar Earned: A Meta-Analysis of School Disparities in Discipline Practice Toward Black Children." *Taboo: The Journal of Culture and Education* 17 (4): 95–112. https://doi.org/10.31390/taboo.17.4.06.

Zembylas, Michalinos. 2007. "The Power and Politics of Emotions in Teaching." In *Emotion in Education*, edited by Paul Schultz and Reinhard Pekrun, 293–309. Burlington, MA: Academic Press. https://doi.org/10.1016/B978-012372545-5/50018-6.

Zhao, Christina. 2018. "'BBQ Becky.'" *Newsweek*, September 4, 2018. https://www.newsweek.com/bbq-becky-white-woman-who-called-cops-black-bbq-911-audio-released-im-really-1103057.

Index

Page references for tables and figures are italicized.

abolition, 5, 121, 150, 163–164; of corporal punishment, 110–11; of exclusionary discipline, 19, *151–52*, 158

achievement gap. *See* opportunity gap

activism, xviii, 50–51, 90, 93, 95, 117, 144; scholar-activism, 163

adultification, xiv, 4–5, 40, 44–48, 54, 72, 91–92

Alabama Appleseed, 29, 125

Alabama Association of School Boards, 62

Alabama Education Association, 62

Alabama State Department of Education (ALSDE): data provided by, 4, 18, 20, 66, 101, 110, 112–13, 125, 137, 139, 142, 150, 156–57; data retrieved from, 4, 29, 131, 155; disciplinary incidents defined by, *13*, 65, 73; documents, 124; reporting system of, 57, 157; request of, 53, 156; system grades assigned by, 58

alternative school, 9, 14, 53, 58, 63–65, *64*, 72, 83, 89, 101, *101*, 140, 156; achievement and, 63; context of, 9, 67, 71–72; discrimination and, 18, 25–27, 44, 76, 84, 99; rationale for, 23–25, *26*, 83, *85*; students in an, 3, 71–72, 76, 78–79, 81, 86–93, 159–60; subjective incidents and, 25–26, 65, *66*, 72–73, 82, 84, *102*, 140, 142, *143*; teaching in an, 1, 71–72, 82, 155–56, 159–60

American Academy of Pediatrics, 115

American Civil Liberties Union (ACLU), 115

antiracism, xi, 98, 127, 162. *See also* equity; justice

Arkansas, 31, 112, 116, 123

arrest, 61, 105, 164; school-based arrest, 9, 28–29, 47, 59, 61, 63, 65–67, 101, 105, 132, 137–39, 156

bias: bias training, 122–23, *151–52*; non-biased, xii; racial bias, xii–xiii, 99, 140;

The Black Belt, xii, 52, 113–15, *114*

The Black Panther Party, 121

brutalization, xiii–xiv, 4, 50, 110–11, 116, 144

California, 123–24, 149

carceral state, 16, 37–38, *151–52*, 164; carceral school climate, 17, 38, 83

Chicago, 123, 130
Chicanx. *See* Latinx
civil rights, 121, 163; advocates of, 51, 121; Center for Civil Rights Remedies, 149; Civil Rights Movement, 51
code of conduct, 57, 132–37, 139
colonialism, 40, 110–11
colorblind. *See* color-evasive
color-evasive, 35n1, 40, 52, 54. *See also* race-evasive
corporal punishment, xii, 14, 31–33, 58, 62, *64*, 109, 156; in the Black Belt, 113–15; discrimination and, 18, 31, 33, 65–66, 112–13; as exclusionary, 9, 14, 67, 109–10; history of, 110–11; law and, 31, 111; parents and, 110–12; racial violence and, 111–12; rationales for, 31–33, *32*, *114*; research about, 110–12; resistance to, 109–10, 115–16; subjective incidents and, 33, 65, *66*, 73, 110, 112–13, 115; trauma and, 50, 150
Cotton County Schools, 57–68
court rulings: Brown v. Board of Education, 39, 41, 50–51; Goss v. Lopez, 49; Milliken v. Bradley, 51; Wells v. Ayers, 111
COVID-19 pandemic, xi, xiv–xv, 50, 165
Creek City Schools, 99–107, *101*, *102*, 122, 126–28, 144
criminalization, 5, 11–12, 43–44, 48, 140, 149–50; adultification and, 44–46, 48; decriminalization, 144, 164; of families, 19; school-to-prison pipeline and, 37; of students, 15, 28, 49, 53–54, 61, 72, 74–75, 86, 90, 92–93, 103–4, 115, 134, *151–52*; of youth, 16;
curriculum, 39, 48, 52, 58, 67, 78–79, 82–83, 98, *151–52*, 160; extracurricular, 1, 52, 58, 65, 88, 160; irrelevance of, 5, 78; tracking of, xiii, 39, 48, 140

decarcerate, *151–52*
The Deep South, 10, 31, 34, 38, 40–43, 50–52, 74, 77, 110–12, 148
defiance, 10, 49, 66, 72–73, 81, 99–100, 122, 124; alternative school and, 3, 83–84, *143*; corporal punishment and, 65, 112, *114*; expulsion and, 65; racialized nature of, xii, 11–12, 22, 72, 74, 115, *151–52*, 165; referral to law enforcement and, 29, 50, *60*, 141; as resistance, 6, 73, 76, 78; state policy about, *13*, 14, 73; suspension and, xiii, 124, *138*, 139
dehumanization, 4–5, 40, 43, 45–46, 93, 144, 150, *151–52*, 163–64
Denver, 123
desegregation, 15, 41, 44, 50–52; orders, 52, 58; resistance to, 51–52. *See also* segregation
deviance, 12, 23, 72, 74–78, 82, 86, 88, 96, 115
differently abled, 31, 113. *See also* disability
disability, 25, 31, 41, 48, 62, 66, 116, 136. *See also* differently abled
disobedience, 10, 49, 66, 72, 81, 122; alternative school and, 3, 23, 83–84, 142, *143*; corporal punishment and, 65, 112, *114*; racialized nature of, xii, 22, 72, 115, *151–52*; referral to law enforcement and, 29, 59, *60*, *141*; as resistance, 6; state policy about, *13*, 14; suspension and, 22, 132, *138*
disorderly conduct, 49, 66, 73, 122; alternative schools and, 3, 142, *143*; corporal punishment and, 65, *114*; expulsion and, 65; racialized nature of, 11, 75, 115, *151–52*; referral to law enforcement and, 59, *60*, *141*, 142, *152–52*; school resource officer and, 28; state policy about, *13*, 74; suspension and, *138*
disruption, 10, 72–73, 96–97, 122; alternative school and, 23, 83–84,

88, 93, *143*; corporal punishment and, 65, *114*; racialized nature of, xii, 11, 44, 46, 74, 103, 115; referral to law enforcement and, *60, 141*; as resistance, 6, 76, 78–79; state policy about, *13*; suspension and, *138*
divestment, *151–52*
dropout, 14, 23, 78, 83, 122, 131, 133, 149. *See also* pushout
due process, 49–50, 125, 132–33, 136

education debt, 48, 63. *See also* opportunity gap
emotions, 117; anger, 40, 127, 162; anxiety, 54; defensiveness, 162; disgust, 40; fear, 40, 43–44, 46, 50–51, 54, 86, 88, 96–97, 99, 106, 110, 159–60, 163; hope, 164; joy, 4, 77, 79, 160, 162
enslavement. *See* slavery
Equal Justice Initiative, 121
equity, 52, 58, 95, 98, 106, 144, 147; audit, 68, 68n1; inequity, 76, 95, 117, 123, 142. *See also* antiracism; justice
expulsion, 6, 14, 22–23, 53, 58, *64*, 67, 83, *101*, 156; achievement and, 63; court rulings and, 49; discrimination and, 12, 18, 22–23, 42, 44, 101, 128; rationales for, *24*; reform and, 124; subjective incidents and, 23, 65, *66*, 73, *102*; zero tolerance and, 15–16, 37

Fighting for Our Rights to Children's Education (FORCE), 133–36
Florida, 27, 149
freedom fighter, 137, 161

gender, 46–48, 53, 66–67, 77, 97–98, 123, 127, 157; gender binary, 107n1
Georgia, 49, 123–24
grammar: of humanity, xv; of school discipline, xvii–xviii, 4–5, 33, 40–41, 54–55, 67, 72–73, 121, 142, 147, 150, *151–52*, 153, 158–59, 162; of schooling, xvii–xviii, 40, 79

humanizing practice, 6, 79, 93, 116, 130, 150, 153, 163–65

incarceration, 37–38, 40, 45, 53; in juvenile justice facilities, 3; mass incarceration, 19, 144; in prisons, 3, 150; in youth development centers, 3;
Indigenous Peoples, xiii, 39, 41, 77
infantilization, 4, 40, 46, 91–93
instruction, xii, xvii, 1, 6, 9, 14, 18, 23, 25, 27, 33, 39, 63, 78–79, 82, *151–52*, 160
integration. *See* desegregation
intersectionality, 11–12, 29, 41, 46

justice, 98, 106, 123, 144, 162; environmental, 82, 121, 160; injustice, 3, 78, 82; justice-orientation, 117; leadership for, 95; racial, xiii, 41, 95–97, 116, 122, 127, 158, 160; reproductive, 39; restorative, 63, 122–24, 127, *151–52*; social, 4, 77, 95, 129, 163. *See also* antiracism; equity
justice system, 91, 121; criminal, 16, 28, 48, 61, 63, 92, 123, 132, *151–52*, 164; juvenile, 14, 28, 37, 61–63, 105, 125, 130, 132, 137, *151–52*, 163. *See also* incarceration

know-your-rights training, 134–35, 140

Latinx, 41, 77
legislation, 17, 22, 39; Alabama SB189, 50; Drug-Free Schools Act of 1986, 16; Gun-Free Schools Act of 1995, 16; Jim Crow laws, 43; Violent Crime Control and Enforcement act of 1994, 16

LGBTQ, 62, 66; genderqueer, 12, 47, 107n1; non-binary, 12, 47, 107n1; queer, 12, 41, 47; transgender, 47
lynching, 18, 112

Maryland, 123
Mississippi, 31, 51, 112, 116
Montgomery Bus Boycott, 121
Muscogee City Schools, 81–87, *85*

National African American Reparations Commission (NAARC), 148
National Association for the Advancement of Colored People (NAACP), 115
National Coalition of Blacks for Reparations in American (N'COBRA), 147
National Education Association, 115
National Women's Law Center (NWLC), 115
net deepening, 16, 49

objective discipline, 10–14, 73
Office of Civil Rights (OCR) data, 4, 18, 20, 22, 25, 29, 33, 53, 59, 65–66, 76, 83–84, 98–99, 101–2, 110, 113, 116, 131, 139–40, 142, 150, 156–57; reporting requirements of, 67, 125, 157
opportunity gap, xiii, 14, 48, 63, 67. *See also* education debt
oppression, 6, 40, 121, 150, *151–52*, 162–64; resistance and, 5, 76–79, 100, 158, 160; school discipline and, 4, 15; schools as sites of, 37, 82–83, 148, 161; stereotypes and, 46

The Parkland Effect, 27. *See also* shootings
patriarchy, 43
Philadelphia, 123
portraiture, 4, 158–59, 162, 164; self-portraiture, 5, 159

positive behavior interventions and supports (PBIS/PBS), 122–23, 128, *151–52*
poverty, xviii, 12, 15, 37, 50, 121, 123, 126
professional development, xviii, 122–23, 126, 136, 140, *151–52*
Public Affairs Research Council of Alabama (PARCA), 54, 131, 157
The Punitive Turn, 16–17, 37
pushout, 1, 12–14, 19, 23, 37, 83, 122, 130–31, 135. *See also* dropout

race-evasive, 54, 97–99, 106, 117, 123, 125–28, 139–40, 142, 144, *151–52*, 157, 160, 163. *See also* color-evasive
racial profiling, xiii, 11, 96, 104, 164
racism, xiv, xv, 41–42, 50, 72, 98–99, 103, 123, 130–31, 140, 144, *151–52*, 155, 158, 163; anti-Black racism, xii–xiv, xviii, 6, 17–18, 34, 40, 42, 45, 48, 50, 53–55, 67, 74, 77, 79, 84, 102, 107, 115, 117, 121–23, 128, 140, 142, 144, 147–48, *151–52*, 153, 155, 159, 162–63; critical theories of, 40, 77; discourse about, 12, 42, 52, 54–55, 95, 126; emotions and, 40, 54–55; environmental, 121; pandemic and, xv; reform and, 140, 142; in research, xiv, 54; sexism and, 11, 46

referral to law enforcement, 9, 14, 27–29, *30*, *31* 53, 58–59, *64*, 66, 101–2, *101*, 139, 142, 155–56; achievement and, 63; arrest and, 63, 65; discrimination and, 18, 44; rationales for, *60*, *141*; subjective incidents and, 29, *66*, 73, *102*, 140–42
reflection, 5, 67, 76, 78–79, 117, 144, 147, *151–52*, 153, 155, 161, 163
rehabilitation, 16
resilience, xiii, xviii, 4, 162, 164

safety, 49; in schools, xii, 17, 19, 45, 47–48, 100, 109, 116
school-based police. *See* school resource officer
school incident report (SIR), *13*, 18, 131, 137, 155–56
school law enforcement officer (SLEO). *See* school resource officer
school/prison nexus, 37, 83, 163–64. *See also* school-to-prison pipeline
school resource officer (SRO), 2, 16–18, 27–29, 39, 47–48, 50, 59–62, 67, 71, 84, 104, 129, 142, 149, *151–52*, 165; National Association of (NASRO), 27–28, 61
school-to-prison pipeline, 11, 37–38, 61, 63, 122, 137, 158, 163–64
segregation, 39, 41, 44, 140; academies, 51–52; of schools, 48, 52–53, 148. *See also* desegregation
Selma Marches, 121
shooting, 44–45; in school, 16, 27
slavery, 39–40, 43, 46, 50–51, 57, 110–11, 114, 147–48; afterlife of, 43; slave codes, 43, 48
Southern Poverty Law Center (SPLC), 121, 124–25, 129–35, 137
stereotypes, xiii, 6, 11–12, 22, 28, 34, 41–42, 49, 74, 76, 84, 87–88, 95–96, 98–99, 104, 106, 117, 128, 163–64; adultification and, 5, 46; criminalization and, xviii, 5, 12, 43–45, 48, 72, 93, 103, 115; gendered, 46, 97; objective incidents and, 11; removal and, 34, 87–88; subjective incidents and, 11, 102–4, 115; surveillance and, 5, 12, 47–48
subjective discipline, *13*, 14, 33, 49, 63, *66*, 67, 73–74, *85*, 101–2, *102*, 122, 131, 135, 140, 157; alternative school and, 25–27, *26*, 65, 73, 82–84, 140, 142, *143*; corporal punishment and, *32*, 33, 65, 73, 110, 113–15, *114*; definition of, 10, 73; discrimination and, 10, 22, 34, 76, 115, 124; expulsion and, 23, *24*, 65, 73; referral to law enforcement and, 29, *30*, *31*, 59, *60*, 65, 73, 105, 140–42, *141*; resistance and, 67, 100; stereotypes and, 11, 22, 72, 115; suspension and, 20–22, *21*, 65, 73, 137–39, *138*
surveillance, xiii, xiv, 3–6, 11–12, 38, 40, 44, 48, 62, 72, 74, 87, 93, 160; adultification and, 45, 54, 72; criminalization and, 43, 48–49, 54, 86, 92; hypersurveillance, 11, 46, 104, 160; incarceration and, 53; infantilization and, 46; police and, 17–18, 27, 53, 62; school administrators and, 97–98; state, 16, 38; stereotypes and, 5, 47–48, 72; technology and, 2, 16, 18, 27, 48, 149, 165. *See also* white gaze
suspension, 6, 12, 14, 18–23, *64*, 67, 76, *101*, 116, 128, 142, 156, 161; achievement and, 19, 63; costs of, 19, 149; desegregation and, 15; discrimination and, xiii, 12, 18, 20–22, 42, 58, 65, 128, 139; dropout and, 131–37, 139; due process and, 131–33, 139; in-school, 3, 9, 19, 20, 44–45, 53, 63, 65–66, 81, 84, 99, *101*, 106, 139; long-term, 49, 130–32, 135, 137, 139; out-of-school, 3, 9, 19, 20, 44, 49, 53, 63, 65–66, 72, 84, 99, *101*, 103, 106, 131, 136, 139; rationales for, 20, *21*, *138*; reform and, 123–25, 127–28, 133–34, 136–37; repeated, 128, 133; short-term, 49; subjective incidents and, 20–22, 65, *66*, 73, *102*, 137, 139; zero tolerance and, 15, 37

Texas, 31, 123, 149
Timber County Schools, 130–44, *138*, *141*
trauma, xv, 12, 111, 150, 162–63

United Nations (UN), 31

violence, xv, 10, 14, 31, 39, 44–45, 50–51, 61, 115; gun, 3, 123; racial, 40, 53, 111–12; state sanctioned, 164. *See also* shooting

War on Crime, 38
War on Drugs, 16
white fragility, 162
white gaze, xiii, 43, 155, 162. *See also* surveillance
whiteness, xi, xiii, xiv, 35n1, 40–43, 49–50, 74–75, 162–63; discourse about, 54; reform and, 41; removal and, 40; school discipline and, xii–xiii, 34; schools as sites of, xii, xiv, 44, 79, 98, 104, 106, 159; stereotypes and, 99, 164; universities as sites of, 161
white supremacy, xiii–xiv, 4, 50, 95, 110, 115, *151–52*, 155, 158, 163; authority, xii; law and, 140; patriarchy and, 43; removal and, 40–42, 150; school discipline and, 35, 41, 142, 147, 163; schools as sites of, xii–xiv, 38, 40–41, 75, 144

zero tolerance, xii, 10, 15–16, 18, 22–23, 27, 37, 48, 83, 104–5

About the Authors

Hannah Carson Baggett is associate professor of educational research in the College of Education at Auburn University. Her scholarship and teaching focus on issues of race and racism in education, educator beliefs and social justice education, and qualitative methods. A former high school French teacher, she continues to work with high school students in East Alabama in formal and informal teaching and mentoring roles.

Carey E. Andrzejewski is professor of social foundations of education and educational research in the College of Education at Auburn University. As a critical scholar of teaching, she explores and facilitates the work of educators toward more socially just schools. In particular, she is interested in how educators develop critical consciousness and how that consciousness shapes their work with students, in schools, and in their broader communities.

Benjamin Arnberg is a storyteller, researcher, philosopher, humorist, and clotheshorse who earned his PhD in higher education administration at Auburn University, where he also teaches social foundations of education and qualitative research methods. His first book *Queer Campus Climate: An Ethnographic Fantasia* was published by Routledge in 2020. He lives in Birmingham, Alabama with his shoes.

Jasmine S. Betties is an educational psychology doctoral student in the Department of Educational Foundations, Leadership, and Technology at Auburn University. Her research interests include multicultural teacher education, with a focus on school discipline policies and practices, and social justice and equity in education.

Sean A. Forbes is professor of educational psychology at Auburn University. His scholarship centers on the integration of biopsychosocial elements in human experience through his direction of O Grows, an expansive community-university food project with the mission to "cultivate community."

Sangah Lee is an educational psychology doctoral student in the Department of Educational Foundations, Leadership, and Technology at Auburn University. Her research interests include multicultural aspects of higher educational systems, equity in education, and motivation in online and statistics education.

Cheryl E. Matias, recipient of the 2020 American Educational Research Association Mid-Career Award for her work on racial justice in teacher education, is professor and director of secondary teacher education at the University of Kentucky. Her research focuses on race and ethnic studies in education with a theoretical focus on critical race theory, critical whiteness studies, critical pedagogy, and feminism of color. Specifically, she uses a feminist of color approach to deconstruct the emotionality of whiteness in urban teacher education and how it impacts urban education. Her other research interest is on motherscholarship and supporting woman of color and motherscholars in the academy. A former K-12 teacher, she earned her doctorate at UCLA with an emphasis on race and ethnic studies in education. She is a motherscholar of three, including boy-girl twins, a runner, an avid Lakers fan, and Bachata ballroom dancer.

Nanyamka A. Shukura is a senior supervising community advocate in the legal department at the Southern Poverty Law Center (SPLC) in Montgomery, AL, with the Children's Rights practice group. For over a decade her work with SPLC has focused primarily on education equity and juvenile justice; the ultimate goal is to dismantle the school-to-prison pipeline affecting too many children across the south. She graduated from Savannah State University, a HBCU in Savannah, GA, in 2010, with a Bachelor of Science degree in sociology and minor in Africana studies and is a 2017 alumnus of the Youth Justice Leadership Institute offered by the National Juvenile Justice Network.

Nicholas P. Triplett is clinical assistant professor of social studies education in the Cato College of Education at the University of North Carolina at Charlotte. His research focuses on educational equity, school discipline, and the role of schools in social class reproduction. He recently published *E(race)ing Inequities: The State of Racial Equity in North Carolina Public Schools*.

www.ingramcontent.com/pod-product-compliance
Lightning Source LLC
Chambersburg PA
CBHW061713300426
44115CB00014B/2662